Geographies of the New Economy

This collection of original essays seeks to provoke debate on the efficacy of the widely used and misused concept of the New Economy. The contributors explore meanings of the 'new economy' at the global scale, from the perspective of advanced, post-socialist, and emerging economies. Also discussed are its socio-spatial consequences, with reference to the nature of work(ers), social polarization, and the impacts of information and communications technology.

Perhaps the New Economy was not that distinctive, but it cannot be written off as merely a redundant episode in the history of capitalism. It has left a legacy that informs our efforts to broaden and deepen understandings of economic change; not least that the New Economy had a distinctive and pervasive geography which coloured both how it emerged and the promises it offered to create a 'frictionless' economy. Conversely, when it failed, geography shaped where the damage was done and where its legacies continue to bring relative prosperity to unexpected locations.

Essential for all those interested in economic geography, this collection reinforces the notion that the New Economy is not only specific to a particular time, when it formed the dominant political and economic discourse, but also to a particular set of places that were home to that ideology. Although it is now more than five years since the New Economy was at its height, this book sheds new light by highlighting its historical and geographical specificity.

Peter Daniels is Professor of Geography and Co-Director of the Services and Enterprise Research Unit at the University of Birmingham.

Andrew Leyshon is Professor of Economic Geography at the University of Nottingham.

Mike Bradshaw is Professor of Human Geography at the University of Leicester.

Jonathan Beaverstock is Professor of Economic Geography at Loughborough University.

Regions and cities

Series editors: Ron Martin, University of Cambridge, UK; Gernot Grabher, University of Bonn, Germany; Maryann Feldman, University of Georgia, USA

Regions and Cities is an international, interdisciplinary series that provides authoritative analyses of the new significance of regions and cities for economic, social and cultural development, and public policy experimentation. The series seeks to combine theoretical and empirical insights with constructive policy debate and critically engages with formative processes and policies in regional and urban studies.

Geographies of the New Economy

Critical Reflections

**Edited by Peter Daniels,
Andrew Leyshon,
Mike Bradshaw and
Jonathan Beaverstock**

Routledge
Taylor & Francis Group

LONDON AND NEW YORK

First published 2007
by Routledge
2 Park Square, Milton Park, Abington, OX14 4RN

Simultaneously published in the USA and Canada
by Routledge

270 Madison Avenue, New York, NY 10016

*Routledge is an imprint of the Taylor & Francis Group, an informa
business*

© 2007 Peter Daniels, Andrew Leyshon, Mike Bradshaw and Jonathan
Beaverstock, selection and editorial material; individual chapters,
the contributors

Typeset in Bembo by Keyword Group Ltd.
Printed and bound in Great Britain by MPG Books Ltd, Bodmin

British Library Cataloguing in Publication Data
A catalogue record for this book is available from the British Library

Library of Congress Cataloging in Publication Data
Geographies of the new economy/edited by Peter Daniels... [et al.].
p.cm.--(Regions and cities)
Includes bibliographical references and index.
ISBN 0-415-35783-7 (hbk: alk. paper)
1. Economic history--1990 2. Economic geography. 3. Technological
innovations--Economic aspects. I. Daniels, P. W. II. Series.
HC59.15.G467 2007
330.9--dc22   2006016001
ISBN10: 0-415-35783-7 (hbk)
ISBN10: 0-203-00389-6 (ebk)
ISBN13: 978-0-415-35783-8 (hbk)
ISBN13: 978-0-203-00389-3 (ebk)

Contents

Contributors

Jonathan Beaverstock is Professor of Economic Geography at Loughborough University, UK. His research focuses on globalization and world cities, and the organizational strategies of transnational professional service firms in international financial centres. He has published widely in international journals, including: *Annals of the Association of American Geographers*; *Environment and Planning A*; *Geoforum*; *Journal of Economic Geography*; *Transactions of the Institute of British Geographers*; and *Urban Geography*.

Mike Bradshaw is Professor of Human Geography at the University of Leicester, UK. His PhD is from the University of British Columbia, Canada. Previously he worked in the School of Geography at the University of Birmingham. His research is on the economic geography of Russia, with a particular focus on the Russian Far East and energy relations with N E Asia. Co-Editor in Chief of *Blackwell Geography Compass*. He is also an Honorary Senior Research Fellow in the Centre for Russian and East European Studies at the University of Birmingham and an Associate Fellow of the Russia and Eurasia Programme at the Royal Institute of International Affairs in London. Publications include: *Regional Economic Change in Russia* (with Philip Hanson, 2000); *The Russian Far East and Pacific Asia: Unfulfilled Potential* (2002); *East Central Europe and the Former Soviet Union: The Post Socialist States* (with Alison Stenning, 2004). He is currently completing a book entitled: *A New Economic Geography of the Russian Federation*.

Julian Cooper is Professor of Russian Economic Studies at the Centre for Russian and East European Studies, University of Birmingham, UK. He researches on the Russian economy, in particular the military sector, information and communication technologies, science policy and foreign trade. He contributes regularly to the Yearbook of the Stockholm International Peace Research Institute. Recent publications include 'Of BRICs and Brains: Comparing Russia with China, India and Other Populous Economies', *Eurasian Geography and Economics*, 2006.

Peter Daniels is Professor of Geography and Co-Director, Services and Enterprise Research Unit, University of Birmingham, UK. He has undertaken research on the service economy, especially producer services as key agents in metropolitan and regional restructuring at the national and international scale. Recent publications include: *Service Worlds: People, Organizations, Technologies* (with J R Bryson and B Warf, 2004); *Service Industries and Asia-Pacific Cities: New Development Trajectories* (ed., with K C Ho and T A Hutton, 2005); *The Service Industries Handbook* (ed., with J R Bryson, in press, 2006); *Knowledge-Based Services* (ed., with J W Harrington, in press, 2006).

Andrew Herod is Professor of Geography and Adjunct Professor of International Affairs and of Anthropology at the University of Georgia, Athens, GA, USA. He is author of *Labor Geographies: Workers and the Landscapes of Capitalism* (Guilford, 2001), editor of *Organizing the Landscape: Geographical Perspectives on Labor Unionism* (University of Minnesota Press, 1998), and co-editor of *The Dirty Work of Neoliberalism: Cleaners in the Global Economy* (Blackwell 2006), *Geographies of Power: Placing Scale* (Blackwell 2002), and *An Unruly World?: Globalization, Governance and Geography* (Routledge 1998). He writes frequently on issues of labour and globalisation.

Michael Leaf is the Director of the Centre for Southeast Asia Research (CSEAR) at the University of British Columbia (UBC), Vancouver, Canada, an Associate Professor in the UBC School of Community and Regional Planning (SCARP), and a Research Associate of the UBC Centre for Human Settlements (CHS). The focus of his research and teaching has been on urbanization and planning in cities of developing countries, with particular interest in Asian cities. Since his original doctoral research (PhD Berkeley, 1992) on land development in Jakarta, Indonesia, Dr. Leaf has been extensively involved in urbanization research and capacity-building projects in Indonesia, Vietnam, Thailand, China and Sri Lanka. The courses he teaches at SCARP covers the theory and practice of development planning and the social, institutional and environmental aspects of urbanization in developing countries.

Roger Lee is Professor of Geography at Queen Mary, University of London, UK and managing editor of *Progress in Human Geography*. His research investigates the nature of economic geographies as social practices and the possibilities of diverse economies. Recent publications include: *Geographies and moralities* (2004 ed., with David M Smith) and *Alternative economic spaces* (2003 ed., with Andrew Leyshon and Colin Williams).

Andrew Leyshon is Professor of Economic Geography at the University of Nottingham. He is currently undertaking research on geographies of financial exclusion and on the geography of musical creativity by way of an analysis of the UK recording studio sector. His publications include: *Alternative Economic Spaces* (edited with R. Lee and C. Williams, 2003); *Bridges into Work? An evaluation of Local Exchange Trading Schemes* (with C. Williams, T. Aldridge, R. Lee, N. Thrift, and J. Tooke, 2001); *The Place of Music* (edited with D. Matless and G. Revill, 1998) and *Money/Space: geographies of monetary transformation* (with N. Thrift, 1997).

Ron Martin is Professor of Economic Geography at the University of Cambridge, where he is also a Fellow of the Cambridge–MIT Institute, and a Research Associate at the Centre for Business Research. His research interests include the geographies of economic growth, finance and labour and the application of economic theory in economic geography. He has published some 26 books and more than 150 papers on these and related themes. Recent books include *Putting Workfare in Place* (with P. Sunley and C. Nativel, 2005), *Regional Competitive Advantage* (with M. Kitson and P. Tyler, 2006) and *Clusters and Regional Development* (with B. Asheim and P. Cook, 2006). Ron is an academician of the Academy of Social Sciences and a Fellow of the British Academy. He is also listed by the American Economic Association as one of the world's most cited economists.

Diane Perrons is Reader in Economic Geography and Gender Studies and Director of the Gender Institute, London School of Economics, UK. She researches the social and spatial implications of global economic restructuring, focusing on employment change and inequality. Recent publications include *Globalization and Social Change: People and Places in a Divided World* (Routledge 2004) and *Gender Divisions and Working Time in the New Economy: Changing Patterns of Work, Care and Public Policy in Europe and North America* (Edward Elgar 2006) an anthology co-edited with colleagues from Oxford and Manchester.

Andrew C. Pratt is Reader in Urban Cultural Economy and Director, LSE Centre for Urban Research, London School of Economics, UK. He has carried out extensive research on the cultural and creative industries (film industry, television industry, music industry, computer games industry, as well as new media industries). He is particularly concerned with international comparative work on these topics. His interests concern three issues: clustering and local interaction, the organisation of production, and industrial and urban policy. He has written many book chapters and articles about these issues, versions of most of these are available for download from http://www.lse.ac.uk/collections/geographyAndEnvironment/whosWho/profiles/a.c.pratt@lse.ac.uk.htm

Matthew Zook is currently an Assistant Professor in the Geography Department at the University of Kentucky, Lexington, KY, USA. His interest centres on the impact of technology and innovation on human geography. Recent publications include 'The Geography of the Internet' in *The Annual Review of Information Science and Technology (ARIST)* (B. Cronin (ed.)) and his book *The Geography of the Internet Industry: Venture Capital, Dot-coms and Local Knowledge* (Blackwell, 2005).

Preface

In a number of disciplines, including geography, sociology, economics, cultural studies, management, psychology and policy studies, there has been a good deal of research devoted to understanding contemporary global capitalisms and the New Economy. The latter, often juxtaposed against the Old Economy is characterised by the de-materialisation of production and a shift away from dealing with raw materials and machines toward dealing with other minds; physical dexterity is still a skills asset but mental processing ability is now often more important. The acceleration of technological change and the associated growth of information available to firms, organisations and other agents are also bound up with growing uncertainty. Economic competitiveness now has less to do with new materials *per se* than with new ways of producing, using and combining diverse knowledges.

The enthusiasm for the New Economy is undeniable but has there been sufficient reflection or debate about what it really represents and whether it is expressed in similar ways, at the same time, in different geographical contexts? Thus, where is the New Economy, especially if diverse regional perspectives are included? If the New Economy possesses a distinctive geography, is it expressed in similar ways in advanced, transition and emerging economies? What determines its characteristics and are these separate (or different) from the Old Economy? What is the New Economy in relation to issues such as the nature of work, social inclusion and exclusion?

These are the themes that have been used to guide the contributions to this book which are all based upon invited presentations that were given during a two-year Seminar Programme on *Geographies of the New Economy* funded by the Economic and Social Research Council (Award R451265035) between 1 July 2001 and 30 June 2003. Four seminars were co-ordinated by Peter Daniels, who hosted the first meeting at the University of Birmingham, with the subsequent meetings hosted by Mike Bradshaw, Jonathan Beaverstock, and Andrew Leyshon. Three overseas participants, Andrew Herod (University of Georgia, Athens), Michael Leaf (University of British Columbia), and Matthew Zook (University of Kentucky, Lexington) joined the Seminar facilitated by the support from the ESRC. This is gratefully acknowledged.

Thanks are due to Mike Bradshaw, who originally suggested the idea for the Seminar, just before he departed the University of Birmingham for the University of Leicester. Colleagues at the Service Sector Research Unit (now the Services and Enterprise Research Unit), University of Birmingham also generously provided comments and suggestions when fine tuning the proposal that was subsequently submitted to the ESRC.

Peter Daniels

March 2006

1 Geographies of the New Economy: an introduction

Andrew Leyshon, Mike Bradshaw,
Peter Daniels, and Jonathan Beaverstock

'That's just so 1997'[1]

One response to seeing a book entitled *Geographies of the New Economy: Critical Reflections* published in the middle of the first decade of the 21st century is to view it as a typical example of academics pronouncing upon an event that is long over and of no further interest. Surely, some critics will argue, the New Economy was at its height between 1995 and 2000: why do we need a book on it more than five years later? Given that as long ago as 2001 one critic was able to confidently and alliteratively claim that the New Economy was 'all over', having been 'scorched, scotched, … scuttled' (Thrift 2001, page 429), why bother raking over the ashes of a period during which many economic actors demonstrated that their capacity for rhetoric vastly exceeded their capacity for action? To some extent, we agree with those who have argued that, in retrospect, the New Economy was not that distinctive, let alone new; in many respects the New Economy resembles all those other 'bubble economies' that litter the historical landscape of capitalism. They too rose rapidly on the back of visions, anticipations and greed, but likewise crumbled when the investments made on the back of such visions failed to materialize quickly enough. Moreover, as is the case with all fads, it is in the period that immediately follows their demise that commentators are most dismissive, the sense of collective embarrassment is at its height, and there exists widespread agreement that the entire episode should be put behind us so that we can move on to something else. As Henwood (2003) has observed, the speed at which the New Economy has been subject to a process of motivated forgetting is remarkable, a process that has been intensified by the spectre of terrorism and geo-political adventures in the Middle East:

> For a while in the late 1990s we had a New Economy. It was the wonder of the world. Computers had unleashed a productivity miracle, recessions were a thing of the past, ideas had replaced things as the motors of economic life, the world had become unprecedentedly globalized, work had become deeply meaningful, and mutual funds had put an end to class conflict. Even to conventional minds, a lot of that sounds embarrassing now. But commentary on

the era usually treats it as a mix of collective folly and outright criminality – never something emerging from the innards of the American economic machinery. And now we're forgetting about it, our amnesia encouraged by the frequent reminders that we're in a state of permanent war. (Henwood 2003, page 1)

We argue that to write off the New Economy as merely an embarrassing and redundant episode in the history of capitalism would be a signal error. The tendency to dismiss the significance of the New Economy is understandable; it may be seen as a welcome antithesis to the thesis of hyberbolic boosterism that was so widely trumpeted in many quarters during the 1990s. For some, the nature of the capitalist economy had changed irrevocably, with 'true enthusiasts [seeing] the New Economy as a fundamental industrial revolution as great or greater in importance than the concurrence of inventions, particularly electricity and the internal combustion engine, which transformed the world at the turn of the last century' (Gordon 2000, Page 47). This prediction was clearly a tad over ambitious (op. cit. 71–72).

Nevertheless, the New Economy, and in particular its rise and fall, has left a legacy that informs our efforts to broaden and deepen understandings of economic change. There are at least three reasons for this. First, the New Economy introduced new modes of economic behaviour that are more persistent than New Economy naysayers appreciate, and has been responsible for introducing a whole range of taken-for-granted business protocols and practices that have changed the nature of economic competition and have now sunk more or less unproblematically into the business background (French *et al.* 2004, Leyshon *et al.* 2005a). Second, a retrospective analysis of the New Economy sheds light on some of the enduring features of a capitalist economy, such as cycles of boom and bust, as well as revealing just how integral the financial system is to wider processes of economic change. Indeed, it is possible to argue that the most important economic force to shape the 1990s was not the New Economy *per se* but, rather, a more powerful and pervasive process of financialization, which in many ways made much of what we understand as the New Economy possible (Feng *et al.* 2001, Williams 2001). Third, and finally, the New Economy had a distinctive and pervasive geography. Although popular accounts and non-geographical academic analyses of the New Economy recognize that it had geographical consequences, this was seen as incidental rather than instrumental to its rise and fall. However, as many of the contributions to this book illustrate, the New Economy was a remarkably geographic phenomenon, which coloured both how it emerged, the promises it offered to create a 'frictionless' economy, but also, when it failed, where the damage was done and, in other cases, where its legacies continue to bring relative prosperity to unexpected locations. In the remainder of this introductory chapter, we shall examine each of these issues in turn, before going on to provide a brief summary of the chapters that follow. However, first we return to the New Economy itself.

The New Economy in retrospect

The origins of the term New Economy are hard to pin down. Like all such descriptive neologisms, they have been in use for much longer than is commonly understood. For example, entering the term into the ISI Web of Knowledge social science database reveals the first use of the term as the definitive article in a paper published in the *Harvard Business Review* in 1967 (Ammer 1967). More recently, it was used regularly in the 1980s in research inspired by the work of Thomas Stanback and Thierry Noyelle, who used the term New Economy to describe service-dominated economies (Stanback *et al.* 1981, Noyelle 1987). However, its use to describe what we now understand as *the* New Economy has been traced back to the venture capital firms of Silicon Valley in the 1990s, being intimately involved in helping new technology firms to establish themselves in the San Francisco Bay Area (Walker 2005). The use of the term gradually escaped its regional origins and gained a wider circulation, then gathered sufficient momentum until it was even used by figures as august as Alan Greenspan, the head of the US central bank, the Federal Reserve (Gordon 2000), to encapsulate what he perceived were fundamental changes underway within the US economy. Speaking in 1999 he commented that:

> A perceptible quickening in the pace at which technological innovations are applied argues for the hypothesis that the recent acceleration in labour productivity is not just a cyclical phenomenon or a statistical aberration, but reflects, at least in part, more deep seated, still developing, shift in our economic landscape. (Greenspan, cited in Gordon, page 49).

On what evidence did normally sober economic commentators like Alan Greenspan make such startling predictions? To some extent it was the increasingly pervasive use of technology within the economy, although there remained considerable scepticism about its actual effect on productivity. Economists had long been cautious about the claims made for technology in the wake of Robert Solow's now famous 1980s pronouncement that the evidence for the significance of computer technology was everywhere except in the productivity statistics. Even though precise measurement of productivity remained elusive, there was agreement during the 1990s that levels of productivity growth were increasing sharply, causing some commentators to argue that the 'Solow paradox' had finally been eliminated (Table 1.1). Indeed, the US Department of Commerce went so far as to define the New Economy as one 'in which IT and related investments [produced] higher rates of productivity growth' (in Temple 2002, page 242), thereby confirming its existence for those easily impressed by such pronouncements. But in addition to higher rates of productivity in the latter part of the decade, the 1990s were also distinctive in that they were characterized by macroeconomic conditions that were more

Table 1.1 US Growth, 1950–2001

	Real GDP growth (per cent)	Productivity growth (per cent)
1950: 2 – 1972: 2	3.9	2.7
1972: 2 – 1995: 4	2.9	1.4
1995: 4 – 2001: 4	3.5	2.4

Source: Temple 2000, 243.

benign than had been the case since at least the 1960s (Temple 2002). The period of US economic expansion between 1991 and 2001:

> …was one of the longest … ever recorded by an industrial country. The rate of inflation remained low throughout, even though the unemployment rate fell to a 30-year low. Faster productivity growth ultimately translated into faster growth in real wages. The incidence of poverty fell and inequality finally stabilized. (Temple 2002, page 241)

Thus, to a very great extent the New Economy was a technological and a macroeconomic phenomenon. However, the extent to which it really penetrated the economy as a whole has been called into question. According to Gordon (2000, page 54) the increases in productivity were mainly delivered within a very narrow part of the economy; that is, those sectors involved in the production of computers and peripherals and the rest of the durable manufacturing sector, which made up only 12 per cent of the US economy in the 1990s. For Gordon, the concentrated nature of such productivity breakthroughs meant that 'the Solow computer paradox survives intact for most of the economy' (op. cit. page 57). (see Martin, Chapter 2)

That the New Economy became such a phenomenon despite being predicated upon such a narrow economic base is revealing. It was not merely an economic process but was also a strongly political and cultural movement, which was ushered into being with no little rhetorical force (Thrift 2001). Thus:

> the idea of the new economy … consists of strong non-inflationary growth arising out of the increasing influence of information and communications technology and the associated restructuring of economic activity. All kinds of other features can be, and usually are, associated with this core definition – for example, the growth of small high-tech firms, the increasing importance of mobile and highly skilled talent, the rise of entrepreneurship and the centrality of venture capital. And it is almost second nature for commentators to produce grand rhetorical flourishes such as the death of the business cycle or virtually unlimited growth. What seems certain is that the new economy is both a description and, at the same time, an assumption of what constitutes a normal future. (Thrift 2001, pages 414–415).

The idea of the New Economy became freighted with a normative vision of an idealized and neo-liberalized economy. In this respect, the New Economy can be seen an example of what Miller has described as virtualism, wherein the real economy is worked upon to increasingly resemble the ideal (Miller 1998, 2000), and of Callon's arguments that economic ideas are performative of the economy (Callon *et al.* 2002). Indeed, Henwood has suggested that the rhetorical movement surrounding the New Economy can be seen as a collective, if haphazard and disorganized, PR campaign on behalf of capitalism and its agents, which in an act of 'spin' sought to accentuate the positives while glossing over the iniquities and exploitative qualities of a competitive and increasingly individualized market economy:

> ... it's tempting to read much of the New Economy discourse as largely ideological, whether conscious (as in propaganda) or not (as in the unreflective enthusiasms of partisans ...). The enthusiasts' claims often look a lot like pre-emptive defenses of capitalism against some of the classic indictments of it...Find capitalism too controlling? No it's spontaneous! Too inegalitarian and exploitative? No, it overturns hierarchies! Vulgar, brutal, de-skilling, and mercenary. Au contraire, it's creative and fun! Unstable? Nah, that's just its miraculous dynamism at work. (Henwood 2003, page 37)

This rampant enthusiasm for business and the celebration of entrepreneurialism in all its forms certainly contributed to the vast amounts of money that flowed into high technology businesses from the mid-1990s onwards, and the encouragement of a series of increasingly ill-judged Internet-based business models that seemed to have no problem in attracting venture capital (Wolff 1998, Malmsten *et al.* 2002).

The legacy effects of the New Economy

While it is true that many of the claims for the New Economy quickly turned to ashes, it would be wrong to argue that the New Economy was nothing but a chimera, and the 1990s a decade of collective economic unreason from which its participants have now recovered and, suitably rehabilitated and supervised, have agreed to work normally within the community. The sheer volumes of money that were invested during the 1990s in search of New Economy dreams have ensured that there are significant legacy effects. On obvious example is the way in which the Internet and e-commerce, unknown at the start of the 1990s, has become so commonplace that it has sunk into the business background. This is now so firmly part of the distribution channels of businesses and organizations that the absence of a customer-facing website is now a subject for comment, rather than the reverse (Leyshon *et al.* 2005a). In some sectors, such as book retailing or travel agencies for example, Internet-based pioneers such as Amazon and Expedia have managed to carve out significant market shares, with substantial implications for market incumbents in many of the ways predicted by New Economy gurus (Evans and Wurster 1999). In other cases, on-line firms have carved out new kinds of markets; most notably the auction sites such as eBay and Craigslist, which have also created opportunities for firms and individuals to earn revenues or even to establish small businesses in new and unexpected ways and places (see Zook, Chapter 5). In the music industry too, the inability of the large companies to see beyond illegal downloading and realize that consumers wanted to listen to music in more flexible software formats created the opportunity for firms such as Apple to move in and grab a share of what was already a shrinking market, with severe consequences for parts of the established musical economy (Leyshon *et al.* 2005b, Leyshon 2006). But in other sectors (e.g. automobiles, non-durable goods retailing), the Internet and e-commerce has not shifted the power of market incumbents in quite the same ways; such developments have, if anything, acted to reinforce market hierarchy and power by adding yet another layer of costs and administration.

The New Economy and financialization

The New Economy is significant in another way too. It has been argued that ultimately what was significant was not so much the orgy of technological invention but the way in which it was funded. As such it was indicative of the latest phase of a longer run process by which capitalism can be seen to have undergone a process of *financialization* (Froud *et al.* 2000, Feng *et al.* 2001, Williams 2001, Erturk *et al.* 2004):

> Financialization is the concept that covers both the routeing of middle-class savings for retirement through the capital market and the stock market's pressure on corporate management for higher rates of return…despite a willingness to 'downsize and distribute', US and UK corporate management found it very difficult to deliver the higher earnings that the stock market required. From this point of view, the new economy represents the next episode in the soap opera of financialization as it offered an unstable and self-defeating solution to the problem of limited corporate earnings at the end of the 1990s. The higher returns could be temporarily generated from capital gains by chasing up the prices of all tech stocks and floating new companies whose product was their own stock, which would make founders rich and venture capital funds superprofitable. (Williams 2001, page 405)

Therefore, it was the process of financialization that drove up the share values of technology companies at the close of the twentieth century. But the wave of money that flowed into stocks and shares, and in particular into the Initial Public Offerings of new technology companies through the 1990s, was given rhetorical justification by the arguments that insisted that capitalism had entered a new and benign era of growth that could sustain price to earnings ratios way in excess of those that had hitherto been normal within the history of capitalism (Thrift 2001) (see Lee, Chapter 3). As a result, the value of stock markets increased precipitously during the 1990s. The US NASDAQ Composite Index, the exchange upon which most technology company shares were traded, ticked up to 500 in Spring 1991, reached 1,000 by the summer of 1995 but reached a record 5,132 at its peak in the Spring of 2000, just before the markets went into reverse (Stiglitz 2003). Thus, although at the time the New Economy was often depicted as being driven by technology and innovation, the 1990s was in reality 'the decade in which finance reigned supreme' (Stiglitz 2003, page xi).

The sheer volume of money flowing through the markets meant that they inevitably influenced the nature of economic development. Helped by a US economic policy which lowered interest rates while continuing to borrow significant amounts of money from the rest of the world (Stiglitz 2003), the 1990s has been described by Brenner as an experiment in 'stock market Keynesianism' (Brenner 2000, 2004). In the USA, the extent to which individuals and households were invested in the rising tide of the stock market has an appreciable impact upon their perceived levels of wealth and economic comfort, which in turn prompted a credit boom and significant equity extraction – or 'cash outs' – which added further impetus to a booming economy (Brenner 2004). By cashing in on assets prices in this way, households were mimicking the behaviour of companies who were similarly riding the wave of rising share prices, using the capital market, rather the markets for their products and services, as the means of ensuring cost recovery (Feng *et al.* 2001). Moreover, as Feng *et al.* argue, the weight of money introduced a new financial ecosystem wherein for the first time a significant amount of research, development and innovation activity was effectively externalized and funded through the capital markets, as investment funds flowed into venture capitalist firms who gambled large volumes of cash on the Internet-focussed business plans of all manner of fledging new companies (Zook 2004). During this decade, most research and development activity was undertaken in-house and funded through the retained earnings of corporations.

The geographies of the New Economy

In all the talk of a generic New Economy, the highly geographical nature of the phenomenon has often been overlooked. At one level it was concentrated in particular cities and regions. Thus, for Walker, the San Francisco Bay Area was the 'Ground Zero' of the New Economy:

> As the world center of high tech in the emerging Internet age, the Bay Area became the paragon of the New Economy and the iconic space of the Neo-Liberal 1990s … The Bay Area's undeniable economic strength and innovative energy was the solid base on which the hyperbole of the New Economy, the American revival, and the Dot-Com dottiness were constructed. (Walker 2005, page 3)

The significance of Silicon Valley as a technology region has been long established (Saxenian 1994, Kenney 2000), and it was from this industrial agglomeration that the larger cultural project of the New Economy arose. That such a project should emerge from what might on the surface have been seen as a milieu of merely technological competence is made more understandable in light of Barbrook and Cameron's claims to have identified what they describe as the California Ideology (Barbrook and Cameron 1995). Written right at the outset of the New Economy, Barbrook and Cameron's thesis points to the rise of what might be described as 'hippy capitalism'; that is, a mixture of left-leaning utopian thinking about the socially liberal – indeed, libertarian – possibilities of electronic information and freedom on the one hand, with right-leaning economically liberal ideas of an electronic market place on the other. What both of these positions share is a disregard for the role of the state, which is ironic given that the technological development that most gave wings to such an ideology was the Internet, which was made possible only by a series of government initiatives, not least by the US Defense Department (Abbate 2000). But what is significant here is that what later became adopted as a general interpretation of economic change can be identified as a particularistic discourse that can be traced etymologically back to the place of its origin, (North) California:

> The Californian Ideology was developed by a group of people living within one specific country with a particular mix of socio-economic and technological choices. Its eclectic and contradictory blend of conservative economics and hippie radicalism reflects the history of the West Coast – and not the inevitable future of the rest of the world. (Barbrook and Cameron 1995)

The Bay Area was also where the material effects of the growth of the New Economy were first manifest. These include booming labour and property markets, as well as the influx of money and finance to underwrite the boom in return for a share in its future profits. As a result the venture capitalist companies of Sand Road Pala Alto (Kenny and Florida 2000) began to forge networks and links with centres of the global financial system, as banks began to channel large investments into the latest new start ups and IPOs (Walker 2005).

The allure of the Bay Area was such that new mimetic spaces of digital growth began to be identified elsewhere, such as Silicon Alley in New York and Silicon Gulch in Austin, Texas (Pratt 2000). As such, the New Economy became less a regional phenomenon, and more a national, geo-economic project which would export the US recipe for economic success to the rest of the world (Gadrey 2003, Stiglitz 2003) (see also Lee, Chapter 3):

> Wherever the myth of US supremacy and capitalist renewal went, the legend of Silicon Valley was not far behind. Everywhere a Silicon Valley, a Silicon Valley for all, a microprocessor in every pot. It didn't hurt that the US government exaggerated the extent and benefits of the boom in terms of computer productivity, the utility of the Internet, and quality of jobs in the New Economy, while minimizing the lag in employment and wages, not to mention the epidemic of overwork, continued fall in unionization, and erosion of benefits. (Walker 2005, page 8)

But of course, as we all know, the bubble economy, and the geoeconomic campaign that was based upon it, was unsustainable, and its more speculative elements began to unravel, most spectacularly from 2000 onwards. As Walker (2005) has argued, it is the bust as much as the boom which reveals how geographically embedded the edifice of the New Economy was. Although the growth of the New Economy was rapid, its collapse was even more precipitous, and the effects of this collapse were highly concentrated. San Francisco and Silicon Valley may have enjoyed the fruits of growth in the 1990s, but in the 21st century it bore the brunt of financial collapse:

> ... the Bay Area's loss of $2.63 trillion on the Chronicle 500/200 amounted to well over one-third of the national total .... When the dust had settled by 2003, the total losses incurred by ... [technology] sectors were equal to all the profits they had rung up by the late 1990s ... hence, stock values fell back to where they had been in 1996–97, before the absurd run-up of the bubble. But in Silicon Valley the debacle was the worst: in one year the top 150 companies lost a combined $90 billion, wiping out all the profits they had made *in the previous eight years.* (Walker 2005, pages 18–19, original emphasis)

This was reflected in job losses: 434,000 layoffs out of a total of 2.45 million jobs lost in the US were in the Bay Area: that is, 17.7 per cent of the job losses were in an area that had less that 3 per cent of the US population. With the dot com boom assigned to history, and with it the twenty-twenty vision that is the benefit of hindsight, this book, and the seminar series that preceded it, reassesses the claims of the New Economy to distil its lasting effects, both in terms of the nature of economic activity in the first decade of the new millennium and in terms of the geographical organization of contemporary developed capitalism.

About this book

The contributions to this volume are arranged as a sequence of couplets that explore the different facets of the New Economy. In Chapter 2, Ron Martin reviews the claims of the New Economy. First he answers the question, what is the New Economy? He then goes on to assess some of the more contentious claims of the New Economy, suggesting that it did not bring the great leap forward in productivity that many of its plaudits claimed. Finally, he considers the spatial consequences of New Economy processes, and critiques the notion that the New Economy brought the end of geography. Far from it, he suggests that it actually reinforced the tendencies toward localization and generated new sources of inequality. He concludes that while it is true that the myth of the New Economy has been translated into a dominant policy discourse, it did also bring about concrete changes in economic practice. These changes present theoretical challenges for who seek to understand contemporary capitalism and also challenges to policy makers whether they are seeking to regulate the New Economy or replicate its essential features. The following chapter by Roger Lee continues the political assessment of the New Economy. First, he questions the very idea of a New Economy. Paralleling Martin's critique of the New Economy, Lee points out that capitalism is constantly remaking itself and thus every economy is to some degree new. The key issue then is the degree of 'newness' associated with the notion of the New Economy. Do the changes associated with the New Economy represent a sea change in the organization of capitalist economies? Lee considers the generic critiques of the New Economy and maintains that when placed in a longer-term perspective the answer is probably not, it does not represent a fundamental change in the process of accumulation and its associated geography. Lee then asks a rather different question; if one were to build a New Economy what might it look like? He argues for a 'moral newness' that takes into account the real costs of accumulation and that recognizes that there is actually more to life than accumulation. Together these first two chapters not only offer a thorough critique of the New Economy and its supposed achievements, they ask us to think beyond the rhetoric to consider whether or not the processes central to the New Economy are having a lasting effect. The two chapters that follow, by Andrew Pratt and Matthew Zook, take up that challenge by looking at some of the core economic activities most associated with the New Economy.

In some ways, by assessing the evidence and concepts associated with the New Economy, Andrew Pratt continues the critique initiated by Martin and Lee; however, he is less concerned about whether or not the New Economy is new and more about the fact that it is much more complicated than suggested in both orthodox and dissenting accounts. According to Pratt, there is huge variation within the range of activities usually associated with the New Economy and that one of the key aspects of its material practices is the shifting of responsibility and risk to those individuals in society who can least afford it. This critique is grounded in an illustrative case study of new media. He notes that one of the most striking features of new media development is its physical location. New media 'clusters' have not developed everywhere; in fact they are confined (concentrated) to a small number of locations across the world. Further, their emergence is not a break with the past, but rather a continuity to the present as the locational assets of particular places are re-worked to serve the purposes of a new group of people whose work practices are substantially different, but whose presence may be fleeting as they personally mature along with the activities in which they are involved. In the second of these empirically grounded chapters, Matthew Zook considers e-commerce, which is supposedly a mainstay of the New Economy. Again, he continues with the theme of continuity versus change, highlighting that there is a lot more to e-commerce than online retailing, which really equates to doing online what we used to do in a shop. For Zook the essential issue is how does e-commerce actually create new value? He suggests that the transformative capacities of the Internet have been greatly exaggerated; too often we are simply doing old things in new ways, rather than creating something that equates with new value, hence his title refers to e-commerce as the 'new old thing'. While the tasks performed in the name of e-commerce may not be new, access to the Internet and the market that it creates is far from ubiquitous. This serves to generate a new landscape of inequality since those on the wrong side of the digital divide, both as producers and consumers, miss out on a new round of opportunities. Again, we are reminded that the New Economy does not mean the end of geography, but rather a re-working of pre-existing patterns of uneven development. The New Economy serves to reinforce existing injustices and inequalities; those who succeeded previously were often best placed to benefit from the opportunities that it offered.

The political and social consequences of the New Economy are the focus of the next two chapters by Diane Perrons and Andrew Herod. Diane Perrons considers the ways in which the economic and social practices associated with New Economy reinforce the widening of social and spatial divisions within (or 'associated with') contemporary global capitalism. The New Economy is associated with widening economic inequality both between and within countries and that these developments are interrelated. It is not only that relatively few places and social groups benefit from the New Economy; it is also that those who benefit can only do so at the cost of others. In her fascinating analysis of 'living and working in a superstar region' she shows how the high flyers can only sustain their work practices and lifestyles by exploiting a low paid and flexible underclass of service workers, who are often migrants with little or no protection or welfare safety net. Thus, the New Economy is dependent upon a very old form of exploitation that has a clear gender bias. Thus: 'the New Economy is characterized by widening social divisions that take a gendered and spatial form'. Andrew Herod continues this assessment of the social consequences of the New Economy by examining the challenges that it poses to labour organizations. Organized labour has traditionally been the mainstay of the industrial and manufacturing economies, activities that have dwindled in relative significance in the advanced economies, which by definition are dominated by service sector activity. Thus, even before the age of the New Economy, organized labour was on the decline. Herod maintains that the telecommunication and transportation technologies associated with the New Economy have enabled corporations to exploit the space–time compressions of the international division of labour. Thus, the model of business organization for many companies has radically shifted to a model of networked firms dependent on subcontracting and associated offshoring to seek out lower cost workers and service providers. These developments pose new challenges to the labour unions and Herod presents eight different models of union campaigning in the New Economy. The particular strategies adopt different conceptions of space and have different implications for the geography of capitalism. In a sense, the challenges described by Herod are a consequence of an internationalizing division of labour that undermines the bargaining capacity of the workforces of the developed economies who are now engulfed in a downward spiral to find cheaper, less organized and less militant workers in other parts of the world. Thus, in parallel to the relationships that Diane Perrons describes within the context of the world city, the changes associated with the New Economy that are taking place in the developed economies are creating dependencies reliant upon the creation and exploitation of a new work force in the emerging economies of countries like India. However, there is another way in which the influence of the New Economy might travel and that is if it were to become the policy prescription for national economic development strategies elsewhere in the world. The final two chapters consider this process in the context of South East Asia and Russia.

Michael Leaf considers whether or not the New Economy offers a viable development paradigm for the nations of South East Asia. As with the following chapter on Russia, there is a problem of definition. It is clear that the positive role of knowledge has now become a central tenet of international development thinking, but is the notion of the New Economy the same as the knowledge-based economy? Likely not, as the New Economy seems more associated with a particular time, the late 1990s, and place, Anglo-America/Western Europe, and with a particular political ideology associated with neoliberalism. However, the essential ingredients of the New Economy and the knowledge economy may be the same. But, in the context of South East Asia, the problem seems to be that you cannot separate the technology from the ideology. As Michael Leaf puts it: 'National Governments may be willing to engage with the material conditions needed for the New Economy, but are they willing to address implicit questions of governance related to informational society and the knowledge-based economy?' The answer is probably not; furthermore the Asian model is one where the state plays a pivotal role, while the New Economy seems a product of a very different political economy. As Julian Cooper and Mike Bradshaw reveal, similar problems exist in Russia, with the added complication of the need to create both a functioning market economy and flourishing/ diversified service sector before developing a knowledge-based economy; an end point that is central to President Putin's economic vision for Russia. At various times in Russia's economic history it has been possible to reap the 'benefits of backwardness' by making short cuts based on the experience and technology of others. However, such leaps are only possible when the material and social requirements of the New Economy are relatively straightforward and the skills required relatively easy to obtain. Neither is true of the knowledge economy and Russia's current political direction is unlikely to nurture an information society; therefore Russia's capacity to create a New Economy by mimicking the experience of others is not only severely limited, it is also seemingly unable to keep up with other emerging markets attempting to develop their own knowledge economies. For Russia the answer may be to seek a new path to a knowledge economy based on its resource wealth.

Both of these chapters reinforce the conclusion that the notion of the New Economy is not only specific to a particular time when it formed the dominant political and economic discourse, but also to a particular set of places that were home to that ideology. Thus, while the technical and material components of the New Economy may be transferred via the policy prescriptions of the knowledge economy, they cannot be replicated because they are embedded in a particular set of political, economic and social relations. In other words the geography of the New Economy is very particular. In this sense, although it is now more than five years since the New Economy was at its height, this book does shed new light by highlighting its historical and geographical specificity. In short, the New Economy was a particular time and place.

Notes

1   This sub-heading is inspired by a description given by an industry practitioner of a research project on e-commerce directed by one of the authors during a music industry convention held in New York in 2002. After some persuasion, the informant was prepared to bring his assessment of the timeliness of the project forward to 2000, but which nevertheless meant that, in the context of what in the 1990s became known as 'Internet time' – that is, an accelerated sense of time, urgent and redundancy – the project was hopelessly out of date and behind the times.

References

Abbate, J. (2000) *Inventing the Internet,* MIT Press, Cambridge, MA.

Ammer, D. S. (1967) 'Entering New Economy', *Harvard Business Review,* 45.

Barbrook, R. and Cameron, A. (1995) 'The Californian Ideology', http://www.alamut.com/subj/ideologies/pessimism/califIdeo_I.html.

Brenner, R. (2000) 'The boom and the bubble', *New Left Review,* II, 5–43.

Brenner, R. (2004) 'New boom or new bubble?' *New Left Review,* 57–100.

Callon, M., Meadel, C. and Rabeharisoa, V. (2002) 'The economy of qualities', *Economy and Society,* 31, 194–217.

Erturk, I., Froud, J., Johal, S. and Williams, K. (2004) 'Corporate governance and disappointment', *Review of International Political Economy,* 11, 677–713.

Evans, P. B. and Wurster, T. S. (1999) *Blown to Bits: how the economics of information transforms strategy,* Harvard Business School Press, Boston, MA.

Feng, H. Y., Froud, J., Johal, S., Haslam, C. and Williams, K. (2001) 'A new business model? The capital market and the new economy', *Economy and Society,* 30, 467–503.

French, S., Crewe, L., Leyshon, A., Webb, P. and Thrift, N. (2004) 'Putting e-commerce in its place: reflections on the impact of the Internet on the cultural industries', in D. Power and A. J. Scott, ed., *Cultural Industries and the Production of Culture,* Routledge, London, pp. 54–71.

Froud, J., Haslam, C., Johal, S. and Williams, K. (2000) 'Shareholder value and financialization: consultancy promises, management moves', *Economy and Society,* 29, 80–110.

Gadrey, J. (2003) *New Economy, New Myth,* Routledge, London.

Gordon, R. J. (2000) 'Does the "new economy" measure up to the great inventions of the past?', *Journal of Economic Perspectives,* 14, 49–74.

Henwood, D. (2003) *After the New Economy,* The New Press, New York.

Kenney, M. ed. (2000) *Understanding Silicon Valley: the anatomy of an entrepreneurial region,* Stanford University Press, Stanford, CA.

Kenny, M. and Florida, R. (2000) 'Venture capital in Silicon Valley: fueling new firm formation', in M. Kenney ed., *Understanding Silicon Valley: the anatomy of an entrepreneurial region,* Stanford University Press, Stanford, CA.

Leyshon, A. (2006) In *School of Geography, University of Nottingham, Nottingham, mimeograph (available from author at andrew.leyshon@nottingham.ac.uk).*

Leyshon, A., French, S., Thrift, N., Crewe, L. and Webb, P. (2005a) 'Accounting for e-commerce: abstractions, virtualism and the cultural circuit of capital', *Economy and Society*, 34, 428–450.

Leyshon, A., Webb, P., French, S., Thrift, N. and Crewe, L. (2005b) 'On the reproduction of the musical economy after the Internet', *Media Culture & Society*, 27, 177–209.

Malmsten, E., Portanger, E. and Drazin, C. (2002) *Boo Hoo: a dot com story,* Random House, New York.

Miller, D. (1998) 'Conclusion: a theory of virtualism', in J. G. Carrier and D. Miller, ed., *Virtualism: a new political economy*, Berg, Oxford, 187–215.

Miller, D. (2000) 'Virtualism: the culture of political economy', in I. Cook, D. Crouch, S. Naylor, and J. R. Ryan, eds, *Cultural Turns / Geographical Turns: perspectives on cultural geography*, Prentice Hall, Harlow, pp. 196-213.

Noyelle, T. J. (1987) *Beyond Industrial Dualism: Market and Job Segmentation in the New Economy,* Westview Press, Boulder, Colorado.

Pratt, A. (2000) 'New media, the new economy and new spaces', *Geoforum*, 31, 425–436.

Saxenian, A. (1994) *Regional Advantage: culture and competition in Silicon Valley and Route 128,* Harvard University Press, Cambridge, MA.

Stanback, T. M., Bearse, P. J., Noyelle, T. J. and Karasek, R. A. (1981) *Services: the new economy,* Rowman and Allanheld, Osmun & Co, Towata, NJ.

Stiglitz, J. E. (2003) *The Roaring Nineties: why we're paying the price for the greediest decade in history,* Penguin, London.

Temple, J. (2002) 'The assessment: The New Economy', *Oxford Review of Economic Policy*, 18, 241–264.

Thrift, N. (2001) "It's the romance, not the finance, that makes the business worth pursuing": disclosing a new market culture, *Economy and Society*, 30, 412–432.

Walker, R. (2005) in *Department of Geography, University of California, Berkeley, (available from author at: walker@berkeley.edu).*

Williams, K. (2001) 'Business as usual', *Economy and Society*, 30, 399–411.

Wolff, M. (1998) *Burn Rate: how I survived the goldrush years on the Internet,* Orion, London.

Zook, M. A. (2004) 'The knowledge brokers: Venture capitalists, tacit knowledge and regional development', *International Journal of Urban and Regional Research*, 28, 621–641.

2 Making sense of the New Economy? Realities, myths and geographies

Ron Martin

Introduction

Change is one of capitalism's constant features. Capitalism cannot stand still. Its central imperative – the search for profit and wealth creation – drives a perpetual process of economic flux. Joseph Schumpeter once described this continual flux as a process of 'creative destruction' which 'incessantly revolutionises the economic structure from within, incessantly destroying the old one, incessantly creating a new one' (Schumpeter 1943, p. 83). Every day, new firms, new techniques, new machines, new products, and new jobs are added to the economy, and old ones disappear. For much of the time this process takes place in a slow, incremental manner, so that there is both change and continuity. As a result, the economy evolves in a gradual, cumulative and path-dependent manner, as a sort of slowly moving equilibrium. This is the view of capitalist evolution that underpins much of conventional economics. For example, Alfred Marshall himself adopted Leibniz' motto, that 'nature does not willingly make a jump' to emphasize his belief that economic evolution was always gradual (Marshall 1919, p. 6).

Yet, standing on the pinnacle of the present and looking back, it is clear that there are also times when economic change is very far from gradual and incremental, but instead rapid and disruptive. Of course, the economy does not 'jump' – there is always continuity with, and dependence on, the past. But the scale of change in these 'disjunctures' is sufficient to generate a major re-orientation of the productive and institutional structures of the economy, an historic inflexion in the pattern, form and sources of economic growth. Schumpeter himself referred to such periodic bursts of economy-wrenching change as 'gales' of creative destruction which, he argued, mark transitions between successive waves or phases of economic development, each phase being stimulated by a new 'technological–industrial revolution'. Seen in these terms, economic evolution is not simply smooth and unilinear, but has an episodic character in which longer periods of 'gradualism' are separated and shaped by shorter periods of 'transformation'. It is a conception somewhat akin to the notion of 'punctuated equilibrium' found in evolutionary biology.

In recent years, this episodic or 'disjunctural' aspect of economic evolution has attracted considerable attention. There is now a widespread view that, since the beginning of the 1980s, capitalism has been experiencing one of the most intensive gales of creative destruction and transformation of its modern history. In most advanced economies there has been immense structural change over the past twenty-five years, involving deindustrialization – the decline in the contribution of manufacturing to national output, jobs and trade – and a rapid process of tertiarization – the growth and economic importance of service activities. At the same time, an historic wave of technological innovation has been gathering momentum, based on computers, telecommunications, biotechnologies, and information processing of all kinds. Equally, numerous so-called 'cultural industries' have assumed increasing importance as loci of growth and employment. Added to these developments, states almost everywhere have been busy withdrawing and redrawing their intervention in the socio-economy in fundamental ways, privatizing whole swathes of state assets and public industries, deregulating product, labour and capital markets, and reforming their welfare systems. And inextricably bound up with these shifts and changes, national economies are rapidly becoming 'globalized', in the sense of an increasing interconnection and inter-penetration of economic activities and economic relations on a global scale, regardless of national borders and boundaries.

Making sense of all this has proved to be a controversial issue. Several different interpretations and characterizations have appeared. There are claims and counterclaims as to the precise nature and significance of the upheaval, and as to what sort of economy is emerging from the turmoil. In part, debate has arisen because it is far from straightforward in the midst of rapid change to separate the transient and ephemeral from the more fundamental and transformative. In addition, different writers use different theoretical and conceptual approaches, each of which provides a somewhat different lens on events. And, inevitably, the passage from one century to another (to say nothing of one millennium to another) has encouraged a flood of hype and hyperbole. During the 1980s and early 1990s, it became highly fashionable in many quarters of the social sciences (and particularly within geography) to view the contemporary upheavals and reorientations as a shift from a 'Fordist' to a 'post-Fordist' form of capitalism, also referred to as 'flexible accumulation'. Another characterization was that we are moving from 'industrialism' to 'post-industrialism'. Yet another was the argument that we were finally leaving behind the age of modernism and entering the 'postmodern' era. These interpretative schemas certainly highlighted some key forces and changes, but also proved problematic. In any case, by the late 1990s, yet another neologism had entered the scene, namely the argument that we are witnessing the advent of the 'New Economy' that, as implied by the very term, is rapidly replacing the 'Old Economy'. However, like other attempts to characterize the contemporary re-orientation of economic life, this notion of the New Economy has itself also proved highly contentious and has attracted diverse definitions and descriptions. Nevertheless, in spite of this, the term has caught and fired the imagination of pundits and policy-makers in a way that the slogans of post-Fordism, post-industrialism and postmodernism have been singularly unable to do, not least of course because the very idea of the 'New Economy' provides politicians and policy-makers with a ready-made slogan for their manifestos and credos.

Indeed, according to Gadrey (2001), politicians and media pundits, not academic economists or other social scientists, have been the primary architects of this New Economy discourse. Both Bill Clinton, whilst President of the United States, and Prime Minister Tony Blair in the UK, have been staunch political exponents of the New Economy 'vision'. And business and market analysts, who are constantly competing to discern the latest business fad or financial fashion, have been highly enthusiastic proselytizers, even claiming to have divined the first signs of the New Economy's birth. Thus, as the editor-in-chief of *Business Week* wrote in November 1997, referring to the New Economy, "This is the sort of thing that economists don't pick up quickly in their models of statistics – and often reject as anecdote. But such changes are precisely what journalists are often first to observe. As the late Washington Post publisher Phil Graham noted, journalism is often 'the first draft of history'." *(Business Week,* 1997). Other US business journalists, economic pundits and IT gurus, such as Stan Davis and Christopher Meyer *(Blur: The Speed of Change in the Connected Economy,* 1998), Kevin Kelly *(New Rules for a New Economy,* 1998), and Bill Gates *(Business @ the Speed of Thought: Succeeding in the Digital Economy,* 1999) were quick to join the growing band of celebratory protagonists. Similarly, in the UK, a whole raft of journalistic proclamations about the advent and supposed benefits of the New Economy have appeared, including Francis Cairncross's *The Death of Distance: How the Communications Revolution will Change Our Lives* (1997), Charles Leadbeater's *Living on Thin Air: The New Economy* (1999), and Diane Coyle's *The Weightless World* (1997), and *Paradoxes of Prosperity: Why the New Capitalism Benefits All* (2001).

Yet, these promissory accounts notwithstanding, debate and disagreement over the New Economy continues, both surrounding its very existence and in relation to its supposed benefits. My aim in this chapter is to provide a critical commentary on these issues, particularly the claims made for the New Economy, including its alleged abolition of the importance of geography.

What is the New Economy?

The use of the term New Economy first emerged in the USA towards the end of 1996 (Weinstein 1997), and then spread quickly to Europe, most especially the UK. Although interpretations of the idea soon multiplied and have broadened in the process (see Table 2.1), two recurring themes have predominated. First, that there are four key forces driving the New Economy, namely an information-technology revolution, accelerating globalization, a new entrepreneurialism, and a new political neoliberalism. Second, that it is a quintessentially 'American growth model', both originating in and being led by the USA (Krugman 1998, Zandi 1998, Zuckerman 1998).

Thus, initially, much of the case for a New Economy was constructed around what was claimed to be an unprecedented phase of US economic expansion (Table 2.1). In 1998 Alan Greenspan, the Chairman of the US Federal Reserve Bank, used the notion to describe what he argued to be a major 'breakthrough'

Table 2.1 Some of the different conceptions of the New Economy

Concept/definition	Alleged key characteristics
'A breakthrough in productivity'	New historic growth path of productivity (e.g. Greenspan 1998). Attributed to the adoption of computers and related technologies
'A new "golden age" of low unemployment-low inflation growth'	Longest post-war phase of uninterrupted US and UK economic growth. Argued to be the new 'American model' of sustainable growth (e.g. Shalman 1999)
'A new paradigm of competition'	Driven by new technologies and globalisation, characterised by new 'system capabilities' (e.g. Best 2001)
'A new information-based, knowledge-driven, networked economy'	Revolutionising effects of new information-communications technologies (ICT) and industries on economy and society (e.g. Greenwood 1997, Castells 1996)
'A new form of dematerialized capitalism'	New model of economic organization, accumulation, work, consumption and regulation based around digital information and processes (e.g. Coyle 1997, Coyle and Quah 2002)
'A new cultural capitalism'	Driven by prominence of cultural production and consumption, a new economy of symbols, signs, and sensations (Lash and Urry 1994, Scott 2000, Du Gay and Pryke 2002)
'A new era of creative capitalism'	The rise of new creative and entrepreneurial classes as the key drivers of innovation and growth (Smith 1998, Norton 2001, Florida 2003)

in the productive performance of the USA, following the languishing of productivity growth from the late-1970s through to the early-1990s. He attributed this 'productivity miracle' in large part to the impact of computers and related technologies. Although Greenspan's argument about the US computer-driven 'productivity miracle' soon provoked controversy, being fervently disputed by writers such as Gordon (1999, 2000), it was nevertheless endorsed and extended by numerous other commentators and observers in the USA. In January 2001, for example, in his Economic Report President Clinton and the Council of Economic Advisors (CEA) proudly announced that 'Over the last 8 years the American Economy has transformed itself so radically that we have witnessed the creation of a New Economy' characterized by 'rapid productivity growth, rising incomes, low unemployment and moderate inflation' (CEA, 2001, p. 20). According to the President and the CEA these 'profound changes in economic trends justify the term "New Economy",' and are explained by 'the mutually reinforcing advances in technological innovation, business practices, and public policy' *(op. cit. p. 20).

A recurring theme in such pronouncements is that new information technologies are the single most important driving force making for a new economic order:

In the *old economy,* information flow was physical: cash, checks, invoices, bills of lading, reports, face-to-face meetings, analog telephone calls or radio and television transmissions, blueprints, maps, photographs, musical scores, and direct mail advertisements. In the *new economy,* information in all its forms becomes digital – reduced to bits stored in computers and racing at the speed of light across networks … The new world of possibilities thereby created is as significant as the invention of language itself, the old paradigm on which all the physically based interactions occurred. (Tapscott 1996, p. 6)

In the past 15 years, a 'New Economy' has emerged in the United States. Among its defining features are a fundamentally altered industrial and occupational order, a dramatic trend toward globalization, and unprecedented levels of entrepreneurial dynamism and competition – all of which have been spurred to one degree or another by *revolutionary advances in information technologies* … In short, a 'New Economy' has emerged: it is a global knowledge and idea-based economy where the keys to wealth and job creation are the extent to which ideas, innovation, and technology are embedded in all sectors of the economy – services, manufacturing and agriculture. (Atkinson, Court and Ward 1999, p. 1).

Indeed, as *Business Week* – the self-styled discoverer of the New Economy – puts it, in distinctly neo-Schumpeterian terms, the true significance of the new technologies is that they are transcendent and transformative in nature, like the railways, the automobile and electricity were before them:

By the New Economy, we mean two broad trends that have been under way for several years. The first is the globalization of business. Simply put, capitalism is spreading around the world – if not full-blown capitalism, at least the introduction of market forces, freer trade, and widespread deregulation. … The second trend is the revolution in information technology. This one is all around us – fax machines, cellular phones, personal computers, modems, the Internet. But it's more than that. It's the digitization of all information – words, pictures, data, and so on. This digital technology is creating new companies and new industries before our eyes. … Furthermore, information technology affects every other industry. It boosts productivity, reduces costs, cuts inventories, facilitates electronic commerce. It is, in short, a transcendent technology – like railroads in the 19th century and automobiles in the 20th. *(Business Week* 1997).

The argument that the concept of the New Economy is more than just a set of new 'high-tech' sectors (such as computers, software, biotechnology and the like), but refers to the way that the new, information-based, technologies are reaching into and transforming all spheres of economic and social life – what some refer to as a new 'general purpose technology' – is particularly important. Much of the hype surrounding the New Economy at the end of the 1990s focused narrowly on the meteoric rise to prominence of myriads of so-called 'dot.com' Internet companies that quickly became the darlings of the investment and financial communities, but which though securing public stock flotations worth $billions had few physical assets and were still to make a profit. Not surprisingly, many of these quickly proved to be unsustainable, and the wave of dot.com failures in 2000–2001, together with the stock market crash that accompanied this shakeout, were taken by critics of the New Economy as evidence of its ephemeral character, its fictitious status. However, for the true believers, the New Economy is a far more fundamental process than the dot.com phenomenon:

> [Is] the New Economy a flash in the pan? Or even worse, a myth spun by an over-imaginative media? Reports of the New Economy's demise have been greatly exaggerated. The New Economy is here to stay … It is an easy but mistaken step to pronounce the death of the New Economy. The fallacy rests on the belief that all the New Economy is about is the Internet and the 'next best thing'. On the contrary, the New Economy embraces more fundamentally a profound transformation of all industries, the kind of transformation that happens perhaps twice a century. The emergence of the New Economy is equivalent in scope and depth to the rise of the manufacturing economy of the 1890s and the emergence of the mass production corporate economy in the 1930s and 1940s. (Atkinson and Gottlieb 2001, p. 2)

In other words, the New Economy is a much more profound phenomenon, nothing less than the passage to a new phase of capitalism.

Some see this new phase as the advent of a 'new paradigm of competition', in which technological change and globalization are both driving and facilitating the development of new 'system capabilities' of continual adaptation to maintain dynamic competitiveness (Best 2001). Others see it as the emergence of a new, networked, information economy and society – variously referred to as the e-economy or i-society – that is, recasting not only the foundations of economic organization, production and exchange, but our forms of consumption, and even our very social identities (Castells 1996, Cohen 2003). Still others see the New Economy as quintessentially knowledge based, and argue that 'knowledge capital' and 'creative capital' have replaced physical capital and human capital as the drivers of wealth generation and prosperity (Burton-Jones 1999). This latter characterization tends to highlight the rising importance of the 'creative' and 'cultural' industries – including not just information and communications technologies such as computer software and the Internet, but a range of 'knowledge intensive' activities for business and consumers, and in particular various 'cultural' industries and services such as media, film, fashion, music, advertising, architecture, and design (Bewes and Gilbert 2000, Gnad and Siegmann 2000). The increasing importance of these sectors of production and consumption has encouraged claims that we have entered the era of 'soft capitalism' (Thrift 1997), 'cultural capitalism' (Scott 2002, Sennett 2005), or 'dematerialized capitalism' (Coyle 1997, Coyle and Quah 2002). And spearheading this new 'creative capitalism', it is argued, is the rise of a new multicultural class of knowledge-intensive, enterprising and talented individuals (Florida 2003).

Whatever the specific epithet employed to describe the capitalism of the New Economy, the common underlying idea is that it is sufficiently distinctive that it can be contrasted with what, by implication, is the outgoing Old Economy. Table 2.2 summarizes some of the contrasts and shifts that various writers have claimed to discern. There is no doubt that many of the shifts and changes that

Table 2.2 From the Old to the New Economy?

Sphere	'Old Economy'	'New Economy'
ECONOMY		
Markets	Stable	Dynamic
Competition	National	Global
Organizational form	Hierarchical bureaucratic	Networked
Structure	Manufacturing core	Services core
Source of value	Raw materials, physical capital	Knowledge and social capital
BUSINESS		
Production	Mass production	Flexible production
Drivers of growth	Capital and labour	Innovation and knowledge/ideas
Technology driver	Mechanization	Digitization
Competitive advantage	Economies of scale	Innovation, quality and speed
Research/innovation	Low–moderate	High
Inter-firm relations	Go-it-alone	Alliances, collaboration, outsourcing
WORKERS		
Skills	Job-specific skills	Broad skills and adaptability
Education needs	One-off craft or degree	Life-long learning
Workplace relations	Adversarial	Collaborative
Nature of employment	Stable and secure	Marked by risk and opportunity
CONSUMERS		
Tastes	Stable	Changing rapidly
Goods/services	Mass, standardized	Customized/ individualized
Consumption	Utility-based and materialist	'Life-style' based and experiential
Financial basis	Cash society	Credit society
GOVERNMENTS		
Political credo	Keynesian–welfarism	Neoliberalism
Business	Impose regulations	Encourage growth opportunities
Regulation	Command and control	Market tools, flexibility
Government services	Nanny state	Enabling state
Policy mechanism	Centralized, top-down	Decentralized, locally delivered

Sources: Based on Atkinson, Court and Ward (1999); Coyle and Quah (2002); Reich (2001).

authors cite are indeed underway. But, as always, such dualistic portrayals should be treated with caution. Not only are some changes much more advanced than others, in many cases the contrasts are exaggerated, and some are based on over-drawn representations of both the Old Economy and the New Economy. Indeed, such dualistic characterizations of the Old and New Economy, like those put for-ward by the Washington-based Progressive Policy Institute (Atkinson *et al.* 1999) and by Coyle and Quah (2002), two enthusiastic British writers on the subject, suffer from the same problems as the oppositional tabulations of postFordism versus Fordism that have been more frequently employed by geographers (see, for example, Harvey 1989), namely: the over-blown image of an historic 'break with the past', the simplified impression of a coherent system-wide transformation, and the construction of over-stylized caricatures of the 'old' and the 'new' that are deliberately intended to play up the differences, and suppress the continuities, between the two. Moreover, the very term New Economy carries the inference that it is necessarily superior to the Old Economy, which by direct implication has been rendered sub-optimal. Thus, so this discourse continues, firms, governments and individuals that do not embrace the new, but cling on to the old structures, practices and ways of doing things, will get left behind in the New Economy:

> This new economy represents a tectonic upheaval in our commonwealth, a far more turbulent reordering than mere digital hardware has produced. The new economic order has its own distinctive opportunities and pitfalls. If past eco-nomic transformations are any guide, those who play by the rules will prosper, while those who ignore them will not. We have seen only the beginning of the anxiety, loss, excitement, and gains that many people will experience as our world shifts to a new highly technical planetary economy. (Kelly 1998, p. 1)

Kelly's sentiments – that there is an ineluctable momentum and trajectory to the New Economy, and that it requires adherence to a 'new set of rules' – resonates closely with the views of many neoliberal observers, including an increasing number of policy makers. Given that the notion and discourse of the New Economy emanated from the United States, and was founded on that country's 'economic resurgence' (Norton 2001) in the 1990s, it is perhaps not surprising that the key 'new rules' held to be driving the New Economy are widely equated with the defining characteristics and alleged superiority of American capitalism: economic liberalism, unfettered free markets, minimal state intervention, a culture of dynamic entrepreneurialism, labour market flex-ibility, deregulated financial markets, and low taxes.

These characteristics have been supported for a long time by advocates of eco-nomic liberalism, but they have found new justification in the supposed proper-ties and imperatives of the New Economy. The New Economy, it is asserted, thrives best in this sort of environment. Thus it is argued that the USA leads in the New Economy precisely because of its highly competitive market economy free of state regulations and state involvement, and the 'market-friendly' nature of its institutions (Shalman 1999, Eichengreen 2004). The advent of the Internet and other ICTs, it is further contended, reinforces this essential primacy of the market, since these technologies offer the prospects for expanding perfect markets and competition to all spheres of socio-economic activity, including culture, leisure, education, and health, and on a truly global basis. As Reich (2001) puts it, rather fancifully (and in typical American parlance), we have entered the 'Age of the Terrific Deal':

> It's based on technology and imagination. Combine the Internet, wireless satellites and fibre optics, great leaps in computing power, a quantum expansion of broadband connection … and you've got a giant real-time, global bazaar of almost infinite choice and possibility .…We're on the way to getting exactly what we want instantly, from anywhere, at the best value for money. (Reich 2001, p. 11)

Although such images are vastly overdrawn, there is no doubt that for many, economic liberalism is viewed the most appropriate, 'best-fit' policy model for the New Economy. For those of neoliberal inclination, the New Economy has become at once both a normative discourse – the desired (and inescapable) path of economic development – and the political justification for the reassertion of pro-market economic ideology. To compete in the globalizing New Economy, it is contended, governments have no choice but to switch their priorities away from expensive welfare provision and social support, to focus instead on promoting innovation, entrepreneurialism, and efficiency. In the neoliberal vision, the role of the state is not only to shape the New Economy, by allowing markets and competition free rein, but also to encourage individuals and firms to help themselves conform to it. Globalization is thus accepted as both inevitable and energizing, a stimulus to dynamic competitiveness and innovation and an opportunity for enterprising behaviour on an unprecedented scale.

There are then, several different but intersecting images or 'models' of the New Economy: those that focus on a renewal of macro-economic performance; those that emphasize the reconfiguration of micro-economic structures and processes; those that point to an historic information-based technological revolution; those that detect the emergence of a new post-industrial, 'dematerialized' cultural capitalism; and those that stress the shift to a new neoliberal political–ideological mode of socio-economic regulation. All of these representations capture certain aspects of what is undeniably a new 'reality', but all do so in a selective way by over-emphasizing particular features of the New Economy, often beyond what is warranted by the evidence, with the result that certain features have been exaggerated, even to the point of caricature. In this way there is as much myth as there is reality about the New Economy (see, for example, Pontin 1997, Siroh 1999, Gadrey 2001, van Reener 2001, Wadhwani 2002).

The contentious claims of the New Economy discourse

Indeed, several contentious claims have been made about the New Economy and its effects (see Table 2.3), each attracting its own counterclaims. One of the

Table 2.3 Some of the claims and counter-claims surrounding the 'New Economy'

Claim	Counter-claim
The New Economy has enabled a productivity miracle	Productivity gains have been much exaggerated, and are confined to just a few sectors. The impact of computers and ICT on productivity is far from clear
The New Economy has signalled the end of the economic cycle	While the cycle has certainly been attenuated in recent years, this does not mean the business cycle is dead. Economic growth remains fragile and unstable
In the New Economy, manufacturing no longer matters	In fact, manufacturing is still the key source of productivity growth, and vital for 'hard goods', many of which are required by high-tech, information-based services and by cultural industries. Reality is that division between manufacturing and services is becoming increasingly blurred
The New Economy has produced a jobs miracle	While employment has expanded, it has also become increasingly polarized, between the technical, highly skilled and professional employment at the one end and large numbers of low-skilled, often insecure and unrewarding, jobs at the other
The New Economy promises prosperity for all	The claim that everyone benefits from the New economy is erroneous. In reality the income distribution has widened and financial gains have been overwhelming appropriated by only a small minority, and 'trickle down' effects have been practically non-existent
In the New Economy, location no longer matters	While ICT and related technologies permit functional propinquity without the need for physical proximity, nevertheless the localization of economic activity is arguably, becoming more, not less important. The qualities of place and individual face-to-face contact have assumed increasing prominence

most debated is the claim that it has underpinned an unprecedented phase of productivity growth and economic prosperity. A key problem here is that both the measurement of productivity growth, and apportioning that part due to capital deepening in the form of investment in IT, are very far from straightforward tasks. Proponents of the view that productivity growth in the US economy accelerated in the New Economy-led boom from 1992 onwards, and especially since 1995, contend that this has indeed been due in large part to investment in IT in industry and services, aided by favourable, pro-market economic policies. For example, according to Jorgenson, Ho and Stiroh (2004) more than half of the average annual growth in US labour productivity over 1995–2003 can be attributed to IT effects (see Table 2.4). Their explanation runs as follows. Fundamental technological progress is the driving force that has allowed each generation of computer equipment and software to outperform prior generations. This technological progress is manifest in Moore's Law, the doubling of computer

Table 2.4 Contribution of IT to USA productivity growth (according to Jorgenson et al. 2004)

Average annual growth rates (per cent per annum)	1959–2003	1959–1973	1973–1995	1995–2003
Labour productivity growth of which	2.21	2.85	1.49	3.06
(1) Capital deepening	1.21	1.14	0.89	1.75
of which IT	0.44	0.21	0.41	0.92
(2) Total factor produc-	0.74	1.12	0.34	1.14
tivity of which IT	0.25	0.09	0.24	0.53

Source: Jorgenson *et al.* (2004).

chip power every eighteen months or so. As a result, the quality of IT has improved even as prices have fallen – a change that is measured as 'total factor productivity' growth in IT production. In response to the enormous relative price declines for IT investment, firms have rapidly substituted IT assets for other production inputs. This massive investment in IT leads to the significant contribution of IT capital deepening to labour productivity growth (see also Temple 2002).

Others, however, contest this interpretation of events. For example, Farrell (2003) argues that the recent improvement in US productivity is almost entirely due to just six sectors, specifically: retailing, securities brokerage, wholesaling, semiconductors, computer assembly, and telecommunications. These sectors account for 76 per cent of the country's productivity gain, but only for 32 per cent of US GDP. Further, she argues that IT *per se* has not been the primary factor in the productivity of these sectors; rather, she contends that intensifying competition has stimulated managers in these activities to innovate aggressively in products, business practices and technology, and it is this that has led to gains in productivity. In other words, she argues that America's New Economy productivity boom has in fact been very uneven, and much more complex in its origins than simply being the result of IT and computers.

But in any case, the basic evidence for the claim that the New Economy is spearheading a productivity miracle is itself contentious. As always when comparing economic performance over time, much depends on the specific periods and start and end dates chosen. Indeed, it is possible to argue that the post-1992 'surge' in US productivity growth is merely a return to its pre-1973 trend. This is evident if we compare the 1992–2000 boom (that is, up to the NASDAQ crash in 2001–2002), with previous economic expansions (Table 2.5). Over 1992–2000, labour productivity grew by 2.12 per cent per annum. While this was certainly an improvement over the two previous boom periods (1976–1979 and 1983–1990), it is in fact less than the growth achieved in the long expansionary period between 1959–1973. Interestingly, Jorgenson, Ho and Stiroh (op. cit.) predict that US productivity will grow at 2.56 per cent over the 2003–2013 decade, which if correct, is again no higher than that achieved over 1959–1973.

Table 2.5 US labour productivity growth over successive economic expansions

	1950–1953	1955–1957	1959–1973	1976–1979	1983–1990	1992–2000
Per cent per annum	3.45	1.97	2.97	1.53	1.83	2.12

Source: US Bureau of Labor Statistics.

All this is not to deny that productivity growth has picked up significantly compared to the stagnant 1970s and 1980s. Nor is to deny that IT may well have played a major part in this recovery. And of course, we do not know what would have happened to productivity growth in the absence of the IT revolution of the past two decades. What could possibly be argued is that the IT-based New Economy has indeed helped to promote a new phase of productivity growth; but it is claiming too much to refer to this new phase as a 'miracle', or to attribute all of the growth to IT and computers.

Equally, and for the same reasons, there is also doubt about claims that the New Economy has so changed the fundamentals and operation of the economy as to have underpinned an unprecedented phase of low-inflation, low-unemployment growth, it has put an end to economic recession. In the UK, for example, the Government (HM Treasury 2005) has boasted that the period of uninterrupted growth since 1997 is the longest period of sustained expansion for 200 years. However, again, the growth record in the USA and in the UK since 1992 has not been much different from the 1959–1973 period, or from 1983–1990. It is true that since 1992 growth has been accompanied by healthy job expansion and low inflation, and that neither country has (yet) experienced a recurrence of the deep recessions of 1974–1975, 1980–1983 and 1990–1992. But, the post-1992 economic boom has not in fact been that exceptional in historical terms (see Table 2.6), and the stock market collapse in 2000–2001 testifies to the latent financial instability of the new capitalism. To be sure, the plummeting of stock values in 2000–2001 did not trigger a more general economic collapse, which some have taken as a sign of the resilience of the fundamentals of the New Economy. But neither is this a valid basis on which to proclaim the 'death of the business cycle'. What the bursting of the dot.com bubble in 2000–2001 demonstrated was that the New Economy is no more immune to instabilities and unsustainable expansions than was the Old Economy. This is not to argue that the New Economy is no different from the Old: patently it is. But it would be premature indeed to insist that it has transcended the inherent rhythmic tendencies of capitalist accumulation.

Similarly bold but suspect claims have been made about the beneficial impact of the New Economy on employment and work. Many economists, technologists and management consultants have argued that the New Economy has unleashed a new phase of employment expansion, involving the creation of millions of new jobs in services, creative industries, and high technology. Furthermore, these same

Table 2.6 An unprecedented growth boom? Average annual changes in real GDP in successive economic expansions in the USA

Per cent per annum	1950–1953	1955–1957	1959–1973	1976–1979	1983–1990	1992–2000
USA	6.2	3.7	4.4	4.7	4.0	3.6
UK	2.3	0.7	3.3	2.9	3.4	3.4

Sources: Based on Harms and Knaff (2003); Economic History Services (www.ch.net/hmit/ukgdp).

commentators predict that the New Economy will liberate the workforce, bringing self-managed work teams, decentralized decision-making, increased self-employment, greater flexibility of working patterns, and significant improvements in work–life balance. Reality, however, is more complicated, and much less reassuring, than these highly positive and optimistic accounts would have us believe.

Both the USA and the UK have indeed generated large numbers of jobs since the early-1990s; non-agricultural employment increased by some 19.2 million (18.5 per cent) in 1992–2003 in the case of the USA, and by 3.2 million (14.7 per cent) in the UK. But the quality, pay and security of these jobs have varied considerably (see for example, Herzenberg, Alic and Wial 1998, Reich 2001, Head 2003). As the pace at which jobs get redefined seems to increase progressively, as firms reorganize work in response to the pressures of globalization and the opportunities afforded by the new technologies, so workers are increasingly being forced to move across firms, and even across types of work. For the higher skilled knowledge classes – professional, technical, scientific, creative and other 'symbolic' workers in high-technology activities, high-end business and personal services, the media and other cultural industries – employment opportunities and conditions have generally improved. Flexibility for such groups often means greater autonomy over working patterns. Yet, at the same time, many of the new jobs have been for those with low skills and qualifications in low wage service jobs with few if any career prospects (Freeman 2002). 'Flexibility' for these types of New Economy workers often means increased insecurity, unsocial working patterns and increased control by employers (Benner 2002).

For example, new business models and the computerization of labour processes have simplified the work of many lower-level (and even some middle-level) employees, fencing them in with elaborate rules and subjecting them to digital monitoring to make sure the rules are obeyed (Head 2003). Thus in the call centre industry workers are subject to the indignity of scripting software that lays out the exact conversation, line by line, with strict time limits, which employees must follow when speaking with customers. In many such cases, computer-routinized and regulated systems devalue rather than enhance a worker's experience and skill, and subject employees to a degree of supervision that is excessive and demeaning. Even in some higher-skill professions (such as health care and education), new computer-driven performance-monitoring and financial-controlling management systems constrain the freedom and flexibility of employees and require a considerable intensification of worker effort (Head op. cit.; Slaughter and Rhoades 2004).

Much of the hype surrounding the 'flexibility' of the New Economy labour market is thus highly one-sided. There are prices to be paid for the 'new flexibility'. It separates workers from the social institutions – long-term jobs, clearly defined skill and occupational structures, predictable incomes, family, and stable communities – that sustained economic expansions in the past. The New Economy may be creating large numbers of new jobs, but it has also ushered in a new age of labour market insecurity and polarization (Elliott and Atkinson 1998, Carnoy 2000).

One dramatic expression of this polarization is the marked widening of income inequalities that has occurred in those countries – like the USA and UK – that have led the development of the New Economy. It has been a recurring claim made about the New Economy that it heralds a new phase of rising prosperity: the very subtitle of Coyle's (2001) book, *How the New Capitalism Benefits All,* clearly conveys this image. If New Economy advocates are correct when they maintain that a new era of prosperity is upon us then we should see strong wage growth across all groups over the most recent expansion (Siroh 2002). The data, however, show something rather different. The overall rise in real wages in both the USA and UK during the New Economy boom of 1992–2000 was in fact modest by historical standards (Table 2.7). In the case of the USA, the negative real wage growth of the 1970s and 1980s may have been reversed, but real wages actually rose more slowly than in the booms during the 1950s and 1960s.

Yet this unremarkable growth in fact conceals pronounced disparities in wage and income gains across different groups of workers. In both the USA and UK, it has been those in the top wage and income bands that have prospered (Aghion and Howitt 2002). These include many working in the creative and cultural industries (the more successful 'celebrities' and 'superstars' in media, sport, music, software, architecture, fashion, and the like), in high-technology sectors, finance, property development, legal and related professions, and in particular many of today's new breed of corporate leaders and CEOs. Both countries have boasted a dramatic increase in the numbers of millionaires, and lists of 'the nation's richest people' have become the focus of regular media attention. Executive pay and benefits have spiralled upwards, not just in salary terms but also in the form of stock options and extraordinarily generous pension handouts. Such handouts

Table 2.7 A new prosperity? Average annual change in real wages in successive economic expansions in the USA and UK

Per cent	1950–1953	1955–1957	1959–1973	1976–1979	1983–1990	1992–2000
USA	2.1	1.6	1.9	−0.2	−0.6	0.5
UK	0.8	1.9	3.5	−0.1	2.5	1.4

Source: Based on Harms and Knaff (2003); Economic History Services (www.eh.net/hmit/ukearncpi).

and annual bonuses for top bosses often exceed what the average worker earns in a lifetime.

It is perhaps no accident that the growth in income inequality has been faster in the USA, the leader in the New Economy. All the indicators point to a dramatic widening of the income distribution there (see Table 2.8). In what is one of the most critical commentaries on this trend, Krugman (2002) argues that the 'new gilded age' of the rich in the USA marks a very disturbing reversal of the post-War commitment, and trend, to greater equality:

> For the past 15 years it has been hard to deny the evidence for growing inequality in the United States. Census data clearly show a rising share of income going to the top 20 per cent of families, and within that top 20 per cent to the top 5 per cent, with a declining share going to families in the middle. Nonetheless, denial of that evidence is a sizable, well-financed industry. Four years ago Alan Greenspan (why did anyone ever think he was nonpartisan?) gave a speech... that amounted to an attempt to deny that there has been any real increases in equality in America ...You might think that 1987, the year Tom Wolfe published his novel *The Bonfire of the Vanities,* and Oliver Stone released his movie *Wall Street,* marked the high tide of America's new money culture. But in 1987 the top 0.01 per cent earned only about 40 per cent of what they do today, and top executives less than fifth as much. The America of *Wall Street* and *The Bonfire of the Vanities* was positively egalitarian compared to the country we live in today. (pp. 2–4)

In the UK, the income distribution has also widened since the 1980s (Table 2.9), albeit not so dramatically as in the USA. Unlike in the USA, the UK Labour Government since 1997 has taken the problem of low incomes and poverty very seriously and has introduced several measures designed to reduce both. Nevertheless, even though these policies have arguably stopped the growth in inequality in recent years, disparities remain noticeably higher than in 1990. Again, as in the USA, the incomes of the top 1 and 5 per cent have pulled progressively ahead of the rest.

Table 2.8 New Economy – new inequality. The growth in inequality of family incomes in the USA, 1980–2001

	Share of income (per cent)					
	Lowest fifth	*Second fifth*	*Third fifth*	*Fourth fifth*	*Highest fifth*	*Top 5 per cent*
2001	3.5	8.7	14.6	23.0	50.1	22.4
1995	3.7	9.1	15.2	23.3	48.7	21.0
1990	3.9	9.6	15.9	24.0	46.6	18.6
1985	4.0	9.7	16.3	24.6	45.3	17.0
1980	4.3	10.3	16.9	24.9	43.7	15.8

Source: United States Census Bureau (www.census.gov/hhes/income/histinc/f02x1.html).

Table 2.9 New Economy – new inequality. Distribution of pre-tax incomes (£) in the United Kingdom, 1990–2003 (by percentile)

	1	5	10	90	95	99	Ratio of 90/10	Ratio of 99/1
1990–91	3,190	3,890	4,650	23,200	30,100	57,200	6.47	17.93
1991–92	3,500	4,250	5,030	24,800	32,100	63,900	6.38	18.25
1992–93	3,630	4,400	5,160	25,500	33,100	62,800	6.41	17.30
1993–94	3,670	4,440	5,220	25,800	33,500	64,800	6.41	17.65
1994–95	3,690	4,460	5,270	26,100	33,700	68,400	6.39	18.53
1995–96	3,760	4,640	5,420	27,100	35,100	69,900	6.47	18.59
1996–97	4,000	4,900	5,650	28,300	37,200	76,100	6.58	19.02
1997–98	4,260	5,220	6,020	29,400	39,000	83,700	6.47	19.64
1998–99	4,450	5,410	6,220	31,100	41,600	90,000	6.68	20.22
1999–00	4,600	5,630	6,570	33,000	44,600	96,400	6.78	20.95
2000–01	4,620	5,520	6,480	34,200	46,700	101,800	7.20	22.03
2001–02	4,780	5,850	6,860	36,200	49,200	107,100	7.17	22.40
2002–03	4,860	5,960	6,970	36,700	49,800	108,300	7.14	22.28
Change 1990–2003 per cent	52.3	53.2	49.8	58.1	65.4	89.3		

Source: Inland Revenue (www.inlandrevenue.gov.uk/stats/income_distribution/menu.htm).

Arguments have raged in the USA over the causes of the new inequality. Both globalization and technological change – the two key driving forces of the New Economy – have played their part (Harms and Knaff 2003), the former by depressing the incomes of low-wage unskilled workers, the latter by rewarding educated and skilled workers demanded in the expanding knowledge-based sectors of the economy. In addition, Krugman (op. cit.) suggests that a 'new culture of greed' – and especially corporate greed – and a new ethos of 'anything goes' have also emerged in US society over the past two decades. Management consultants, many economists, numerous politicians, even the media, seek to legitimize and justify previously unthinkable levels of pay for celebrities, executives and the like in terms of 'leadership' – meaning personal charismatic leadership – and the need for incentives to attract and promote the best, from managerial expertise to sporting talent, especially now that we are in a global marketplace. But this shift in culture and ethos is itself closely related to, and supported by, the neoliberal political ideology that has thrived around the New Economy. Through tax cuts and the celebration of enterprise and wealth creation, over the past two decades US and UK governments have fuelled the new social norm of greed. High incomes at the top, we are told, are the result of a free-market system that provides huge incentives for performance. And the system delivers performance, which means that greater wealth at the top doesn't come at the expense of those lower down in the income distribution: everyone is better off. Why the wealthy and successful should need ever-greater incentives is not adequately explained. Nor is there evidence of any real 'trickle down' of wealth and income to other groups.

Claims that the New Economy means 'prosperity for all' have to date proved utterly unconvincing.

Where is the 'New Economy'? The exaggerated death of geography

It is with respect to geography and location that, many claim, the New Economy will have the most potentially destabilizing implications, for, according to such commentators, together the new technologies and globalization are expunging local difference and rendering space and place irrelevant. The claim – the myth – is twofold: first, that the New Economy signals the 'death of distance', and second, that because location no longer matters, all areas and places can share in the growth that the New Economy brings: in effect that the New Economy at last spells the end of spatial economic disparities.

In its extreme versions, this argument sees no role for geography. Thus in the words of the cyber-guru, William Gibson, 'the Internet could one day be seen as being something terrifically significant, something akin to the building of cities. It's postnational and postgeographical' (1996). In somewhat similar vein, Quah – one of the initial expositors of the notion of the 'weightless economy' – argues that 'dematerialised commodities show no respect for space or geography' (1996). This he contends is due to a property he calls 'infinite expansibility', that is the idea that the use of a dematerialized object by one person does not prevent a multitude of others using it, even simultaneously, regardless of their different locations. Trade in such goods and services is not an exchange, in the conventional socio-economic sense, but nearly costless reproduction, again regardless of location. This property of an increasing number and variety of goods and services is thereby taken by some commentators to signal the imminent 'death of distance', the 'fate of location', at the hand of the new ICT economy. Here, for example, is Cairncross, claiming in prophetic tones that:

> The death of distance as a determinant of the cost of communicating will probably be the single most important force changing society in the [twenty-first] century. Technological change has the power to revolutionize the way people live, and this one will be no exception. It will alter, in ways that are only dimly imaginable, decisions about where people work and what kind of work they do, concepts of national borders and sovereignty, and patterns of international trade. Its effects may well be as pervasive as those of the discovery of electricity, which led in time to the creation of the sky-scraper cities of Manhattan and Hong Kong, and transformed labour productivity in the home. (1997, p. 1)

The prediction is that in the New Economy location will no longer be key to most business decisions. Companies can now locate any screen-based activity anywhere on the globe, wherever they can find the best bargain of skills and productivity. The trend towards the off-shoring and out-sourcing of many online services to developing countries – from monitoring security screens, running help-lines, call centres, writing software and so forth – is considered to be merely one aspect of an accelerating 'annihilation of distance' (Dore 2001) by the globalizing power of ICT and the Internet. Indeed, given that the skill required for the provision of many of these online services is relatively straightforward and can be easily and quickly learnt, the range of locations for these activities is potentially huge. At the same time, as an increasing proportion of households become connected to the Internet, and especially broadband, so they can access these online services regardless of where they, or the service providers, are located.

There is no need for geographical proximity between the customer and the service. Moreover, this New Economy of online services 'de-spatializes' labour markets and communities of practice in that the 'horizontal bonds among people performing the same job in different parts of the world will strengthen. Common interests, experiences and pursuits rather than proximity will bind these communities together' (Cairncross 1997, p. xii). In the New Economy, the new information technologies confer functional propinquity without the need for spatial proximity.

Thus, a central hallmark of the New Economy, we are told, is the 'delocalization' of socio-economic activity, the lifting of economic relationships out of local knowledge networks and circuits of exchange:

> It means the displacement of activities that until recently were local, into networks of relationships whose reach is distant or worldwide. Domestic prices of consumer goods, financial assets such as stocks and bonds, even labour – are less and less governed by local and national conditions (Gray 1998, p. 57)

> In the emerging global bazaar, distance is on the way to all but vanishing. The economy is moving from things towards weightless services that can be transmitted anywhere around the world, at almost no cost. With everything a click away, there's less reason to shop locally. Local economies won't vanish anytime soon, but the Internet will steadily erode them. You will no longer need the local pharmacist to fill your prescription, or even a local doctor to give you one … you'll circumvent local car dealers and garage mechanics. … An ever larger proportion of international television shows, news, designs, software, and business services (management consulting, marketing, financial legal, engineering) that no longer need to be located near their clients. (Reich 2001, pp. 16-19)

Some do not stop there but indulge in even more fanciful flights of imagination, pronouncing the coming of some sort of telecosmic utopia of unlimited and ubiquitous bandwidth, wherein the world wide web not only erases the limits of geography but even physicality itself:

> Within the market space of the net, anyone anywhere can issue a petition or publication, utter a cry for help, broadcast a work of art. Anyone can create a product, launch a company, finance its growth, and spin it off into the web. Imagine that a worker could collaborate with any other worker at any time. Imagine the

mesh of lights − the radiance of sine waves − as an efflorescence of learning curves as people around the world launch projects and experiments without requiring any physical plant and equipment and regimented workers in Adam Smith's factory. Without the overhead and entropy, noise and geographical friction, entrepreneurial creativity takes off. (Gilder 2000, pp. 259–264)

A frequently implied corollary of all this is that in a world where the need for physical proximity in economic relationships is rapidly being lessened, even eliminated completely, and where many of the services and products consumed are essentially nonmaterial in nature, and do not require large capital equipment, economic activities are free to locate almost anywhere. As such, the conventional location attraction factors and the most favoured locations of the Old Economy no longer exert the pull they once did, and now all regions, cities and localities can in principle participate in and benefit from the New Economy. The image, to adapt Reich's phrase, is that of a 'locational bazaar'.

This in turn is taken by some to imply that in the New Economy we should expect spatial inequalities in economic growth and prosperity to narrow appreciably, as lagging regions, cities and localities find they can more easily catch up with the prosperous regions, cities and localities in this 'location-neutral' digital environment. The presumption is that most regions and cities can access and insert themselves into the 'soft world' of the digital and culturally orientated economy.

Other observers, including almost all geographers, contest this prognosis. However, the counter-arguments take somewhat different forms. In his monumental work on the Information Age, Castells puts forward the view that the explosion in interaction made possible by the new information technology revolution is forging a new spatial logic to socio-economic activity, a logic he terms a 'space of flows' that is dialectically opposed to the historically rooted spatial organization of our common experience, the 'space of places':

> The emphasis on interactivity between places breaks up spatial patterns of behaviour into a fluid network of exchanges that underlies the emergence of a new kind of space, the space of flows. Thus the network of communication is the fundamental spatial configuration: places do not disappear, but their logic and their meaning become absorbed in the network. The technological infrastructure that builds up the network defines the new space, very much like railways defined 'economic regions' and 'national markets' in the industrial economy. (Castells 1996, pp. 398, 412).

At its most fundamental, according to Castells, this new space of (information) flows is a virtual geography of the electronic impulses that are the Internet and other forms of electronic telecommunications. The same basic idea has been a key theme in the related literature about the globalization of money, where it is argued the new information technologies have revolutionized the nature and operation of the transactional spaces of global financial markets, indeed the nature and meaning of money itself. Thus, Kobrin describes the world financial system as a construct 'in electronic space rather than geographic space ... a network integrated through electronic information systems' (1997a, p. 158; see also 1997b). Similarly, Cohen (1998) actually uses Castells' notion of the 'space of flows' in his 'flow-based' characterization of the new geography of money.

What connects such counter-arguments is perhaps not the idea that geographical space is now irrelevant, but that for an increasing array of socio-economic activity the nature of geographical space has changed, from a fixed physical metric to a relational entity, defined and constantly redefined, by flows of information and electronic communication. But this is not to suggest that the space of places no longer matters. Even the 'virtual space' of Internet flows has a geography (Dodge and Kitchin 2000, 2005). Indeed, data on Internet traffic and connectivity reveal distinct geographies to the new space of flows. At one level, maps of global Internet traffic reveal how these flows are overwhelmingly concentrated between the three major trading blocs of Western Europe, the USA and Japan–South East Asia (Telegeography Research 2005): just as these blocs dominate world trade, so (unsurprisingly) they also account for the bulk of Internet flows. At another level, the maps of connectivity within major blocs and countries, such as Western Europe and the USA, reveal how Internet service and bandwidth providers (ISPs and BPs), network access points (NAPs) and Internet exchange points (IXPs), cluster in and around the major cities (see Table 2.10). These cities are the hubs and nodes of the largest networks (the 'backbone'), that own or lease international and national high-speed fibre optic networks and deliver Internet and broadband services around the world for the many smaller networks. In most cases these backbone hubs also reach businesses and consumers directly by operating their own vertically integrated ISPs. Research suggests that spatial proximity and face-to-face contact actually play a key role in the locational behaviour of ISPs, geographical agglomeration serving to reduce transaction costs, facilitate 'peering agreements' between networks, and help verify brand reputation and trust in cyberspace (Giovannetti *et al.* 2003). Place matters even for the Internet.

As Castells himself acknowledges, the 'space of flows' of the Information age is anchored in, articulated by, and constituted through its physical nodes and hubs: the electronic network links up specific places, which have different roles

Table 2.10 Major bandwidth provider nodes in the USA and Europe, 2004 (top five cities)

Europe		USA	
City	*No of bandwidth providers*	*City*	*No of bandwidth providers*
London	33	New York	32
Frankfurt	32	Chicago	24
Paris	24	Atlanta	24
Amsterdam	24	Los Angeles	23
Stockholm	20	Dallas	23

Source: Telegeography Research (2005).

in this global cyberspace. Some places are exchanges, communication hubs coordinating the interaction of the elements integrated into the network. Other places are the nodes of the system, the locations of strategic functions that build up a series of locality-based activities and organizations around a key function in the network. For example, the global financial centres (London, New York, Tokyo, Hong Kong, Singapore, Paris, Frankfurt, Milan, Sydney, and certain other cities) that organize and control the virtual network of international money transactions confirm that even in Castells' new 'space of flows', places (locations) remain of key importance. The annihilation of space, of distance, by the digital revolution has most certainly not rendered place irrelevant.

In fact, localization appears to be a characteristic feature of most New Economy industries and services, whether high-tech activities (such as computers, software, biotechnology), or so-called creative and cultural industries (such as fashion, design, media, music, and the like). Thus while globalization and the new information and communication technologies are rendering the 'national economy' increasingly 'borderless' and problematic as a concept, it seems that economic production and organization are becoming increasingly localized. As the geographer Allen Scott puts it:

> ...with the wholesale resurgence of localised production systems, national economies are starting to look more and more like loose confederations of regional economies. ... Even if the continued existence of national monetary and fiscal systems means that it is still meaningful to speak of national economic aggregates, what is important for our purposes is that *systems of production and exchange* are increasingly being reconfigured at geographical scales of operation other than the national. (1998, p. 22; emphasis as in the original)

And, similarly, according to the business management guru Michael Porter:

> In a global economy – which boasts rapid transportation, high speed communications and accessible markets – one would expect location to diminish in importance. But the opposite is true. The enduring competitive advantages in a global economy are often heavily localised, arising from concentrations of highly specialised skills and knowledge, institutions, rivalry, related businesses, and sophisticated customers. (1998, p. 90)

Porter's own, highly influential 'cluster' concept has rapidly become the standard lexicon used to describe and analyse these localized concentrations of economic activity. The more so because the concept has become increasingly associated with New Economy activities and the 'new competition' these are allegedly driving (Porter 1998b, Porter and Ackerman 2001). Norton (2001), for example, argues that the global leadership of the USA in the New Economy derives precisely from the growth there of a number of dynamic clusters of innovative entrepreneurialism. Emblematic New Economy activities that conform to this clustered mode of development include computers, software, and biotechnology. Innovation in these sectors appears to be a distinctly localized phenomenon, deriving from the intense inter-firm rivalry and inter-firm knowledge spillovers that spatial clustering tends to produce. But clusters are also to be found in a whole range of other knowledge-intensive and 'creative' sectors, such as media, film, fashion, design, finance, and the like. Many cities in particular are witnessing a resurgence of vitality and growth based on a new urban economy of cultural production (Scott 2000, Power and Scott 2004). In the view of writers such as Florida (2003), a new 'creative class' is on the rise, and it is those cities and regions that are able to attract such people that are leading the New Economy. He identifies two 'major trends':

> The first is a new geographic sorting along class lines. Different classes have long sorted themselves into neighbourhoods within a city or region. But now we find a large-scale resorting of people among cities and regions, nationwide, with some regions becoming centres of the Creative Class, while others are composed of larger shares of Working Class or Service Class. ... The second is that the centres of the Creative Class are more likely to be economic winners. ... The emerging geography of the Creative Class is dramatically affecting the competitive advantage of regions across the United States. Significant competitive advantage goes to regions that are home to substantial concentrations of this class, whereas regions that are home to large concentrations of the working and Service Classes are by and large being left behind. (Florida 2003, pp. 234, 243).

Florida's depiction of the 'new class structure' of the creative economy can be questioned on several fronts, for example: the criteria used to distinguish his 'creative' class from the 'service' and 'working' classes; his depiction of the spatial 'sorting' of these different classes as some sort of voluntaristic process; and the somewhat stylized geography of creativity that he invokes, which seems to ignore the interdependencies between his three classes, and their frequent co-existence in the same city or region. Nevertheless, what is all too evident is that the New Economy is forging a new landscape of development no less spatially uneven than that of the Old Economy that it is replacing: a New Economy maybe, but capitalism as usual as far as geographically uneven development is concerned. In both the USA and the UK, particular cities and regions appear to have secured a clear 'first mover advantage' in the New Economy. Various rankings of cities and regions on various New Economy knowledge and competitiveness indices testify to this (see Atkinson *et al.* 1999, Atkinson and Gottlieb 2001, Atkinson 2002, Robert Huggins Associates 2003, 2004, 2005, and Local Futures 2005). And there is evidence to suggest that the cities and regions leading the process are also among those that are enjoying the fastest economic growth and highest wealth creation (see Tables 2.11 and 2.12, and Figure 2.1). But, as the data also reveal, the mapping between the geographies of the New Economy and the geographies of economic prosperity is by no means exactly one-to-one.

In fact, even those cities and regions that have been identified as spearheading the New Economy contain their own distinctly uneven socio-economic

Table 2.11 The top twelve 'New Economy' cities in the US, 2001 (rankings out of 261 metropolitan areas)

	The digital economy	Knowledge jobs	Innovative capacity	Globalization	Economic growth (GDP)
San Francisco	1	7	2	4	1
Austin	2	4	3	12	9
San Diego	3	11	6	6	6
Washington DC	4	1	8	14	22
Denver	5	2	7	48	2
Dallas	6	27	25	25	13
Seattle	7	6	9	1	5
Los Angeles	8	49	28	22	16
Salt Lake City	9	10	11	28	15
Atlanta	10	15	22	21	10
Phoenix	11	38	27	13	8
Kansas City	12	36	41	22	20

Source: Atkinson and Gottlieb (2001).

geographies. Almost all such 'success story', 'high-tech' and 'creative' regions, cities and clusters contain social groups and local communities that thus far have failed to share in and benefit from the wealth and prosperity that the New Economy is claimed to bring. Just as the New Economy has widened income inequalities across society, so it has opened up and accentuated spatial inequalities in incomes and welfare. For example, take the case of London. This city stands out as the core centre of the UK's knowledge economy, and overall has

Table 2.12 The South and East lead Britain's New Economy, 2002 (regional rankings)

	Knowledge business	R&D spending per worker	Innovation rate	E-commerce	Venture capital	Growth in GDP per head
London	1	6	6	1	1	3
South East	2	2	2	2	2	2
South West	3	4	3	4	9	6
Eastern	4	1	1	5	3	1
North West	5	3	5	11	5	10
E Midlands	6	5	4	6	8	9
W Midlands	7	7	7	7	6	5
Yorks–Humb	8	10	10	8	7	4
Scotland	9	8	9	10	4	11
North East	10	11	8	3	10	12
Wales	11	9	11	12	12	8
N Ireland	12	12	12	9	11	7

Source: Robert Huggins Associates (2004, 2005), ONS, British Venture Capital Association, European Commission.

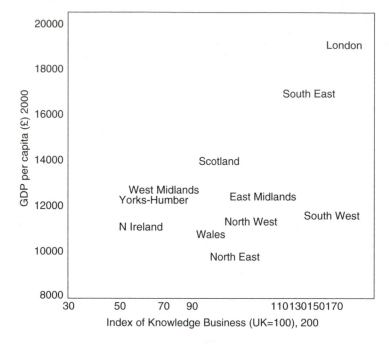

Figure 2.1 The New Economy and regional prosperity in the UK. Source: Huggins
        (2003), ONS.

the highest GDP per head (Figure 2.1). But not only does it have some of the richest postcode areas in the UK, it also has internal social divides that are not simply the result of certain groups – such as Florida's 'service classes' – being excluded from or bypassed by the New Economy, but in some cases are a direct product of the very concentration of New Economy activities in these areas. Thus, the growth of a local population of high-earning technological, knowledge and creative workers itself produces a corresponding growth of low-wage, low-skilled activities – from cleaning, to security – to service the business and personal needs of the New Economy enterprises and classes. High levels of social and wage polarization can thus be found even within the exemplar New Economy success regions. Further, the problems facing the low-skill, low-wage service workers in such areas are in fact exacerbated by the impact that the high wages of the elite symbolic and technical workers have on local house prices.

At all spatial scales, therefore, geography is intimately and inextricably bound up with the processes at work shaping the New Economy. Contrary to those who predict the 'end of geography' and the 'death of distance' at the hand of the new information technologies and globalization, we are witnessing the reassertion of location and place, albeit in different ways, and with different roles from those of the past. Space, place and location have undoubtedly become much more relational in nature and function. However, what is happening is not the demise of geography in economic life, but the reconfiguration of its meaning and role, rendering it far more complex in the process. We have barely begun to decipher and understand this new complexity.

New Economy – new challenges?

So where does all this leave us? A basic point is that this is not the first New Economy. There have always been 'new economies' – the concept is not tied to any one particular time or technology. Throughout history there have been periodic transformative developments in technology and economic organization – 'gales of creative destruction' – that have brought radical changes to market boundaries, expanded the scope to exploit intellectual capital, created new industries, services and products for major sections of society as new customers triggered off significant changes in the interactions and operating principles of enterprises, and redefined the relationship between customers and suppliers, and between the state and the economy. The advent of steam power had this effect, enabling knowledge embedded in engineered products to replicate itself on a mass production scale. The spread of the railroads subsequently produced yet another major shift, creating and linking large integrated markets in many countries, and opening access to products to millions of people. The invention of electricity and the petrol engine then spawned another phase of economy-wide and society-wide reorganization. And now developments in information communications technology are once again leading to a new regime of economic accumulation and social regulation. In each of these historic inflections, the key catalyst for change has been the emergence and diffusion of a 'general purpose technology' that not only spawns new industries, activities and products, but which eventually reshapes the principles and operation of everyday socio-economic life.

This is not to deny that many of the claims made for the contemporary New Economy have been highly extravagant and exaggerated. To the contrary, a large body of myth has quickly built up around it. The term has been a rhetorical device, a script used by business, media and politicians alike to hype, promote, subscribe to and live out a particular model of capitalism. Little wonder that many commentators see it largely as a form of discourse:

> What seems certain is that by the mid 1990s the new economy had already become a stable rhetorical form, in common usage in business and government and seeping into popular culture. In effect the new economy had become a kind of *brand,* compounding in one phrase the attraction and rewards of a new version of capitalism. (Thrift 2005, p. 114)

Yet to interpret the New Economy as a whole simply as a discursive, cultural or even mythical construct, would be to ignore the fact that key economic materialities – the state of technology, the nature of capital accumulation and investment, the flow of circulating capital, the nature of work, the inequalities of rewards – are undergoing real and profound change:

> Certainly, words and language are a critical moment in the circuit of mediations through which economic reality operates, and there can be no doubt that many unique effects are set in motion at this particular level of analysis … [But] there are also deeply-rooted economic logics and dynamics at work in the contemporary space economy, and at least some of these require investigation on their own terms above and beyond invocations of the causal powers of discourse and culture. (Scott 2004, p. 490)

Indeed, even Thrift is forced to acknowledge that there is more to the New Economy than just discourse:

> It is easy to be cynical about the new economy. … But I think it is important not to be quite so dismissive. … To write it off as simply a discourse is to misunderstand discourse's materiality. To begin with, it is by no means certain that the widespread adoption of technologies and new modes of industrial organization over the past five years has not generated growth in the output produced from a given amount of labour and capital. Then, a global software industry has been produced in a quite remarkably short space of time. And, as Chandler and Cortado (2000) point out, software is profoundly discontinuous with the past, not only in how it has appeared in the economy, but in how it sold and what it is … Most importantly of all, though many of the investments in the new economy will be written off, many of the practices and products of the new economy will carry over into what follows. … Most particularly, the extraordinary wave of investments in that splashed out all over North America and parts of Europe has produced a flood of innovations whose effects will be with us for a long time to come. (Thrift op. cit., p. 129).

But to accept that the New Economy has real substance, and is not all just hype, also means it is necessary to confront the numerous challenges it poses, both intellectual and political. Three of these are worth highlighting here.

First, there is the question of how we measure the New Economy. Many aspects of the new information-driven economy remain imperfectly measured. Some activities are entirely new, while others are inherently difficult for statistical authorities. For example, the measurement of the knowledge available to an enterprise is much harder and less developed than measuring its physical assets or its number of employees. Likewise, national economic accounting systems, designed to measure the output of the standardized mass production economy of the post-war era, fail to capture the value and circulation of intangible assets such as knowledge (Coyle and Quah 2002, Rowlatt, Clayton and Vaze 2002). How do we value and monitor information flows, Internet trade, knowledge production, and the like?

Second, do we need a new economic theory to understand the New Economy? In large part, the answer to this question depends on whether one takes the view that the New Economy is simply the latest 'surface' expression of what is still, underneath, a quintessentially capitalist system (some might argue even *more* capitalist), driven by the core imperatives of profit and accumulation; or whether the very nature of the New Economy, with its critical dependence on information, knowledge capital and cultural capital, renders our existing theories of economic growth and distribution, theories devised to explain and regulate the industrial economy, increasingly outmoded. But in part the answer also depends on one's view of theory, on whether and to what extent it is feasible and meaningful to construct theory that is ahistorical, or transhistorical, or whether theory itself must adjust to the changing circumstances of time and place. To a certain degree, the contemporary flux within the economics discipline is a reflection of these issues. While it is the case that the past twenty years or so have seen the increasing prominence of mainstream, neoliberal economics, and – as we have noted – this body of theory is viewed by many to be the 'natural' counterpart to the globalized, competitive New Economy, nevertheless other schools of economics have also emerged to contest the hegemony of the mainstream, such as evolutionary economics, with its emphasis on technological innovation, and institutional and social economics, with their focus on the contextual, relational and cultural bases of economic organization.

Likewise, recent theoretical and conceptual developments in economic geography also partly reflect attempts to grapple with the complexities and shifts of the new age. The rapid growth of such fields and topics as 'regional innovation systems', 'high-tech milieu', 'creative cities and clusters', 'learning regions', and cultural and relational economic geography, is surely no accident. These are all in large measure a reaction to new emerging realities in the economic landscape. Even the discovery of geography by the new 'geographical economists' (led by Krugman) and business cluster economists (led by Porter), can be read in this way, as part of a growing recognition of the role of localized increasing returns in high-technology, innovation-based economic growth and productivity advance.

What seems indisputable is that to achieve a proper understanding of the New Economy, our theories need to assign central significance to knowledge, its production, application, consumption, and circulation. Peter Drucker, one of the most enduring and prophetic management thinkers, argued this more than a decade ago:

> We need an economic theory that puts knowledge into the centre of the wealth-producing process. Such a theory alone can explain the present economy. It alone can explain economic growth. It alone can explain innovation. So far there are no signs of an Adam Smith or a David Ricardo of knowledge … [it is] crystal clear that the knowledge-based economy does not behave the way existing theory assumes an economy to behave. We therefore know that the new economic theory, the theory of the knowledge-based economy will be quite different from any existing economic theory, whether Keynesian or Neo-Keynesian, Classical or Neo-Classical. (Drucker 1993, pp. 167–168)

Although there have since been various explorations into the 'economics of knowledge' and the 'geographies of knowledge', Drucker's call for a theory of the knowledge-based economy still stands.

Third, what should be the policy responses to the New Economy? Does a new phase (or possibly a new model) of capitalism require a new mode of state regulation and intervention? According to the Washington-based Progressive Policy Institute (a proselytizer of 'Third Way' politics) the answer to this question is clear:

> Over time, policy frameworks must adapt to changing underlying economic and social realities. Turn-of-the-century industrialization triggered the development of new institutions and policies in the Progressive Era. Likewise, the rise of a national mass production, industrial economy in the 1940s led to the emergence of the post-New Deal, Keynesian policy framework. But during the rocky and turbulent transitional period from the mid-1970s to the mid-1990s – when the old economy was collapsing but the New Economy had not yet emerged – that consensus broke down. Now that the New Economy has emerged, we must foster a new consensus around a new framework for government and public policy. This framework must be consistent with the unique properties and logic of the New Economy. These characteristics include an increase in knowledge-based jobs, higher levels of entrepreneurial dynamism and competition, reduced delays between design and production, faster times to market, increased product and service diversity, constant technological innovation, the advent of the Internet and the information technology revolution, globalization, the replacement of hierarchical organizational structures with networked learning organizations, and relentless economic churning. These are more than economic fads or passing trends; they go to the heart of how the New Economy works. (New Economy Task Force 1999, p. 1)

The Institute goes on to suggest ten guiding principles for governing the New Economy (Table 2.13). Despite the Institute's proclaimed Third Way inclinations, however, these principles have an obvious neo-liberal thrust – pro-market, pro-flexibility, pro-competition, pro-privatization, pro-deregulation – and resonate strongly with New Labour's programme in the UK. The need to ensure that vulnerable, less advantaged groups, regions, cities and localities are not left behind in the rush to promote the New Economy is recognized, but the overwhelming message is clear: the new policy framework 'must be consistent with the unique properties and logic of the New Economy'. Yet this implies that the role of policy is simply to respond to and facilitate a set of forces that are somehow 'out there' and to all intents and purposes ineluctable. But as economic history shows, policy is not merely a reactive and facilitative process; rather, it is an active and causative determinant of the trajectory and nature of economic development. There is nothing inevitable or even necessarily 'best-fit' about a neoliberal policy stance towards the New Economy. It is simply what the USA and UK in their respective ways have chosen to follow. And as we saw

Table 2.13 The progressive policy institutes ten principles for governing the New Economy

Governing principle	Main thrust of policy
Spur innovation to raise living standards	Government must be on the side of policies that boost innovation and foster higher productivity and against policies that seek only to divide a slowly growing pie, protect or reward special interests at the expense of overall economic progress, or slow down the process of change. But at the same time, government must play a key role in providing workers and communities with the skills and tools they need to successfully navigate turbulent waters and prosper.
Expand the winners' circle	As the economy has become increasingly volatile and knowledge-based, success for people, organizations, and entire communities is more than ever determined by the ability to learn and adapt. Government needs to counterbalance the tendency toward a new division of society around learning and skills.
Invest in knowledge and skills	To spur innovation and equip citizens to win in the New Economy, government should invest more in the knowledge infrastructure of the 21st century: world class education, training and life-long learning, science, technology, technology standards, and other intangible public goods.
Grow the net	Policymakers should craft a legal and regulatory framework that supports the widespread growth of the Internet and high speed 'broadband' telecommunications, in such areas as taxation, encryption, privacy, digital signatures, telecommunications regulation, and industry regulation (in banking, insurance, and securities, for example). However, they must do so in ways that are fair and responsible.
Let markets set prices	In the absence of clear market failures, markets, not governments, should set prices of privately provided goods and services. At the same time government must strive to reduce or eliminate the tariffs, unnecessary price regulations, and the array of government protections that protect entrenched interests without increasing the economy's innovative or productive capacity.
Open regulated markets to competition	Government should move away from regulating economic competition among firms and instead promote competition to achieve public interest goals of lower costs, new products and greater consumer choice.
Let competing technologies compete	Technological innovation has now become central to addressing a wide range of public policy goals, including better health care, environmental protection, a renewed defence base, improved education and training, and reinvented government. We should look for technology-enabled solutions to public problems, but not so that today's winners are frozen in place at the expense of tomorrow's innovators.

Continued

Table 2.13 The progressive policy institutes ten principles for governing
the New Economy—cont'd

Governing principle	Main thrust of policy
Empower people with information	Governments should encourage and take advantage of this trend to address a broad array of public policy questions by ensuring that [everyone] has the information they need as consumers and citizens. Making a wide range of government information available over the Internet could lead to more open and accountable government.
Demand high-performance government	Government should become as fast, responsive, and flexible as the economy and society with which it interacts. The new model of governing should be decentralized, non-bureaucratic, catalytic, results-oriented, and empowering. Procedurally, governments should use information technologies to fundamentally re-engineer government and provide a wide array of services through digital electronic means to increase efficiency, cut costs, and improve service. Digitizing government is the next step in re-engineering government.
Replace bureaucracies with networks	Rather than acting as the sole funder and manager of bureaucratic programs, New Economy governments need to co-invest and collaborate with other organizations – networks of companies, universities, non-profit community organizations, churches, and other civic organizations – to achieve a wide range of public policy goals. Government needs to co-invest in these efforts and foster continuous learning through the sharing of best-practice lessons. Most importantly, the collaborative network model requires government to relax its often overly rigid bureaucratic programme controls and instead rely on incentives, information sharing, competition, and accountability to achieve policy goals.

Source: New Economy Task Force (1999).

above, it is surely no accident that these two countries have also witnessed the most marked widening in income disparities and job and skill inequalities. While both countries' governments – and especially New Labour governments – have sought to protect and support those who are being left behind, how to make the New Economy socially and spatially inclusive remains a key policy challenge.

References

Aghion, P. and Howitt, P. (2002) Wage Inequality and the New Economy, *Oxford Review of Economic Policy,* 18, 306–323.

Atkinson, D. (2002) *The 2002 New Economy Index,* Washington: Progressive Policy Institute.

Atkinson, R.D. and Gottlieb P.D. (2001) *The Metropolitan New Economy Index,* Washington, DC: Progressive Policy Institute.

Atkinson, R.D. Court, R.H. and Ward, J.M. (1999) *The State New Economy Index: Benchmarking Economic Transformation in the States,* Washington, DC: Progressive Policy Institute.

Bailey, M.N. (2002) The New Economy; post-mortem or second wind? *Journal of Economic Perspectives,* 16, 3–22.

Bailey, M.N. and Lawrence, R.Z. (2002) 'Do we have a New E-conomy?' *American Economic Review,* 91, 308–312.

Benner, C. (2002) *Work in the New Economy,* Oxford: Blackwell.

Best, M. (2001) *The New Competitive Advantage,* Oxford: Oxford University Press.

Bewes, T. and Gilbert, J. (2000) *Cultural Capitalism: Politics after New Labour,* London: Lawrence and Wishart.

Braunerhjelm, P. (2000) *Knowledge Capital and the 'New Economy',* Dordrecht: Kluwer.

Burton-Jones, A. (1999) *Knowledge Capitalism: Business, Work and Learning in the New Economy,* Oxford: Oxford University Press.

Business Week (1997) 'The New Economy: What it Really Means', *Business Week,* 11 November (www.businessweek.com/1997).

CACI (2004) *Wealth of the Nation Report, 2003,* London: CACI.

Cairncross, F. (1997) *The Death of Distance: How the Communications Revolution will Change our Lives,* London: Orion Books.

Cantner, U., Dinopoulos, E. and Lanzilloti, F. eds, *Entrepreneurship, the New Economy and Public Policy,* Berlin: Springer-Verlag.

Carlsson, B. (2002) The New Economy: what is new and what is not, Paper presented at the DRUID Summer Conference on Industrial Dynamics of the Old and New Economy, Copenhagen.

Carnoy, M. (2000) *Sustaining the New Economy: Work, Family and Community in the Information Age,* New York: Russell Sage Foundation.

Castells, M. (1996) *The Rise of the Network Society* (Vol 1 of The Information Age: Economy, Society and Culture), Oxford: Blackwell.

Caves, R.E. (2000) *Creative Industries: Contact between Art and Commerce,* Cambridge, MA: Harvard University Press.

Cohen, B. (1998) *The Geography of Money,* Ithaca: Cornell University Press.

Cohen, D. (2003) *Our Modern Times: The New Nature of Capitalism in the Information Age,* Cambridge, MA: MIT Press.

Council of Economic Advisors (2001) *Economic Report of the President: The Making of the New Economy,* Washington: US Council of Economic Advisors.

Coyle, D. (1997) *The Weightless World,* Oxford: Capstone Publishing.

Coyle, D. (2001) *Paradoxes of Prosperity: Why the New Capitalism Benefits All,* London: Texere Publishing.

Coyle, D. and Quah, D. (2002) *Getting the Measure of the New Economy,* London: Work Foundation/iSociety.

Daveri, F. (2000) 'The New Economy in Europe, 1992–2001', *Oxford Review of Economic Policy,* 18, 345–362.

Davis, S. and Meyer, C. (1998) *Blur: The Speed of Change in the Connected Economy,* New York: Addison-Wesley.

Department of Trade and Industry (1998) *Our Competitive Future: Building the Knowledge Driven Economy,* London: HMSO.

Dodge, M. and Kitchin, R. (2000) *Mapping Cyberspace,* London: Routledge.

Dodge, M. and Kitchin, R. (2005) 'The role and value of maps of Internet infrastructure', in *Moving Goods, People and Goods and Information in the Twenty First Century: Urban Technology, the New Economy, and Cutting-Edge Infrastructure,* New York, Spon Press.

Dore, R. (2001) Making sense of globalisation, *Discussion Paper 16,* Centre For Economic Performance, London School Of Economics.

Drucker, P. (1993) *Post-capitalist Society,* London: Butterworth Heinemann.

Du Gay, P. and Pryke, M. (2002) *Cultural Economy: Cultural Analysis and Commercial Life,* London: Sage.

Eichengreen, B. (2004) Productivity growth, the New Economy and catching up, *Review of International Economics,* 12, 243–245.

Elliott, L. and Atkinson, D. (1998) *The Age of Insecurity,* London: Verso.

Farrell, D. (2003) 'The Real New Economy', *Harvard Business Review,* October, pp. 1–9.

Fingleton, E. (1999) *In Praise of Hard Industries: Why Manufacturing, not the New Economy, is the Key to Future Prosperity,* London: Orion Publishing.

Florida, R. (2003) *The Rise of the Creative Class,* New York: Basic Books.

Freeman, C. (2002) The labour market in the New Economy, *Oxford Review of Economic Policy,* 18, 288–305.

Gadrey, J. (2001) *New Economy, New Myth,* London: Routledge.

Gates, B. (1999) *Business @ the Speed of Thought: Succeeding in the Digital Economy,* London: Penguin Books.

Gibson, W. (1996) 'The Net is a waste of time … and that's exactly what's right about it'. *New York Times Magazine* 14 July 1996. Available at: http://www.voidspace.org.uk/cyberpunk/gibson_wasteoftime.shtml.

Gilder, G. (2000) *Telecosm: How Infinite Bandwidth Will Revolutionalise Our World,* New York: The Free Press.

Giovannetti, E., Neuhoff, K. and Spagnolo, G. (2003) Agglomeration in the Internet: Does Space Still Matter? Paper presented at the Conference *Economics for the Future,* Cambridge, September.

Gnad, F. and Siegmann, J. (2000) eds, *Culture Industries in Europe: Regional Development Concepts for Private Sector Cultural Production and Services,* Düsseldorf: Ministry for Economic and Business, State of Westphalia.

Gordon, R.J. (1999) Has the 'New Economy' rendered the productivity slowdown obsolete? Draft (May) available at www.econ.northwester.edu/faculty-frame.html.

Gordon, R.J. (2000) 'Does the 'New Economy' measure up to the great inventions of the past?' *Journal of Economic Perspectives,* 14, 49–74.

Gray, J. (1998) *False Dawn: The Delusions of Global Capitalism,* London; Granta Books.

Harms, J.B. and Knapp, T. (2003) 'The New Economy: What's New, What's Not', *Review of Radical Political Economics,* 35, 413–436.

Harvey, D. (1989) *The Condition of Postmodernity,* Oxford: Blackwell.

Head, S. (2003) *The New Ruthless Economy: Work and Power in the Digital Age,* Oxford: Oxford University Press.

Herzenberg, S.A., Alic, J.A. and Wial, H. (1998) *New Rules for a New Economy: Employment and Opportunity in Postindustrial America,* Ithaca: Cornell University Press.

H.M. Treasury (2005) *Enterprise and Economic Development in Deprived Areas,* London: H.M. Treasury and Stationery Office.

Jorgenson, D.W., Ho, M.S. and Stiroh, K. J. (2004) 'Will the US Productivity Resurgence Continue?' *Current Issues in Economics and Finance, 10, 13,* Federal Reserve Bank of New York (December).

Kelly, K. (1998) *New Rules for a New Economy,* London: Fourth Estate.

Kellner, R. and Young, G. (2001) 'The New British Economy', *National Institute Economic Review,* 177, 70–84.

Kobrin, S. (1997a) 'The architecture of globalisation: state sovereignty in a networked global economy', in J. Dunning, ed., *Governments, Globalisation, and International Business,* Oxford: Oxford University Press, 146–171.

Kobrin, S. (1997b) 'Electronic cash and the end of national markets', *Foreign Policy,* 107, 65–77.

Krugman, P. (1998) 'America the boastful', *Foreign Affairs,* 77, 32–45.

Krugman, P. (2002) 'For Richer', *New York Times Magazine,* October, 1–11.

Lash, S. and Urry, J. (1994) *Economies of Signs and Space,* London: Sage.

Leadbeater, C. (1999) *Living on Thin Air: The New Economy,* London: Viking Books.

Local Futures (2005) *State of the Nation; The Geography of Opportunity in 21st Century Britain,* London: Local Futures Group.

Lundvall, B-A. (2004) Why the New Economy is a learning economy, *Working Paper 04-01,* Danish Research Unit for Industrial Dynamics.

Marshall, A. (1919) *Principles of Economics,* London: Macmillan.

Neef, D. (1998) *The Knowledge Economy,* Oxford: Butterworth-Heinemann.

New Economy Task Force (1999) *Rules of the Road: Governing Principles for the New Economy,* Washington: Progressive Policy Institute.

Norton, R.D. (2001) *Creating the New Economy: The Entrepreneur and the US Resurgence,* Cheltenham: Edward Elgar.

Oakley, K. (2004) 'Not so Cool Britannia: The Role of the Creative Industries in Economic Development', *International Journal of Cultural Studies,* 7, 67–77.

OECD (2000) *A New Economy; The Changing Role of Innovation and Information Technology in Growth,* Paris: OECD.

OECD (2001) *The New Economy: Beyond the Hype,* Paris: OECD.

Pontin, J. (1997) 'There is no New Economy', *Red Herring Magazine.* http://www.redherring.com/

Porter, M. E. (1998a) *On Competition,* Cambridge: MA; Harvard Business School Press.

Porter, M. E. (1998b) 'Clusters and the new economics of competitiveness', *Harvard Business Review,* December, pp. 77–90.

Porter, M. E. and Ackerman, F.D. (2001) *Regional Clusters of Innovation,* Washington: Council on Competitiveness.

Power, D. and Scott, A.J., eds, (2004) *Cultural Industries and the Production of Culture,* London: Routledge.

Quah, D. (1996) 'The invisible hand and the weightless economy', *Discussion Paper 12,* Centre for Economic Performance, London.

Reich, R. B. (2001) *The Future of Success: Work and Life in the New Economy,* London: Random House.

Robert Huggins Associates (2003) *World Knowledge Competitiveness Index,* Robert Huggins Associates, Pontypridd.

Robert Huggins Associates (2004) *World Knowledge Competitive Index,* Robert Huggins Associates, Pontypridd.

Robert Huggins Associates (2005) *UK Competitiveness Index: The Changing State of the Nation, 1997–2005,* Robert Huggins Associates, Pontypridd.

Rowlatt, A., Clayton, T. and Vaze, P. (2002) 'Where, and how, to look for the New Economy', *Economic Trends,* 580, 29–35.

Schumpeter, J.A. (1943) *The Theory of Economic Development,* Oxford: Oxford University Press.

Scott, A.J. (1998) *Regions and the World Economy: The Coming Shape of Global Production, Competition and Political Order,* Oxford: Oxford University Press.

Scott, A.J. (2000) *The Cultural Economy of Cities: Essays on the Geography of Image-Producing Industries,* London: Sage.

Scott, A.J. (2004) 'A perspective of economic geography', *Journal of Economic Geography,* 4, 479–499.

Sennet, R. (2005) *The Culture of New Capitalism,* London: Yale University Press.

Shalman, W.A. (1999) 'The New Economy is Stronger than You Think', *Harvard Business Review,* 1 November.

Siroh, K. (1999) 'Is there a New Economy'? *Challenge,* 42, 82–101.

Siroh, K. (2002) 'Are spillovers driving the New Economy?', *Review of Income and Wealth,* 48, 33–57.

Slaughter, S. and Rhoades, G. (2004) *Academic Capitalism and the New Economy,* Baltimore: Johns Hopkins Academic Press.

Tapscott, D. (1996) *Digital Economy: Promise and Peril in the Age of Networked Intelligence,* New York: McGraw Hill.

Telegeography Research (2005) *Global Internet Geography: International Internet Statistics and Commentary* (www.telegeography.com)

Temple, J. (2002) 'The assessment: the New Economy', *Oxford Review of Economic Policy,* 18, 241–264.

Thrift, N. J. (1997) 'The rise of soft capitalism', *Cultural Values,* 1, 29–57.

Thrift, N. J. (2005) *Knowing Capitalism,* London: Sage.

Townsend, I. (2004) *Income. Wealth and Inequality,* Research Paper 04/70 House of Commons, London.

Van Reener, J. (2001) 'The New Economy: Reality and Policy', *Fiscal Studies,* 22, 307–336.

Wadhwani, S.B. (2002) 'The New Economy: myths and realities'. *Bank of England Quarterly Review,* 42, 2.

Weinstein, B. (1997) 'Welcome to the New Economy', *Perspectives,* 12, 1–4.

Zandi, M. (1998) 'Musings on the New Economy', *Regional Financial Review,* March, 4–10.

Zuckerman, M. (1998) 'A second American century', *Foreign Affairs,* 77, 18–31.

3   The Old Economy[1]

Roger Lee

[T]he years 2000–01 witnessed the end of the opposition between the 'new' and the 'old' economies

Robert Boyer (2004, 151)

Introduction

A recent paper by one of the foremost commentators on the New Economy began by exclaiming:

> What, another paper on the new economy? When financial markets are raking through the debris of $7 trillion of lost equity values and '.com' is a reviled four-symbol word, a paper on the impact of the new economy...would seem as welcome as an analysis of the role of whales in the lighting revolution.

Despite this, publication was justified by the author on the grounds that 'the new economy ... continues to raise important puzzles' (Nordhaus 2002, 211). And it still does – not least those of productivity (Jorgenson *et al.* 2004), profitability (Nordhaus 2004), the future of growth and regimes of growth (Boyer 2004) and, of course, of geography (see, for example, Zook *et al.* 2004). Such 'puzzles' have unleashed a storm of publications[2] in a seemingly self-perpetuating debate. But this debate has left the question of the 'new' in the New Economy largely unquestioned. Even asking 'What's new about the new economy?' (Audretsch and Thurik 2000) leaves all the important terms in the questioned unproblematized. So, this paper attempts to push a little further: to ask in what senses can economies/economic geographies[3] be new.[4]

In attempting to offer the beginnings of an answer, the first section of this chapter asks a necessarily prior question: what are economies/economic geographies? The second section considers a range of 'old' debates on the New Economy. They are described as old in that they do not question the issue of newness itself. But this section concludes with some more generic and radical critiques of the New Economy. Section three of the chapter tries, briefly, to point to at least one answer to the question of how economies/economic geographies might, more genuinely, be new. The argument here is for a shift from a view of economies as the means of producing commodities by commodities, to a view which, in Robert Boyer's (2004, xv–xvi) memorable shorthand, understands economies as 'the production of humans by humans.'

What are economies/economic geographies?[5]

Economic geographies are circuits of value. They involve intentional – if not always successful – exploitative[6] relations and practices of the consumption, exchange and production of value sustained across space and time (see Figure 3.1a). The imperative of circuits of value in the sustenance of social life provides the criteria and framing of the regulatory template of economic geographies (see Figure 3.1b). And this imperative of value also marks the economy/ economic geography as distinct from, and irreducible to, social and cultural relations, notwithstanding the inseparability of economy/culture/society. Thus, unless circuits of value are sustained – can be reproduced – economic geographies do not exist. In this sense, then, the notion of a New Economy is an impossibility. Economic geographies are singular entities: either they are or they are not.

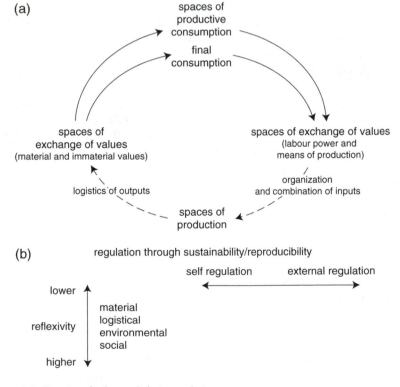

Figure 3.1 Circuits of value and their regulation.

But the material practices of economic geographies are meaningless outside a frame of social relationships – what can be called social relations of value. Economic geographies are set in motion, defined, given meaning and momentum and, most significantly, evaluated and regulated by the norms and practices associated with the social relations of value through which they take place.

The recognition that economic geographies cannot be other than simultaneously social *and* material and the consequent struggles over the meaning, organization and objectives of circuits of value, and the social relations of value which shape them, together mean that the establishment of different forms of economy is hardly a foregone conclusion. Whilst capitalism (or a certain variety of it; see, for example, Figure 3.2) may be treated by some as the end of history, the obscene consequences of its uneven development – along with their profound moral and geo-political implications – and the variety of the mechanisms of its regulation and normalization, which contribute to the struggles over the meanings and objectives of circuits of value, suggest otherwise. But these contested processes of social construction do not disturb the conclusion that economic geographies are singular entities.

Thus the possibilities for economic–geographic newness are limited by the material singularity of economic geographies and the social meanings endowed by social relations of value. Within capitalism – which dominates the circuits of value through which the vast majority of the world's population now struggles to make a living or, despite the struggle, is unable to do so – the possibilities for diversity are limited by the powerful symbolic and material relations and regulations of its reproduction.

'Old' critiques of the 'New' Economy

Can the New Economy be identified?

Despite such limitations, what sorts of newness are possible within economic geographies? Conventionally, economic newness is recognized as one or more of a range of economic transformations. Examples include changes in production processes and products (innovations), the organization and scale of production, the balance of power between consumption and production, the conduct of exchange mechanisms (and, in particular, the degree of freedom of market forces), the nature of regulatory regimes and, perhaps most intriguing, the speed and compression of space–time in consumption, production and exchange. Newness has also come to be associated, more problematically, with the so-called 'knowledge economy' (see, for example, Hudson 2005, chapter 4).

By contrast, the New Economy in the literature to which Nordhaus (2002) refers is associated with a narrower range of variables. It is frequently interpreted as the coalescence of four strands of change that were thought to come together most noticeably in the USA of the late 1990s: (1) the death of the business cycle, associated with; (2) the responsive operation of capital markets, especially venture capital – at least with respect to IT but perhaps also to biotechnology and nanotechnology; (3) historically significant productivity

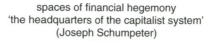

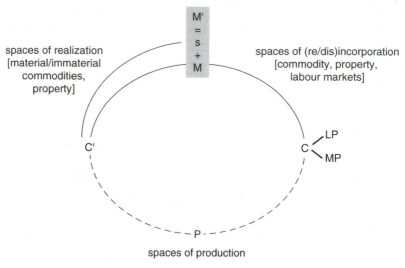

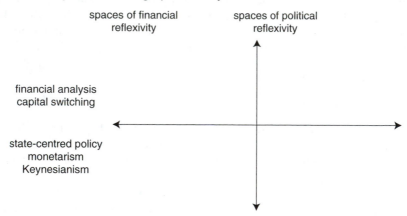

Figure 3.2 Circuits of capital and their regulation.

changes associated with new technologies – and especially; (4) information technology – which is thought not only to generate its own high rates of productivity but, potentially, at least to jack up productivity in the rest of the economy.

For Boyer (2004), the New Economy involves three sets of relational transformation – increasing returns and the learning curve effects of hardware and infrastructure, standardization of competition associated with software, and managed competition facilitated by portals. A simple comparison between these lists reveals immediately the diverse ways in which the New Economy is categorized. And, as Boyer argues, such diversity contributes to the difficulty of finding a 'canonical organisational model ... to represent the "new economy"'. What is more, without working systematically through the lists, there are also indications that many changes associated with the New Economy of the late 1990s have been short-lived and/or of relatively limited significance in long-run historical perspective.

Old new?

For Robert Boyer the New Economy is already passé. 'Why', he asks (2004, xi), 'dwell on the concept of a "new economy" that many people now consider to be a thing of the past?' Two indications of what is, arguably, now an old New Economy must suffice here. First, in terms of media representation (Figure. 3.3), the term 'the new economy' began to appear in the early 1990s but was very much at its zenith in 2000 and had all but disappeared from the financial media by 2002. Intriguingly, Boyer (2004, Graph 9.1, 146) offers a similar analysis based on academic publications which shows a very similar pattern. But academic output is, less interesting in terms of the shaping of economies by economics than that of influential media. Of course, the rapid rise and fall in media interest could simply be because, after 2000, the notion no longer sold column inches – but in the self-reflexive world of financial journalism that is itself a significant indication of decline. Alternatively, it may indicate that the New Economy was no longer 'new' – but then this, too, would indicate that its supposedly widespread and radically transformative effects were short-lived

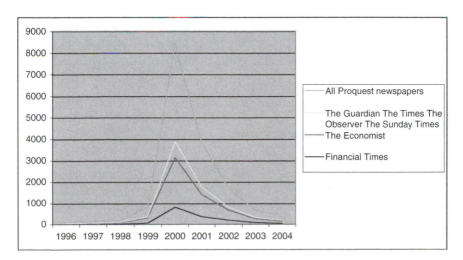

Figure 3.3 Media accounts of the New Economy (media mentions of 'the New Economy' UK 1992–2002).

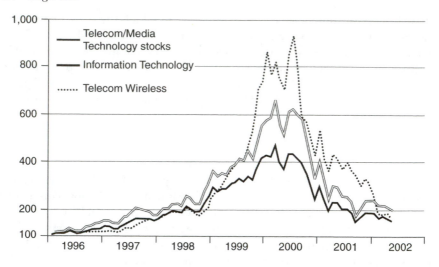

Figure 3.4 Financial evaluations of the New Economy USA 1996–2002.
Source: Thomson Financial Datastream *Financial Times* 22 May 2002, 23

and, in the event, not especially significant. In this respect, at least, the New Economy is already old.

And, secondly, this history of its representation is paralleled by the history of its financial evaluation during the 1990s (Figure. 3.4). Doubtless, media representations and financial evaluations of the New Economy are mutually formative – the rise and fall of one is reflected in the rise/fall of the other. But, again, this two-way relationship between representation and financial evaluation is indicative of the extent to which the New Economy remains practically significant – or not – for economic actors and financial investors.[7] Indeed, it is arguable that a far more genuinely New Economy now reflects the oldest and most fundamental economic relationship – that with the physical environment – currently manifest in the diverse array of pressures on natural resources (Lee 2005a, Morrison and Brown-Huhnes 2005).

The old economics of the New Economy

Similarly, the presumption that globalization and associated increases in the flexibility of labour and capital markets, along with the rise of monetarism and neo-liberalism, had effectively killed off the business cycle, misunderstands the continuing cyclical significance of lumpy investments, of 'herd behaviour' and – more than a little ironically in view of the claims made for their transformative effects in the New Economy – of Kondratieff-style systemic innovations and Schumpeterian creative destruction in the generation and sustenance of business cycles. And, whilst growth was certainly rapid from 1980–1998 (from the bottom to the top of the cycle), it was far from unprecedented in

Figure 3.5 Long run business cycles 1883–2002. S&P Composite Index in 2002 prices, deflated by the consumer price index. Source: *Financial Times* 19 June 2002, 23.

cyclical terms. The annual rate of growth in the S and P index was 12 per cent from 1982–2000 but this compares with, for example, an annual – albeit clearly unsustainable – growth rate of 20 per cent over the nine years from 1920–1929 (see Figure 3.5).

Furthermore, the much vaunted productivity miracle based on new ITs may not be so significant in the long-run. Aggregate US data doubtless demonstrate that productivity growth in the period of the New Economy since 1995 has been 'more than twice the average of the previous two decades' (Jorgenson *et al.* 2004, 1) and that capital deepening and total factor productivity made the largest contributions to this growth. Thirty-five per cent of the latter was accounted for by IT production and 60 per cent of capital deepening was attributable to IT goods. But to assume that a given input of IT has a direct and instant impact on productive practice, rather than being refracted through the perpetual processes of corporate reorganization and retraining, is grossly to simplify the dynamics that have always been characteristic of capitalist economies.

Robert Gordon (2000, 72) argues that the 'new' ICT-related economy is limited by diminishing returns and so, despite its dramatic aggregate effect on productivity in parts of the US economy, cannot measure up to the 'great inventions that constitute what has been called the Second Industrial Revolution.' Equally, long run growth data show that recent developments are far from exceptional[8] and certainly cannot compare with the long wave of post war growth (Table 3.1). Notwithstanding rapid growth in the late 1990s – especially in the USA – the exceptional period of growth in GDP per capita over the period 1950–2001 took place from 1950–1973 rather than from 1973–2001.

Furthermore, and zooming in more closely on the age of the New Economy, work by the McKinsey Global Institute (www.mckinsey.com accessed 18 10 2001) questions the role of the New Economy in driving the growth in

Table 3.1 Long run global growth rates 1500–2001 (average annual compound per capita
　　　　growth rates)

	1500–1820	1820–1870	1870–1913	1913–1950	1950–1973	1973–2001	1995–2001
Western Europe	0.15	0.95	1.32	0.76	4.08	2.45	2.37
former USSR	0.10	0.63	1.06	1.76	3.36	-0.84	2.72
USA	0.36	1.34	1.82	1.61	2.45	2.41	2.36
Japan	0.09	0.19	1.48	0.89	8.05	2.89	0.85
World	0.05	0.53	1.30	0.91	2.93	1.70	2.06

Source: Data calculated from Maddison (2001) table B-22 265, Maddison (2003) tables 2c 89
5c 184 7c 234.

productivity experienced in the USA between 1995 and 2000. Around 60 per cent
of the increase in US productivity across the whole economy at this time was
accounted for by wholesaling and retailing, and over 99 per cent of the increase
in productivity was accounted for by just six sectors: wholesale, retail, securities, electronics, industrial machinery and telecoms. Of course, investment in IT
played a major part in the development of logistics in firms such as Wal-Mart
but, in the 70 per cent of the US economy outside the 6 high productivity sectors, investment in IT did not increase productivity significantly. Thus the
53 remaining sectors in the study accounted for 62 per cent of the increase in
IT spending but contributed only 0.3 per cent of the productivity growth.
Indeed, productivity declined over the period across about one third of the US
economy (see Figure. 3.6).

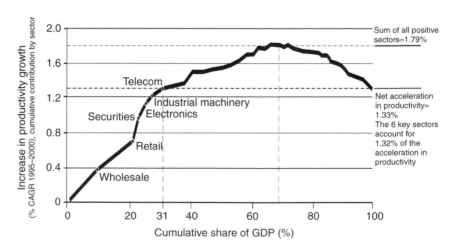

Figure 3.6 Sectoral contributions to productivity growth USA 1995–2000. Source:
　　　　Bureau of Economic Affairs; McKinsey Global Institute *Financial Times* 17
　　　　October 2001, 15.

The old history and geography of New Economy

Not only is the New Economy arguably already old, it is also limited in significance in terms of both temporal and spatial change, at least from a global and long-run perspective on world economic geography. The dramatic growth of the world economy from the end of the 18th century is well known. As represented over a time-scale of 1000 years, growth has been continuous and rapid ever since. But this stands in marked contrast to the static trajectory of growth during the previous 800 years (Figure 3.7).

Although there are clearly many caveats that must be drawn around such long run data, they give cause for caution in identifying any significant shifts apparently associated with a New Economy emerging at the end of the second millennium. And the claim here is not that the New Economy is invisible in such a long-run global perspective – it is almost certain to be so at this temporal scale – but rather that the stress on the notion of economic newness is misplaced. Furthermore, one of the most dramatic geographical transformations of the past half century is hardly new either. At the outset of the last millennium, Asia (excluding Japan) accounted for over two thirds (67.6 per cent) of the value of total global production.[9] By 1820, this share was still as high as 56.2 per cent, whilst that of the West (western Europe and its global offshoots – the USA, Canada, Australia and New Zealand) had grown from less than one tenth of the global total in 1000 to over a quarter in 1820. Then, despite the fact that between 1820 and 1998 the value of global production grew at an annual rate ten times that of the preceding 800 years, growth in Asia was scarcely half that of the West over the period.

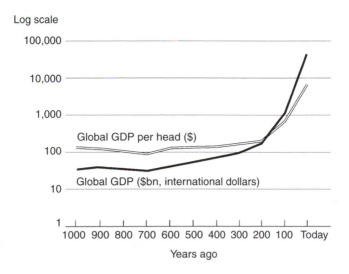

Figure 3.7 1000 years of economic growth. Source: de Long B (http://econ161.berkely. EDU/TCEH/1998_Draft/ worldGDP/Estimating_World_GDP.html) *Financial Times* 8 September 1999.

Thus, whereas Asia's share of global production was only 15.5 per cent in 1950, that of the West was 56.9 per cent – almost the mirror image of the shares of these two regions in 1000. However, from 1950 onwards, Asia began to move back to its previous dominance. During the second half of the twentieth century, production in the region grew at three times the rate of the West so that by 2001 Asia accounted for 38 per cent of global production compared with the 45 per cent located in the West. The contemporary geography of global development is moving back to a pattern more reminiscent of the early-nineteenth than the mid-twentieth century. Again, however, the argument here is not for some sort of economic geographical inevitability or see-sawing but, rather, that geographically uneven development is hardly new either in its occurrence or in its geography.

And, of course, this changing global geography reflects long-established economic relationships involving highly uneven and exclusionary geographies of profitability and productivity and not just newly emergent spaces of economic growth based on novel productive principles and relations of economic activity and location. How, for example, did sub-Saharan Africa and much of east-central Europe – and especially Russia – benefit from the New Economy? The answer is not very well. Excluding South Africa (ranked 34), only one sub-Saharan country – Botswana (ranked 50) – appears in the top 50 in the World Economic Forum's (WEF 2005) rankings of 104 countries by the Networked Readiness Index. By contrast 11 sub-Saharan countries fall into the lowest quintile in the rankings. Faring little better, the Russian Federation is ranked 62nd, up only one place from 2004, and is out-performed by 9 countries from east-central Europe, although none appear in the top 20.

In short, the New Economy works through a rather less than dramatically new geography. And, at the same time, the New Economy is not a simple outcome of particular 'new' geographies of economy created through the diffusion of 'a new productive paradigm. A study of the geography of the merging ICT-based growth regimes … requires going beyond Silicon Valley for insights' (Boyer 2004, 145). Cooperation as well as competition and high and egalitarian access to education are also conditions in which the New Economy can take place and prosper. Thus Singapore is ranked 1st in the 2005 index, the USA falls to 5th, four Scandinavian countries appear in the top 10, and a further five 'old' European countries are ranked in the top 20.

The point of this commentary on the old historical geography of the New Economy is that the complex geographies of uneven development, social relations and materialities of economic growth disrupt, divert and delay any simple model in which investment in IT (including investment within the IT industries themselves) leads to increases in productivity. At the same time, old economic geographies continue to provide the conditions of existence and to shape the geographies of the new.

Generic critiques of the New Economy

Whilst the New Economy has generated an enormous literature, most accounts – especially the most cited references – are concerned with specific facets rather than with a more generic perspective. Three of the most notable exceptions in this regard emanate from Europe or are written by Europeans: Manuel Castells (1996, 2001), Jean Gadrey (2002) and Robert Boyer (2004). And, from one perspective or another, they all question the newness of the New Economy.[10]

Information and the continuing significance of time and space path dependence

Manuel Castells (1996, 1) claims nothing less than that a 'technological revolution, centered around information technologies, is reshaping at an accelerated pace, the material basis of society'. Further he argues that, in what he calls the informational society, information is central in driving productivity. '[T]he term informational indicates the attribute of a specific form of social organisation in which information, generation, processing, and transmission become the fundamental sources of productivity and power ...' (21, fn 33) However, he is more circumspect (92) both about what it is that has changed and the extent of that change:

> What has changed is not the kind of activities human kind is engaged on, but its technological ability to use as a direct productive force what distinguishes our species as a biological oddity: its superior capacity to process symbols.

And he is careful to point out (31) that 'information, in its broadest sense, e.g. as communication of knowledge, has been critical in all societies, including medieval Europe' and that what he refers to as the two Industrial Revolutions (late eighteenth century and latter half of the nineteenth century) both relied on information and the diffusion of knowledge. Thus, like other more sceptical commentators (e.g. Gordon 2000), Castells sets his understanding of the transformations involved in Information Technology Revolution firmly in the context of those of earlier Industrial Revolutions. 'Information technology is to this revolution what new sources of energy were to successive Industrial Revolutions ...' (Castells 1996, 31). 'The internet is', he asserts (Castells 2001,[11] 1), 'the fabric of our lives' and IT 'is the present-day equivalent of electricity in the industrial era.'

Boyer (2004, 14), too, is sceptical of the newness of the information economy. He argues that:

> [It] would be wrong to say that the importance of information was only discovered in 1995. With the historical rise of commercial, and subsequently of industrial and, even more importantly, financial capitalism, information became a key component in the organisation of trading and production, and in the functioning of credit and securities markets.

And, as with the continuing influence of the historical geography of capital-ism, the geography of the network society is both formative and uneven. Castells (1996) stresses 'the critical role played by milieus of innovation' and the continuing significance of geographically diverse 'history, culture, and institu-tions' in the conduct and success of the revolution and points to the 'large areas of the world, and considerable segments of the population, switched off from the new technological system'(34).

Growth

Robert Boyer (2004, xi) points to the irrationality of the 'many economists' who 'became convinced by the emergence of a new growth regime, one driven by information technology.' His critique stems from a scepticism about the ability of ICT to drive a new growth regime. Thus, although some (e.g. Oliner and Sichel 2000, 21) would claim that 'the now larger share of total output produced by this dynamic sector would provide an ongoing boost to productivity growth for the economy as a whole' and, though more qualified, 'that the growth contribution from information technology capital – including both its use and its production – will stay relatively strong for the next few years', Boyer (2004, 43) argues that 'it would be wrong to extrapolate anything from the productivity and growth rates that were observed between 1995 and 2000.' This is because 'the specificity and cost structure of a given environment will continue to give rise to innovation strategies that make differentiated use of ICT's capabilities' (42). Thus, rather less than '[P]aradoxically …' – as Boyer would, paradoxically, have it (99) – '… the "old economy" was more stable then the "new", the end result being that the sudden deceleration of the ICT sectors did not lead to a severe recession.'

New or old?

Manuel Castells' account of 'the rise of the network society' is unambiguous about the emergence of something economically new and significant. 'A new economy has', he argues (1996, 66), 'emerged in the last two decades on a worldwide scale'. Castells also points (33) to the 'lightning speed' with which the 'new information technologies have spread throughout the globe' such that 'dominant functions, social groups, and territories across the globe are con-nected by the mid-1990s in a new technological system that, as such, started to take shape only in the 1970s (34).

This speed may be 'new' but Boyer is ambivalent about the significance of the 'new technologies'. He distinguishes between a *generic technology* (such as that which, he argues, underpins the New Economy) hyped by 'financialisa-tion', manifest most notably, perhaps, in the dynamics of venture capital – and the 'power of Wall Street' (Boyer 2004, 149) which 'had a greater effect on stock price inflation and the creation of over-capacities than in encouraging the rest of the economy to use equipment and software more efficiently' (99) on the one hand, and a *radical technology* involving economy wide restructuring and a new growth regime on the other. In short, 'the 1990s were more about finance than about an information and real growth economy.' (xv). Stressing as it does 'old' financial norms and criteria of evaluation,[12] this conclusion points, once again, to the limited significance of the New Economy. Jean Gadrey (2002, ix) agrees. Not only was finance the determinant influence on the rhetoric and development of the 'new' economy but, whilst:

> it is true that the Internet and the software revolution have introduced new elements, ...we are very far from a radical change in economic practices, production, consumption and ways of life.

Thus, what, for Boyer (2004, 14, 15), is 'new' in recent years is the 'digitalisation of information' and 'information processing ... organised as a network, both inside and outside of production units.' Together, these developments led to '*a transformation of competition* ...' against which 'the distinction between the new and the old economy ...' is 'a misleading issue, one of little relevance indeed' (17, italics in original). Thus the end of the clear distinction – and opposition – between the 'new' and the 'old' economies leaves 'little doubt' that we need 'to recognize the multiple nature of the factors that have shaped the trajectory of OECD economies' (151). The difference of the New Economy is, thereby, diminished – almost to the point of invisibility.

'Old' Europe and New Economies?

New models of growth?

Speculating on an agenda for the future of economic growth, Robert Boyer (2004, 144) proposes a wager:

> ... if we were to bet on the model which is most likely to emerge as the winner over the next few decades, we would probably have to take a close look at the 'production of humans by humans' and to start exploring the institutional environment that will allow this to happen.

The reasons for the likely success of his bet are straightforward and well known:

> Once essential needs are satisfied (food, clothing, housing, transport), both public and household budgets shift towards a type of spending that specifically ensures anthropogenetic reproduction from one generation to the next.

Further, as well as the limited possibilities for productivity increases in medical care and education:

> technological progress has a very different meaning in hospitals from that in the manufacturing forum. Whereas the secular orientation of manufacturing

industries seeks to save work by applying increasingly efficient technical processes and organisational forms, medical advances have had the effect of eradicating diseases that are relatively easy to heal or prevent. What arises instead are ailments that are more serious and crippling and where no satisfactory treatment exists. … In addition, technological progress in the medical field has increased the number of analyses and security tests, hence the volume of services provided for a given health problem. Lastly, with populations ageing there has been a whole range of new illnesses which require major care …

Thus public health innovations exert a direct influence on demographics and on the quality of life, whereas industrial innovations only (sic) affect these variables indirectly by means of an improvement in living standards, a reduction in working times, the development of leisure and the like (139–140).

Although straightforward in its employment of changing income elasticities of demand, this account of economic growth goes well beyond notions of endogenous growth founded on the knowledge economy – 'the production of ideas by ideas' – as it recognizes that 'education, health and culture represent crucial components in the production, and especially in the shaping, of lives and lifestyles' (Boyer 2004, 137). In other words, it reintegrates the corporeality and materiality of human being into abstracted, virtual, notions of economic growth and so begins to reverse the oft-times simply presumed relations of economic purpose *from* people for economy, *to* economy for people.[13] This really is potentially new and has (or should have) profound implications for macro-economic policy – not least fiscal and public expenditure policy.

The flip-side of Boyer's search for a new model of economic growth is the subversion of the old models by the negative effects of material progress on the apparent positives of that progress. The widening gap between the growth of GDP and broader conceptions of material well-being (as measured, for example, by the Index of Sustainable Welfare (Daly and Cobb 1989) or the Genuine Progress Indicator;[14] see Figure. 3.8) which modify GDP by subtracting a range of 'bads' (e.g. expenditure on the effects of crime, accidents or pollution) and adding 'goods' (such as voluntary work in the community) is well known. Value created through circuits of consumption, exchange and production is diminished, not least as a consequence of the costs of material progress.

Three questions arise from this simultaneous accumulation of wealth (in the global north) and diminution of value: How to manage it in order to enhance genuine progress (above all, in the global south)? What to do with the wealth? and, relatedly, What is the purpose of economic activity? This latter question is both implicit in, and central to, Boyer's attempt to identify a sustainable economic future based upon an anthropogenetic model of growth.

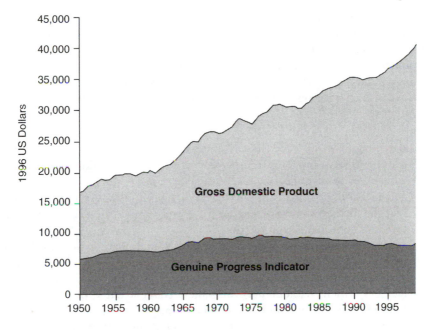

Figure 3.8 GDP and GPI USA 1950–2000. Source: *Redefining progress* 2003
http://www.rprogress.org/projects/gpi.

From model newness to moral newness

In the preface to his critique of the New Economy, Jean Gadrey (2002, xii) is
fully aware that, from the point of view of:

> the new stock exchange capitalism made in the USA, it might be concluded
> that my book is little more than a collection of precautionary advice ... hostile
> to 'inevitable' changes, conservative even.

But, he goes on:

> If we are talking about preserving an inherited set of moral values that extends
> beyond the mere maximisation of individual interests to embrace non-
> economic goals and social protection arrangements that reduce inequality and
> insecurity, then I accept this version of conservatism and lay claim to it as a
> defence against the apostles of the new economy.
>   The purpose of this essay is ... to focus attention upstream of ... political
> debates to identify the principal characteristics of this technologically driven,
> free-market model .... The task of politicians and other decision-makers ...
> would then be to ... create the conditions under which those who would seek
> to put economic and technological factors in their place as resources for social
> and human development rather than inescapable constraints with all the force
> of laws of nature ... (3)

In systematically challenging the benefits presumed by, the causal links assumed in, and the conditions of existence of the New Economy, Gadrey's concern is with the construction of a moral economy and, in this, he points to a more genuinely new economic geography.[15] He outlines three precautionary principles designed to address the 'question of the risks inherent in applying competitive market relationships to all social transactions' (77). In particular, he highlights:

- the production of knowledge, culture, creativity and biodiversity on the grounds that 'in the long-term interest of economic development itself ... a huge area of scientific research ... [should] ... not ... [be] ... bound by laws and reckonings of markets ...' (79). He is careful, however, not to suggest that the market is entirely inappropriate and to note the dangers in other forms of coordinating production
- activities serving the common good. His example here is the Post Office which, he argues does not merely provide a logistical service but 'a neighbourhood service open to all' (86). And the same could be said of many facilities which, without necessary intent, offer a range of benefits well beyond their narrowly instrumental functions
- the need to socialize the 'laws of the market' (Callon 1998) and, in particular the social costs arising from narrowly financial evaluations and decisions on social development.[16]

Such precautionary principles go some way to addressing the questions posed by the simultaneous growth in wealth and decline in genuine economic progress. But they address the question of the purpose of economic growth only tangentially. The concern for the morality and ethics of economies – what they are for, as well as what they do – which underlies all three European critiques of the New Economy, may provide a more fruitful way into thinking about a more genuinely New Economy.

Moral newness?

Keynes' grandchildren: What are (really new?) economies for?

As Keynes (1930) argued as early as 1928, it is not necessary to re-calculate GDP in social and environmental terms to show that there is a contradiction created by compound rates of growth. Keynes calculated that, with a growth rate of 2 per cent pa, the capital equipment of the world would increase by 50 per cent in 20 years and by 750 per cent in 100 years:

> this means in the long run *that mankind is solving its economic problem* (325) and that, therefore:
> the economic problem is not ... *the permanent problem of the human race* (326)

And this claim has a wide provenance and long pedigree. Economic progress had been dramatic (and new) a century and a half before Keynes' calculation:

> some time in the 1780s, and for the first time in human history, the shackles were taken off the productive power of human societies, which henceforth became capable of constant, rapid and, up to the present, limitless multiplication of men (sic), goods and services. (Hobsbawm 1962, 29)

The question is what has this (highly uneven) growth of wealth and productive power done for those who have created it? For the one third or so of humanity who are, in effect, economically dispossessed, the answer is worse than nothing. The world around them changes in ways over which they have no control are, at the very least environmentally questionable and, geopolitically highly de-stabilizing. And for those who have access (albeit, again, highly uneven access) to this wealth, the consequences are far from sanguine:

> Those who believe we should pursue the goal of economic growth should be made to sit and stare at the time trends in reported happiness ... In a country like the US, the trend is systematically down. Billions of hamburgers and sports utility vehicles have proved useless – indeed worse than useless.
> Some economists and policy designers will go to their deathbeds ignoring these data. The numbers are too scary. They imply that clever people have for decades given the wrong advice to governments and citizens.
> Yet the best evidence now suggests that growth does not work. This opens up an extraordinary hole in the middle of textbook economics. It also puts generations of policymaking intellectually out of business. (Oswald 2005, 42).

This is a devastating critique. It points to the reductive failure of economics not only to get beyond abstraction, method and measurement, and so of its failure to think about the geographical and social realities through which economies take place but – and even more fundamentally – its failure to think about purpose.

But this is not only a catastrophic failure of economics. Prevailing social relations of value shape the thought of non-economists as well as that of economists. Thus, mindful of the increasing significance and influence of the emergent 'headquarters of capital' (Schumpeter 1961; see Figure 3.7) and foreshadowing Gadrey and Boyer, Keynes (1930, 38) predicts that:

> The strenuous purposeful money makers may carry all of us along with them into the lap of economic abundance.

And so he advocates (329, 330, 331) both a critical engagement with:

> the true character of this purposiveness [which, in financial interpretation] means that we are more concerned with the remote future results of our

> actions than with their own quality or their immediate effects on our own environment ... jam is not jam unless it is a case of jam tomorrow and never jam today ...

and a:

> return to some of the most sure and certain principles of religion and traditional virtue ... [to] value ends above means and prefer the good to the useful.

Thus:

> it will be those peoples, who can keep alive, and cultivate into fuller perfection, the art of life itself and do not sell themselves for the means of life, who will be able to enjoy the abundance when it comes. (328)

This profoundly conservative and geographically introverted prospectus begs a range of questions. These include the prevailing and ongoing grossly uneven relations of class power, divisions of labour and distributions of income (c.f. e.g. Esping-Anderson 1993, Savage 2000, Wills 2002, Skeggs 2004); the economic and financial significance of the evaluative norms of social relations of value (c.f. e.g. Lee 2003); and the notion that white, male, middle class values are universal but that gender relations are given and unproblematic (c.f. e.g. McDowell 2003). Furthermore, although sagacious about the growing power and influence of spaces of hegemony, Keynes does not recognize the powerful symbolic role of financial markets or foresee the multiplicity of temporalities – and, in particular the possibilities of instant judgements and actions – through which modern financial markets work.

Conclusion: stasis or change in a New Economy?

Notwithstanding its remarkably conventional limitations, Keynes' advocacy of a New Economy for his grandchildren does have the great advantage of recognizing, like Adam Smith writing at the point of inflection of the new late eighteenth century economy, that there is more to economic life than accumulation; that the purpose of economic activity is more than instrumental; and that the possibilities enabled by the solution to the economic problem may be genuinely radical and new.[17] Eric Hobsbawm (2005, 19) has recently argued that this sort of disjunction is:

> crucial for the understanding of homo sapiens. It is the conflict between the forces making for the transformation of homo sapiens from neolithic to nuclear humanity and the forces whose aim is the maintenance of unchanging reproduction and stability in human social environments.

But is a New Economy a force for change or stasis?

The purpose of this essay has been to argue that such a question should – always – lie at the heart of any kind of economic analysis. Only by recognizing the purposes to which economic geographies are put and by identifying their unchangeable socio-material characteristics can a critical analysis proceed. Without such, it is impossible to perceive of economic transformation in anything other than a superficial fashion. The material and social imperatives of economic geographies are what drive and shape them. These imperatives constrain any notion of newness and yet they are themselves shaped by the moral geographies that both emerge from and come to define prevailing social relations of value. If for no other reason than this, a constant reference to Karl Marx and Adam Smith – for whom the question of the purpose of economy was the point of their work – is absolutely essential in economic geography. In this fundamental sense, then, old economic geographies are the new new. That there is, always and everywhere, a profound but complex ethical and moral framing of economic life (Lee and Smith 2004) means that there is also, always and everywhere, the possibility of change and of a real New Economy.

Acknowledgements

So many thanks are due, as ever, to the friends and colleagues who helped me to see what it was that I was trying to say in this essay. Peter Dicken, Andrew Leyshon, Phil Kelly, and Adrian Smith – along with the members of the Spaces of Inequality and Development research group at QMUL – all offered both generous and highly perceptive critiques. Whilst I know what I have learned from them, I fear that this is far from apparent in my attempts to respond to their comments. Thank you, too, to Ed Oliver who, as always, dealt with my endless technophobic adjustments to the diagrams with his enviable combination of patience and efficiency. Finally, a massive thank you to Peter Daniels, Jonathan Beaverstock, Mike Bradshaw and Andrew Leyshon for organizing the ESRC seminar on *Geographies of the new economy* in 2003 and, remarkably, for inviting me to participate in it.

Notes

1 An earlier version of this paper was presented at the ESRC seminar Geographies of the new economy, University of Nottingham, 16 April 2003.
2 scholar.google.com lists over 390 000 entries for 'the new economy' (accessed 8 February 2005).
3 An argument that economies cannot be other than economic geographies is developed in Lee 2005.
4 Thus it is not primarily concerned with questions of definitional detail (see, for example, Stiroh 1999, Castells 1996, 30–31); nor with what the 'new' economy may – or may not – do economically; or with how it works. As long ago as 1997, some enthusiasts had already promulgated 'rules' or 'laws' for the 'new' economy on the grounds that '[T]hose who play by the rules will prosper; those who ignore them will not'! (Kelly 1997). Given this threat of social exclusion it is surprising that, to date, only 211 people had consulted the paper for advice. See also Kelly 1998.

5   This section of the paper draws on the fuller answer to this question in Lee 2005b.

6   These relations are exploitative in the sense that they must involve the creation and extraction of value.

7   And see recent claims that the 'new' economy – now referred to as 'the technology sector' – 'is gearing up for another boom five years after the bubble burst.' (Pesola 2005, 3).

8   Except, perhaps for the former USSR. The data in the table under-estimate the collapse of the Soviet economy whilst the more recent recovery is probably exaggerated. In any event, the uneven geography of global development reflects old, rather than new, economic dynamics.

9   Data calculated from Maddison (2003, Table 7b, 233). For some discussion, see Lee (2005). A far fuller account of the historical geography of the world economic geography is offered in Dicken (2003).

10   Others, of course, have written more devastating critiques, some elements of which are reflected in those discussed below. See, for example Frank (2000).

11   However, it is, surely disingenuous to propose such an equivalence? IT is one of the very many transformations enabled by the economy-wide consequences of electricity. Whilst IT is a 'generic' technology, electricity is 'radical'.

12   See Lee (2005b) for a discussion of these evaluative norms.

13   See, for example, Lee (1995).

14   See www.rprogress.org/projects/gpi accessed 17 March 2003.

15   In doing so, he reflects an earlier critique 'that the informational activities and the growing stock of instrumentation around us are attributable, in large part, to the economic, political and cultural pressures and strains produced by the general crisis of the world market system' (Schiller 1986, xii).

16   Lee (2005b) has more to say on this.

17   A recent example of this kind of radical thinking on the purpose of economic activity is offered by the recent economic interest in happiness. Much of this work is founded on revisiting a paper, now over thirty years old (Easterlin 1974). For more recent developments see Layard (2005); Oswald di Tella and MacCulloch (2003).

References

Audretsch, D. and Thurik, A.R. (2000) 'What's new about the new economy? Sources of growth in the managed and entrepreneurial economies', Erasmus Research Institute of Management Report Series *Research in Management*, www.erim.eur.nl downloaded 23 November 2004.

Boyer, R. (2004) *The future of economic growth as new becomes old*, Edward Elgar, Cheltenham.

Callon, M. (1998) *The laws of the markets*, Blackwell Oxford.

Castells, M. (1996) *The rise of the network society*, Blackwell: Cambridge, MA.

Castells, M. (2001) *The internet galaxy: Reflections on the internet, business and society*, Oxford University Press: Oxford.

Daly, H.E. and Cobb, J.B. Jr. (1989) *For the common good: Redirecting the economy toward community, the environment and a sustainable future*, Beacon Press: Boston, MA.

Dicken, P. (2003) *Global shift*, Sage: London, 4th edition.

Easterlin, R.A. (1974) Does Economic Growth Improve the Human Lot? Some Empirical Evidence. In: David, P.A. and Reder, M.W. eds, *Nations and Households in Economic Growth: Essays in Honour of Moses Abramovitz*, Academic Press: New York and London.

Esping-Andersen, G. (ed.), (1993) *Changing classes: stratification and mobility in post-industrial societies*, Sage: London.

Frank, T. (2000) *One market under God Extreme capitalism, market democracy and the end of economic democracy*, Doubleday: New York.

Gadrey, J. (2002) *New economy, new myth*, Routledge: London.

Gordon, R.J. (2000) 'Does the "New Economy" measure up to the great inventions of the past?', *The Journal of Economic Perspectives*, 14, 4.

Hobsbawm, E.J. (1962) *The age of revolution Europe 1789–1848*, Weidenfeld and Nicholson: London.

Hobsbawm, E. (2005) In defence of history, *The Guardian*, 15 January.

Hudson, R. (2005) *Economic geographies Circuits, flows and spaces*, Sage: London.

Jorgenson, D.W., Ho, M.S. and Stiroh, K.J. (2004) 'Will the US productivity resurgence continue?' Federal Reserve Bank of New York, *Current Issues in Economics and Finance*, 10, 13.

Kelly, K. (1997) 'New rules for the new economy', *Wired News*, 5.09 September www.wired.com/wired/5.09/newrules_pr.html downloaded 23 November 2004.

Kelly, K. (1998) *New rules for the new economy: 10 radical strategies for a connected world*, Viking: New York.

Keynes, J.M. (1930) Economic possibilities for our grandchildren, In: *Essays in persuasion*, W. W. Norton: New York.

Layard, R. (2005). *Happiness: Lessons from a new science*, Allen Lane: Harmondsworth.

Lee, R. (1995) 'Look after the pounds and the people will look after themselves: social reproduction, regulation, and social exclusion in western Europe', *Environment and Planning* A, 27, 1577–1594.

Lee, R. (2003) 'The marginalisation of everywhere? Emerging geographies of emerging markets', ch 4. In: Peck, J. and Yeung, Wai-Cheung, H. eds, *Remaking the global economy: Economic-geographical perspectives*, Sage: London.

Lee, R. (2005a) 'Production'. In: Cloke, P., Goodwin, M. and Crang, M., eds, *Introducing human geographies*, Arnold: London.

Lee, R. (2005b) The ordinary economy (draft manuscript available from the author).

Lee, R. and Smith, D.M. eds, (2004) *Geographies and moralities: International perspectives on development, justice and place*, Blackwell Publishing: Malden MA and Oxford.

Maddison, A. (2001) *The world economy: A millennial perspective*, OECD: Paris.

Maddison, A. (2003) *The world economy: historical statistics*, OECD: Paris.

McDowell, L. (2003) *Redundant masculinities? Employment change and white working class youth*, Blackwell: Oxford.

Morrison, K. and Brown-Huhnes, C. (2005) On the climb: a natural resources boom is unearthing both profits and perils, *Financial Times*, 11 April, 19.

Nordhaus, W.D. (2002) 'Productivity growth and the new economy', *Brookings Papers on Economic Activity* 2, 211–265 [including Comments and Discussions: William, D. Nordhaus; Robert James Gordon, Daniel E. Sichel].

Nordhaus, W.D. (2004) 'Schumpeterian Profits in the American Economy: Theory and Measurement NBER', *Working Paper*, w10433.

Oliner, S.D. and Sichel, D.E. (2000) 'The resurgence of growth in the late 1990s: Is information technology the story?' *The Journal of Economic Perspectives*, 14, 4.

Oswald, A. (2005) Burgers and SUVs do not make us more happy *Financial Times*, 17 March.

Oswald, A., di Tella, R. and MacCulloch, R. (2003) 'The Macroeconomics of Happiness', *Review of Economics and Statistics*, 85, 809–827.

Pesola, M. (2005) End in sight to dotcom's five years of doubt, *Financial Times*, 7 March.

Savage, M. (2000) *Class analysis and social transformation*, Open University Press: Buckingham.

Schiller, H. (1986) *Information and the crisis economy*, Oxford University Press: Oxford.

Schumpeter, J. (1961) *The theory of economic development*, Transaction Publishers: New York.

Skeggs, B. (2004) *Class, self, culture*, Routledge: London.

Stiroh, K. (1999) Is there a new economy? *Challenge*, July–August; 1999.

WEF (2005) *Global information technology report*, World Economic Forum: Geneva.

Wills, J. (2002) 'Bargaining for the space to organise in the global economy: A review of the Accor–IUF trade union rights agreement', *Review of International Political Economy*, 9, 675–700.

www.findarticles.com, downloaded 23 November, 2004.

Zook, M., Dodge, M., Aoyama, Y. and Townsend, A. (2004) 'New Digital Geographies: Information, Communication, and Place', in S.D. Brunn, S.L. Cutter, and J.W. Harrington, eds, *Geography and Technology*, Kluwer: Netherlands, 155–176.

4 The New Economy, or the Emperor's new clothes?

Andrew C. Pratt

Introduction

The idea of the New Economy is at once both an attractive and problematic one. Without doubt, there have been significant events that have constituted some dramatic economic turbulence in recent years, notably in the 2000–1 period and the formation of the so-called 'dot com bubble'. This 'bubble' is not unique and has a lot in common with previous speculative investment events. It may be that the bubble, and crash afterward, has been bigger or had more widespread fallout than previous events. It is not clear whether this restructuring constitutes another round of market speculation where the mode of speculation is the novelty and not the commodity being speculated on (see Feng *et al.* 2001); or, a view more commonly found in the literature, a change in some fundamental values that would indicate a step change for the economy. Second, and related, evidence for the emergence of a New Economy is commonly indexed to particular technologies: namely, computers and the Internet. We should be wary of the technological determinist overtones of much discussion here and point to the gap between what might be a twinkling in the eye of futurologists and what is actually happening. Third, hitched to debate about the New Economy are a host of social/economic/political rhetorics about 'new business practices', (de-)regulation (Kelly 1998), and latterly a new work–life balance (Reich 2000). Fourth, and perhaps most crucially, there is the issue of what the New Economy actually is: a new phase that the whole economy is in; or, a sub-sector of the old economy? Fifth, if it is the latter, how precisely is the New Economy to be defined: does it include all of those activities that use computing or Internet technologies, is it only those businesses that conduct all of their activities 'on-line', or is it something else altogether? Sixth, and finally, what is the causal process that is embodied in the New Economy, and 'what changed' to differentiate it from the 'old economy'? Is it a matter of degree, or something new entirely?

This paper does not seek to answer all of these questions in detail; many are picked up in other chapters of this book. This chapter is sceptical of the notion of the New Economy altogether, however it does accept that there is something worthy of further investigation, although this 'something' is not described adequately as the New Economy, the causal processes implicated by most New Economy writing are not very robust, and neither are these processes universal as is commonly implied. The objective of this chapter is to take a careful look at what is called the New Economy. The New Economy is a slippery term. This chapter focuses on new media because at least this can be defined and is a part of what is implied by the New Economy. By new media we mean those activities embedded in a common sector of economy activity. Although this is a new sector of the economy, one enabled by particular technologies, it cannot be reduced to these technologies, nor can its particular form and practices be explained away by macro-economic changes. At least three modalities of new media can be noted: real-time interaction; on demand services, and hybrids of on-demand and interaction, and; material and immaterial goods. Whilst there is not a necessary organizational or spatial form associated with new media, some rather particular (micro-scale) forms can be observed at present: namely, the spatial clustering of some production activities and a rich socio-economic networking of producers and consumers. In opposition to much of the debate about the New Economy by its cheerleaders and fellow travellers, the macro-economic sceptics (see for example Temple 2002) and the critical discourse of macro-economics (for example Williams 2001), this chapter seeks to be precise about its object and repositions analyses on the micro-scale and empirical practice rather than generalization, and in so doing focuses on the situated nature of production and consumption.

The New Economy: evidence and concepts

Here we will review what might count as evidence of a New Economy, and what its effects could be, and whether these might be considered 'more of the same', or a 'step change'. As is usual such an exercise also discloses that any evidence is only as robust as the conceptualization of the objects that it seeks to represent.

We can begin by reviewing the initial analyses of the impact of high-technology, or computing, on the economy. The data from the USA are fairly conclusive; namely that despite the huge investment in IT there is not a discernable productivity effect (Box 4.1). (See, for example, Gordon 2000, Jorgensen and Stiroh 2000, Oliner and Sichel 2000.)

These types of analyses shed light on the problem of assessing the impact of the New Economy, and they are based upon a number of assumptions that may detract from their potential use or power of explanation. A review of the underpinning assumptions of what have become orthodox analyses of the New Economy can be simply stated. The first point concerns what precisely is understood to constitute the New Economy. It is quite clear that some commentators use the term to refer to the application of computers to conventional activities. From this they assume that any impact of such applications, or 'pay off', can be arrived at through a correlation between investment in computers and growth. Thus, the relevant data for such analyses are spending on

---

Box 4.1 The theory of the New Economy

'The argument was that factors peculiar to technology, particularly the plummeting cost of information processing power, helped to make organizations vastly more efficient. To put it another way, technologically increased productivity and global competition had held down inflation, which means that growth could be higher without the need to choke off inflationary pressures with higher interest rates. Advocates of the notion of a new economy cited supporting factors uniquely combined in the US economy, particularly minimal government, high levels of competition, encouragement of entrepreneurship, and access to venture capital. What gave the theory bite, was the vision that the widespread diffusion of new technology had permanently changed the way economies worked for the better.'

Source: Coyle and Quah (2002, p. 4)

---

computers and output data from firms, which are assumed to be positively correlated. Although advocates of the productivity effect have argued that since spending on IT began to accelerate in the early 1980s, it did take the best part of 20 years for the productivity effect to be realized. Thus, to these mainstream commentators the New Economy can be elided with investment in technology and computers[1] (see David 1999 and Temple 2002 for overviews of the orthodox). This seems to be a remarkably blunt conception, and one that arguably does not touch upon the specific changes (notably, the Internet) and the claims for 'a new business model' and 'new forms of organization' that many see as defining the New Economy (see Feng *et al*. 2001).

Alternatively, orthodox economist dissenters, or 'visionaries' such as Coyle and Quah's (2002), claim that some new measures and indices are required to prove the hypothesis. They include a raft of consumption measures to help to get a sense of the ways in which both production and consumption are influencing one another. Unfortunately, their pragmatic response is to use almost every indicator of new media consumption and use. There is no hint of factors being prioritized (aside from technology) or, a causal model aside from the assertion that the 'weightless economy' will privilege on-line transactions at the expense of face-to-face ones.[2] Unfortunately, for these writers such a simple assertion can be resoundingly undermined with empirical evidence even using simple measures such as employment and location (see Pratt 2000).

What both of these analyses lack – both orthodox and dissenting – is an insight into process and the precise ways in which particular digital technologies can be harnessed to create new products and markets. Economic commentators are generally concerned to look at macro/whole economy measures to identify an outcome and a key variable, such as technology, in the hope that these will 'explain' the New Economy effect. As computers are found in all aspects of the economy this becomes an increasingly diffuse measure. Moreover, many orthodox commentators are wedded to the idea that a revolution is happening, and that a break point with the past can be identified. A common approach of economists is to seek out extant data sets that can be calibrated against their models. Unfortunately, such data are not available. If we sought out either employment or output measures we would need to rely upon standard (old) industrial taxonomies. There is no industrial classification for new media, let alone the New Economy. Analysts are forced back onto the use of inadequate surrogate and secondary measures. The only option would seem to be to suspend judgement on whether such a revolution has occurred until some substantive primary data collection has been carried out, and until we have a clear notion of what 'the New Economy' is, and thus what effects and processes it might produce.

Another core idea that is linked to the notion of a New Economy is that it is different from the 'old economy'. Clearly, the vagueness of these categories makes such a claim difficult to establish. Interestingly, Atkinson and Court's (1998) definition of the New Economy, which Coyle and Quah use in their study, looks remarkably like the transition between Fordism and Post-Fordism, or the transition to flexible specialization augmented by 'high tech rankings'.[3] There is insufficient space to debate the conceptual underpinnings and weaknesses of the transitional arguments offered by the post-Fordist or Flexible Specialization schools of thought here, but it is critical to note that they pose neither computers nor 'new technology' as determining agents (see Piore and Sabel 1984 on Flexible Specialization; see Lipietz 1992 on Post-Fordism). So, despite the apparent similarities between post-Fordism and the shift from an old to a New Economy, there is no substantive conceptual comparison; we are still back to the mono-causal 'factor x: technology'.

A more specific dimension of the process change implied by the New Economy or hi-technology theorists is the impact of instantaneous communications (see Cairncross 1998, Coyle 1998). Once again, one is led to ask 'what is new here?' The telephone and the fax, let alone the telegram and the letter post, all gave rise to similar possibilities. The shift from fax to email, or even video conferencing, whilst different in degree is not revolutionary.[4] Moreover, as Boden and Molotch (1994) have discussed, the 'compulsion of proximity' has not disappeared, rather, it is stronger than ever. We can point also to the fact that the volume of travel, local and international, has never been greater and continues to grow. We should perhaps not dismiss this issue of the 'death of distance' out of hand, it is clear that there has been a shift towards a finer technical division of labour in the service sector, and a strategic relocation of that labour, facilitated by technology. The rise of the remote call centre is a prime case in point (see for example Graham and Marvin 2001, chapter 7). At the same time, there is a more intense interaction of non-routinized – what the Japanese appropriately term 'high-touch' – activities in core urban areas. So, we can find evidence of two types of outcomes: dispersal and agglomeration. This polarization looks suspiciously like the organizational restructuring that was seen in the manufacturing industries (see Dicken 2003), and it seems that at its core it too has the same dynamics.

The third dimension commonly spoken about with regard to the New Economy is the 'network economy' organizational form (Castells 1996). Without doubt there are changes that are occurring in business organization as firms explore new ways to play off economies of scale and scope. We can point to accounts of flexible specialization, which certainly pre-date the New Economy, that seem to offer an account of a shift toward more fragmented, articulated and networked organizational structures. These forms themselves, as Piore and Sable (1984) observed, offer a return to a craft mode of organization that existed before the 'blip' of mass-production. Additionally, some of the newer issues about cross-firm networking and institutions have been evident for many years, it is only since the blinkers of neo-classical economists, whose conceptual concern is with the atomistic and sovereign firm, have been lifted from our eyes that we have begun to recognize these interactions within and across firms and to give them the attention that they deserve.

Fourth, we might consider the issue of falling transport costs associated with products that are digital: the so-called 'weightless economy'. Here, once again, analysts have fallen foul of a partial vision: often extrapolating what is happening in a particular technical division of labour to a whole labour process and whole industry. First, whilst it is possible to download software anywhere there is a telephone connection or Wi-Fi base station, there are not yet (ro) 'bots' that will self-write programs for us, so, it still requires human labour to write them. This is labour-intensive work; coders need managing, a place of work, and somewhere to live, etc. Analyses of the software production industry has shown it to be subject to internationalized mass production techniques (Cusumano 1991), as well as specialized craft production (Pratt 2000). In the latter case (an exceptional, but nevertheless important segment) particular concentrations of labour and unusual labour processes tend to result in localized production. Second, the notion that digital products can be distributed and consumed free is not sustained by the facts; at the very least it relies upon users having hardware, skills and software to play the new product; as well as there to be an effective demand. Much of the New Economy is not pure software but has a material element. Amazon, darling of the New Economy, rests upon the efficiency of its warehouses, logistics and trucks to get products to customers, much as any other business: so-called 'bricks and clicks' businesses (see Dodge 1999).

Box 4.2 A weightless economy?

Even *Wired* magazine, mouthpiece of the digital revolution − where I serve as one of the editors − does not approach the idea of an intangible company. *Wired* is located smack in the middle of an old-fashioned downtown city [South of the Market, San Francisco], and in one year turns 8 million pounds (or 48 railway trucks) of dried tree pulp, and 330,000 pounds of bright coloured ink into hard copies of the magazine. A lot of atoms are involved. [not to mention distribution of the magazine].

(Kelly 1998, p. 4)

Fifth, we can consider the argument of Reich (2000), who terms the New Economy 'the age of the great deal'. By this he means the ability of re-contract for the provision of services at minimal notice or cost. Reich points to the huge instability that this creates for employment, social reproduction and the economy. He has a point. However, the observed processes are reliant upon a pervasive and sustaining neo-liberal market ideology. Moreover, there is evidence of institutional rigidities of the providers of a service,[5] and conservatism (or lack of time) on the side of the consumer. Consider the problems involved in switching a bank account or the small 'churn' between competing providers that is found in the utilities markets. The question remains: is this a sufficient 'step change', or is it an intensification of existing process?

Finally, we have to consider the social aspects of the New Economy; the most widely discussed dimension of which has been the so-called 'digital divide'. Once again, we can point out that the digital divide discriminates against the same kinds of people that experience social exclusion in the analogue world. The difference is that the usual techno-universalist discourse blinds us to the fundamentals that cause such division. In fact, as has been well illustrated, the digital divide is about delivering a 'double whammy' to deprived communities. First, people are unable to, or have little incentive to, gain access to online resources even if they are provided at no charge. This is because web resources are primarily based on consumption (if you have little or no money there is less incentive to learn how to access resources on line, many of which are linked to buying products). Second, off-line resources (such as banks, for example) are withdrawn first from deprived communities (as this is where the least profitable clients are[6]). Added to which on-line businesses offer discounts to those on-line, and compensate by adding charges onto the off-line: effectively this benefits the rich even more. The UK Online initiative to deliver

---

Box 4.3 The age of the Terrific Deal

'The world is in the midst of another great opening: the Age of the Terrific Deal. It started in America several decades ago and has been gathering momentum ever since. It's about to accelerate very sharply. It's based on technology and imagination. Combine the internet, wireless satellites, fiber optics, great leaps in computing power (through circuits no wider than a few atoms), a quantum expansion of broadband connection (transmitting more and faster digital data into homes and offices through networks of fiber-optic cables and constellations of satellites), a map of the human genome and tools to select and combine genes and molecules – and you've got a giant, real-time, global bazaar of almost infinite choice and possibility.

Finding and switching to something better is easier today than at any other time in the history of humanity, and in a few years, will be easier still. We're on the way to getting exactly what we want instantly, from anywhere, at the best value for money.'

(Reich 2000, p. 15)

public services via the Internet has been, at least in part, an exercise on cost-saving with regard to local authority delivery of services. The logic of cost saving is undermined if one has to, say, produce a small run of leaflets (where the cost saving is in volume) to serve those not on-line. Commercial logic is to withdraw the analogue route to encourage 'migration' to digital access. Public bodies can claim free access and availability of information; in practice usage is related to access and motivation: the result is a widening digital divide (see Perrons 2002).

The message from the critical points raised above is one of profound scepticism of anything beyond an intensification of already on-going processes. In this sense agreement is reached with Williams (2001) in his diagnosis of 'business as usual'. Above and beyond this the object New Economy is far more variegated than many of its promoters suggest. It is not reducible to (one) technology, and it is closely bound up with the particularities of the production process (and hence, variable). Moreover, any instance of the New Economy is profoundly interwoven with an emergent mode of governance, manifest as neo-liberalism or simply an ideology of entrepreneurialism (Armstrong 2001). The material practices of the New Economy lead to the individuation of subjects, and the shifting of the responsibility, and risk, to the lowest levels of society: commonly to individuals who can least afford it. The power of this neo-liberal rhetoric is that the presumed effects of the New Economy are commonly presented as a neutral and natural characteristic of particular technologies. In this context it is not surprising that such issues of collective and individual rights and ownership have become one of the new points of contestation in the new world/economy order (see Lessig 2004).

In an attempt to bypass some of the excesses of New Economy rhetoric, and the tendencies to universalize its supposed outcomes, there follows an analysis of one industry: new media. Without doubt, new media would be included in everyone's definition of the New Economy; however, no claims will be made as to the wider generalization of new media activities.

New media: definitions

There is no space here to do more than scratch the surface of the growth and development of the new media industry (see Braczyk *et al.* 1999, Pratt 1999, Scott 2000, Perrons 2003b). The first question that we have to answer is, 'What is new media?' A refreshing riposte to New Economy hyperbole is suggested by Crosbie (2002) who argues that there is much confusion between the media and the medium. Crosbie states that what most people think of as media are actually vehicles within a medium. In other words, a personal computer or the Internet are not media, nor is a magazine: they are all vehicles within a particular medium. Crosbie argues that there are two communications media: mass (many to many) and interpersonal (one to one). The new medium is defined as one whereby 'individualized messages can be simultaneously delivered to an infinite number of people; and, each of the people shares reciprocal control over that content'. Moreover, this new medium is totally dependent on technology, and is not an extension of the previous two media (mass and interpersonal). It is out of this technological capability, and on the back of necessary infrastructures and training, that new forms of organization, business models, and products can be fashioned. In this sense, they are grafted onto and develop out of existing practices. For example, shopping online for a product is similar, but different, from visiting a shop. The requirements for distribution systems and stockholding do not necessarily change with these new purchasing modes. What might be different is the personalized recommendation for new purchases based on previous purchases; or, specialized offers and personalized services. The sophistication of data reconciliation between consumer past behaviour and current orders is what gives on-line shopping a real edge.[7]

In practical terms we can identify three modalities of new media. First, interactive screen-based interfaces: these include web design, and integrated logistics and stock control that enable on-line, automated, Business-to-Business (B2B) and Business-to-Customer (B2C) interactions. Second, hybrids that link material products and virtual resources, for example computer games: whilst these have been, and will increasingly be, played on-line, their characteristic form is a free-standing 'box', or a box incorporated into a personal computer (PC). They are essentially personalized 'arcade machines'. As a business model, computer games are very much like buying records, videos or CDs. Historically,

---

Box 4.4 Defining a new medium

[Those] who truly understand this New Medium and its possibilities to simultaneously deliver an infinite number of individualized messages while providing equal control over that content refer to the New Medium as the *'many-to-many'* medium – to distinguish it from the 'one-to-one' (Interpersonal) or 'one-to-many' (Mass) media.

Mistakes, misnomers, and misperceptions of the New Medium are easy to make because the vehicles of this New Medium are only starting to appear, as are the true capabilities of this New Medium… . Just consider the converged technologies that make this New Medium possible…

Imagine that when a person visits a newspaper Web site, he sees not just the bulletins and major stories that he wouldn't have known to request information about but sees the rest of that edition customized to his own unique needs and interests. Rather than every reader seeing the same edition, each reader sees an edition that has simultaneously been individualized to his interest and generalized to his needs …

[T]hese New Medium forms of content inherently are forms of mass customization, something impossible with either the Interpersonal Medium or the Mass Medium. The existence of this New Medium will catalyze, economize, and popularize entirely new vehicles for production and distribution, just as the invention of the medium of air did for transportation. And it will create entirely new concepts in and forms of content.

Source: Crosbie (2002) (gender as in original)

the proprietary 'platform' or player has been an important element of structuring the market. Third, and finally, broadband, on demand, services: these include downloads in real time, or time-shifted, film, music and other information. The flow is predominantly one-way, from producer to consumer. For a time (in the late 1990s) it looked as if Peer-to-Peer (P2P) file-sharing might constitute a new hybrid of interactive and on-demand models; however, most have been incorporated into the third business model (but see Leyshon 2003). Thus, really, the third modality is an extension of the distributional possibilities of existing technologies; and the second is materially constrained to particular hardware. The first mode is the only true 'new media'; however, there is a strong potential for modes two and three to migrate to mode one.

Whilst there has been much academic debate about the consumption of new media, there is precious little about its production (it is almost as if researchers are taken in by the 'weightless economy' myth). What follows will highlight this overlooked production side of the argument. At present, the institutional structure of the entertainment industries is not conducive to the shift to purely on-line activity, although it is technically possible. Nevertheless, all three modalities share similar (though different) characteristics of their production.

The growth of the industry has been accompanied by the development of specific sub-markets and, more critically, institutions associated with their production and distribution. In the case of computer games, the memory and data transfer limitations of the Internet and home computing have meant that they remained linked to a proprietary technology, playback and distribution structure. Even with the advent of computer games on PCs (albeit modified with sound and video cards and faster processors) this production structure remains. The nature of games, the market, and the investment required to develop them has created specific conditions associated with their production. There is no space to explore this issue in any depth here, but the games industry has had a distinctive trajectory and quickly developed an institutionalized industrial structure that is very similar to the (old) music industry. Likewise, the possibilities of convergence (facilitated by media migrating from analogue to digital technologies) have meant that a substantial part of the music industry, and increasing parts of the film and factual broadcasting and newspapers are also within the ambit of new media (mode 3). Likewise, in the near future, mobile telephony will increasingly be drawn into this nexus.

My definition of new media concerns what used to be called multimedia (Pratt 2000), namely a combination of sound, text and images (moving or still), usually delivered in real time. Thus, in the early 1990s, this included a range of technologies that delivered digital content (and hence, they are distinguished from tools such as programming). Such software was usually distributed on CD-ROMs, tapes and floppy disks. However, with the development of the Graphical User Interfaces and web browsers from 1992 onwards, the dominant form of distribution has been the Internet. As Crosbie notes, the Internet adds a new dimension of interactivity and customization to multimedia, making it fully fledged new media. This interactivity is captured by the common terms (in the late 1990s) of B2C and B2B. Put simply, this is the development of web sites, web design, and web businesses. One of the issues I have raised with interviewees in San Francisco, New York, Berlin, Tokyo and London during field research has been how they define 'new media'. Usual responses are about 'opposition' to old media and market opportunity, drawing attention to what they felt was the uniqueness of their business. In a sense, early businesses had a distinctive cultural approach to business that stressed individualism and creativity. Most confirmed Crosbie's point about the 'on-line' and interactive nature of their activities: in traditional terms this offered the possibility of reaching new markets and better integrated logistics, both tailored to a variety of customers. The key element seemed to be to use technologies and substantive content to deliver surfers to sites, and to transact business there.

One of the enduring challenges for new media businesses is the search for a business model that will allow money to be made (see Pratt 2000, Feng *et al.* 2001). Most firms did not start with a 'product' and a 'market'; they saw the possibility of a niche, or a new way of attracting customers. As the interactivity occurs, businesses change their focus moving in whichever direction offered greatest potential profitability. Until such profitability can be found there is often a huge sunk investment; but, in the mid- and late-1990s business investors and/or venture capital were not hard to find. Thus, many firms were living in a game of 'pass the parcel' where the music never stopped, and the money never had to be paid back. This was a problem for investors, if not for firms. The publicity that was linked to the rise of new media helped to direct a huge stream of external funds into new media businesses. Not surprisingly a market solution was found, venture capital, and later a promised public listing where shares we sold to investors to underpin long-term development. Given that few companies actually registered a profit these investments were akin to trying to fill a sieve with water.[8] Critically, early employees were held to the company with offers (or, more correctly, promises), of 'stock options' on vesting (when the shares were actually listed for the company at the Initial Public Offering). The geography of the new media venture capital business is important in sustaining local clusters of businesses (Pratt 2000, Pratt *et al.* 2000, Zook 2002, 2004).

A striking feature of new media development is its physical location.[9] New media 'clusters' have not developed everywhere, or only in locations close to labour environmental preferences, as was suggested by those who predicted workers would work at home in 'tele-cottages' (Toffler 1980). In fact they have developed in a small number of locations across the world. The surprising point is that, according to some economists who hail the New Economy, clusters should not have developed at all (see Quah 2000). That clusters did develop highlights the peculiarities of the production process of new media as well as the continuities, rather than breaks, with the old economy. The key elements in the development of new media concern the unusual organization of production and the structure of labour markets which are dominated by freelance and serial project working. This state of affairs is referred to as 'boundaryless careers' or 'portfolio careers' within project-based enterprises (Jones 1996). The emergent effects are very tight co-location based upon face-to-face interactions (Grabher 2001, 2002). Firm formation is on the basis of a specific, time-limited, project for which key people are recruited. The small-scale operation and short time scale of such projects was initially – in new media at least – based upon 'flat firms' with little or no hierarchy with an expertise-based division of labour (such that there was much team work). It was only later that specific 'job descriptions' emerged, and as they did so they echoed those found within the advertising, film and television industries. Even today training is de-institutionalized with individuals responsible for their own development, in their own time (Christopherson and Van Jaarsveld 2005).

Studies have found that employees were recruited from diverse communities (coding; artistic and business) with project management and a 'directorial' role deemed to be a key skill. In the earlier years, when the labour market was buoyant, employees were either freelancers or self-employed, and as such firms had to 'add value' for employees if they were to attract and retain staff. As employees were usually on temporary contracts, they were always looking for the next job, thus networking was vital to find out who was hiring next. As analysts of the film and television labour markets have argued, workers in this sphere use jobs as steps in their career development (Blair 2001, Blair *et al.* 2001). Such a strategy requires high quality, fresh gossip and information exchange. Thus, physical co-presence is required. Accordingly, new media companies were not only found clustered in particular cities, but actually within a small number of specific streets and buildings.

Moreover, project-based firms also require to be 'in the loop' in order to pick up their next contract. Studies have gathered significant examples of firms acting like individuals, moving from one contract to another in a 'learning curve'. Sometimes this learning involved the firms 'migrating' between different technologies and markets, commonly from web design to business consultancy. Being 'in the loop' for such companies meant just the same intense information exchange as that of individuals and hence they tended to locate themselves in a community setting (with other companies, clients and lenders), as well as with employees (past, present and future). Often, employees were an embodied form of information exchange. Within the workplace, large open plan offices/lofts were commonly preferred so that work process could be fluid. That is, they could be re-organized at short notice. Office communication was often on the basis of a 'shout' for assistance from colleagues: this necessitates working in the same room. In the short term, the social nature of business led to instances of 'borrowed' and 'shared' equipment and personnel (often from the company 'down the hall'). Again, issues of physical proximity were salient (Wittel 2001, Pratt 2002).

Finally, we can note that the 'bulimic' nature of work (see Pratt 2000) leads to 'crunch periods' (often requiring 24/7 shifts) that have severe impacts on home–work relations or social reproduction (Perrons 2003a, Jarvis and Pratt 2005). We found few examples of the idealized 'live–work' settings of new media companies in lofts where they also lived (aside from those set up by housing providers, to make a killing in the property market). As Florida (2002) has noted, many creative and high technology workers like to live in culturally rich and diverse areas. Taken together this has created inflationary pressure on locales where new forms of cultural production take place, and in many cases it has created severe housing market stress for both new media workers (and for company principals) who have been priced out of 'gentrifying' neighbourhoods.

It might be argued that both boundaryless careers and project-based firms are evidence of a youthful industry and immature firms: to this extent they are found in all micro enterprises. However, if we look to the film, television and advertising industries we can see that such a temporal maturity narrative will not hold. First, 'deregulation' (or rather new regulatory structures) has been the driver of such organizational fragmentation (Christopherson 2002). Second, it may be that instead of 'growing out of it', that is small firms getting bigger and more 'normal', that an unusual organizational structure is maintained for particular reasons (associated with intense competition and innovation). Clearly, more detailed qualitative research is required to establish this point.

Revolution, business as usual, or something else?

The big question remains: is there anything unique or revolutionary about new media that might at least count as evidence for the claims about a 'New Economy'? The first point has to be a definitional one. Most definitions of the New Economy are so wide and all encompassing that even if there *were* anything going on it is likely that it would be swamped by the 'noise' of contradictory activity. Second, using self-fulfilling definitions of the New Economy such as those of the US Department of Commerce does not promote critical scholarship. Third, better definitions, more macro scale analyses, and secondary analyses, would not help us to analyse this area of the economy as the basic data available, namely the industrial classification codes used to classify it, are many years out of date and simply do not measure the object of interest: New Economy or new media: it is 'below the radar'. Thus, we have to begin from the bottom up, with detailed analyses of what is going on in emergent economic sectors. This has been my objective here to avoid idealization and generalization and to peel off an area of economic activity and examine it in detail.

One characteristic of new media is that it is part of a wider production process, one that is constantly being re-articulated as new products, markets and means of distribution are envisaged. In part this is due to re- and dis-intermediation that is a significant potential of the medium (in another context see French and Leyshon 2004). We have to look at the whole production network/chain to see what is behind the screen. We need to see the connections between infrastructure (wires and roads) and products, to see the hybrid nature of these systems, and the complex and emerging division of labour. It is in these novel formations that work practices emerge. In some cases, such as those that I have explored, the organization of production is tightly constrained to place and people.

In each of the modalities of new media, relationships to customers or with other producers varies. As most of the businesses have a 'chart mentality' (that is they are driven by 'hits') they are extremely sensitive to market fluctuation change and potential change. In order to address this challenge they commonly seek to create a feedback loop with clients *and* customers that will hopefully calibrate precisely the *qualities* of what is produced (not simply *quantities* as in the old economy), at particular times, and in specific places. The general 'buzz', or more specifically the local gossip, may provide access to 'the next big thing' for those attuned to understand it, and thus cultural producers more generally, and new media producers in particular, cannot afford to drift outside of this charmed circle.

Even if it is a passing phase, or an immature phase, the recent form of new media businesses is worth looking at (particularly as there are some striking parallels with other 'cultural industries'; a sector of the economy that is growing rapidly in the developed world). The project-based firm, and a fluid labour market, as well as the lack of capacity to 'learn systemically', creates an unstable and perhaps unsustainable structure; learning is individualized (at firm and worker level): in the end the potential to add value is both carried in the gossip and embodied in the people active in new media and associated industries in these districts (Pratt 2002). This is a situated and embodied interaction: it is the practice of 'embedding' for this industry. Consequentially, property price rises, takeovers, firm migrations, etc., all pose threats for such regions. Moreover, there are maturity issues. A workforce mainly comprised of '20-somethings' cannot forego security indefinitely. As age catches up the need to either pay a mortgage or form a family (or both) constrains the room to manoeuvre for many. Due to the freelance nature of work there is little visibility of the 'lay-offs' common in the manufacturing industries. People are simply not re-hired. There are also a number of labour market effects. Gill (2002), for example, notes how the de-institutionalization of media labour markets has specific gender, age and race implications. These effects are mainly about discrimination as a result of recruitment through informal friendship-based networks. This makes it particularly hard for 'outsiders' to break in and reinforces privilege.

Related and overlain on all of this is the way that the new media story meshes so successfully with the shift to neo-liberal governance in US and UK society: a shift to individual responsibility, and a minimal role for the state and other social actors. The initial promotion of the New Economy seemed to emerge from the pages of *Wired* and (US) government advisors; it was a story about technological utopianism and libertarianism. As Armstrong (2001) notes, the unexamined myths or idealizations of entrepreneurship need to be checked against empirical practices; which is what this chapter has sought to achieve.

So, it is not a revolution, however, whilst it may be business as usual as far as the macro economy goes, there are some unusual day-to-day practices going on that make new media (at least) different to our expectations. There are some interesting things that are going on for specific reasons; they are worthy of attention and note. They may, or may not, be subject to generalization, but they do deserve further investigation. If nothing else they need attention as the 'prophets' of the business world seem to be selectively plundering the sector for examples upon which to base a new social and political philosophy. For all its hard technology and cyberspace, new media is a very 'touchy–feely' business.

Further reading

Many of the key references are clearly signposted in the chapter. The aim of this chapter has been to take readers away from secondary data and idealizations of work practice and toward an appreciation of the material practices that constitute it. A very comprehensive analysis of the development of New Media in New York can be found in Mike Indergaard's (2004) *Silicon Alley*. An ethnographic study of Silicon Valley provided by English-Lueck (2002), is indicative of where I think future work could be directed. Finally, a novel by Ellen Ullman (1997) captures the issues and dilemmas of work in new media. Her book, *Close to the machine: technophilia and its discontents* documents life as a software coder in San Francisco's 'multimedia gulch' in the mid-1990s.

Notes

1   In a somewhat teleological statement given the dominant hypothesis of technology-led growth the US Department of Commerce (2002) defines the New Economy as 'an economy in which IT and related investments drive higher rates of productivity growth'. Furthermore, such a definition elides technology with IT and the rest of the economy.
2   The weightless economy is based upon two principles (enabled by the Internet): cost-free reproduction of goods, and zero distribution costs (see Quah 1999).
3   That is they explicitly privilege the impact of one technology over another.
4   The reader can ask themselves the question: 'what can be communicated by email but not fax?'
5   Institutional contrasts also account for the different form and impact of new media in Europe compared to the US (Watson 2001).
6   Of course loans to the poor are generally very profitable for lenders as such high rates of interest are charged in exchange for high risk (Leyshon *et al.* 2004). However, in aggregate terms banks achieve greater income and profits dealing with the rich.
7   A good example is the store affinity card. The on-line example is the 'recommendation' offered on a purchase on Amazon.
8   The popular terminology of the time was the 'burn rate' of companies (how long it took them to exhaust all of the investment capital).
9   This is something shared in similar but diverse ways with film and television production, computer games and advertising.

References

Armstrong, P. (2001) 'Science, enterprise and profit: ideology in the knowledge-driven economy' *Economy and Society,* 30, 524–552.

Atkinson, R. D., Court, R. (1998) *The New Economy Index: Understanding America's Economic Transformation,* Progressive Policy Institute: Washington.

Blair, H. (2001) '"You're only as good as your last job": the labour process and labour market in the British film industry' *Work, Employment and Society,* 15, 149–169

Blair, H., Grey, S., Randle, K. (2001) 'Working in film – Employment in a project based industry', *Personnel Review*, 30, 170–185.

Boden, D., Molotch, H. L. (1994) The compulsion of proximity in *NowHere: space, time and modernity*, R Friedland, D Boden, eds, University of California Press, Berkerley 257–286.

Braczyk, H. J., Fuchs, G., Wolf, H.-G., eds. (1999) *Multimedia and regional economic restructuring* Routledge, London.

Cairncross, F. (1998) *The death of distance: How the communications revolution will change our lives* Harvard Business School Press: Boston.

Castells, M. (1996) *The rise of the network society*, Blackwell, Cambridge: MA.

Christopherson, S. (2002) 'Project work in context: regulatory change and the new geography of media', *Environment and Planning A*, 34, 2003–2015.

Christopherson, S., van Jaarsveld, D. (2005) 'New media after the dot.com bust: The persistent influence of political institutions on work in the cultural industries', *International Journal of Cultural Policy*, 11, 77–94.

Coyle, D. (1998) *The weightless economy*, Capstone, London.

Coyle, D., Quah, D. (2002) *Getting the measure of the new economy*, Work Foundation: London.

Crosbie, V. (2001) *What is new media?*. www.digitaldeliverance.com/mT/archives/000622.html accessed 8 July 2005, since unavailable. Copy available at www.sociology.org.uk/as4mm3a.doc accessed 4 October 2006.

Cusumano, M. (1991) 'Factory concepts and practices in software development', *Annals of the History of Computing*, 13, 3–32.

David, P. (1999) *Digital technology and the productivity paradox: After ten years what has been learned*, Department of Commerce, Washington DC.

Department of Commerce (2002) *Digital economy 2002*, Department of Commerce, USA, Washington DC.

Dicken, P. (2003) *Global shift: reshaping the global economic map in the 21st century*, Sage, London.

Dodge, M. (1999) *Finding the source of the Amazon.com: examining the hype of the earth's biggest bookstore*, University College London, London.

English-Lueck, J. A. (2002) *Cultures@siliconvalley*, Stanford University Press, Stanford.

Feng, H.Y., Froud, J., Johal, S., Haslam, C., Williams, K. (2001) 'A new business model? The capital market and the new economy', *Economy and Society*, 30, 467–503.

Florida, R. L. (2002) *The rise of the creative class: and how it's transforming work, leisure, community and everyday life*, Basic Books, New York.

French, S., Leyshon, A. (2004) 'The new, new financial system? Towards a conceptualization of financial reintermediation', *Review of International Political Economy*, 11, 263–288.

Gill, R. (2002) 'Cool creative and egalitarian? Exploring gender in project-based new media work in Europe', *Information, Communication and Society*, 5, 70–89.

Gordon, R. (2000) 'Does the new economy measure up to the great innovations of the past?', *Journal of Economic Perspectives*, 14, 48–74.

Grabher, G. (2001) 'Locating economic action: projects, networks, localities, institutions', *Environment and Planning A*, 33, 1329–1331.

Grabher, G. (2002) 'Cool projects, boring institutions: Temporary collaboration in social context', *Regional Studies*, 36, 205–214.

Graham, S., Marvin, S. (2001) *Splintering urbanism*, Routledge, London.

Indergaard, M. (2004) *Silicon Alley: the rise and fall of a new media district*, Routledge, New York.

Jarvis, H., Pratt, A. C. (2006) 'Shifting and grounding the work–life balance: an exploration of San Francisco's new media households', *Geoforum* 37, 331–339.

Jones, C. (1996) Careers in project networks: the case of the film industry in *The Boundaryless Career* M B Arthur, D M Rousseau, eds, Oxford University Press: New York.

Jorgensen, D., Stiroh, K. (2000) 'Raising the speed limit: US economic growth in the information age', *Brookings Papers on Economic Activity,* 31, 125–211.

Kelly, K. (1998) *New rules for the new economy,* Fourth estate: London.

Lessig, L. (2004) *Free culture: how big media uses technology and the law to lock down culture and control creativity,* Penguin: New York.

Leyshon, A. (2003) 'Scary monsters? Software formats, peer-to-peer networks, and the spectre of the gift', *Environment and Planning D-Society & Space,* 21, 533–558.

Leyshon, A., Burton, D., Knights, D., Alferoff, C., Signoretta, P. (2004) 'Towards an ecology of retail financial services: understanding the persistence of door-to-door credit and insurance providers', *Environment and Planning A,* 36, 625–645.

Lipietz, A. (1992) *Towards a new economic order: postfordism, ecology and democracy,* Polity: Cambridge.

Oliner, S., Sichel, D. (2000) 'The resurgence of growth in the late 1990s: is information technology the story?', *Journal of Economic Perspectives* 14, 13–22.

Perrons, D. (2002) The new economy, labour market inequalities and the work life balance in *Geographies of labour market inequality* R Martin, P Morrison, eds, Routledge, London.

Perrons, D. (2003a) 'The new economy and the work life balance. A case study of the new media sector in Brighton and Hove', *Gender work and organisation* 10, 65–93.

Perrons, D. (2003b) 'The new economy and the work-life balance: Conceptual explorations and a case study of new media', *Gender Work and Organisation,* 10, 65–93.

Piore, M. J., Sabel, C. F. (1984) *The second industrial divide: possibilities for prosperity,* Basic Books, New York.

Pratt, A. C. (1999) *Technological and Organisational Change in the European Audio visual Industries: An Exploratory Analysis of the Consequences for Employment,* European Audio Visual Observatory: Strasbourg.

Pratt, A. C. (2000) 'New media, the new economy and new spaces', *Geoforum,* 31, 425–436.

Pratt, A. C. (2002) 'Hot jobs in cool places. The material cultures of new media product spaces: the case of the south of market, San Francisco', *Information, Communication and Society,* 5, 27–50.

Pratt, A. C., Ramsden, P., Peake, L. (2000) *Financing new media: a report for banking on culture,* North West Arts Board: Liverpool.

Quah, D. (1999) *The weightless economy in economic development,* London School of Economics and Political Science Centre for Economic Performance, London.

Quah, D. (2000) 'Internet cluster emergence', *European Economic Review,* 44, 1032–1044.

Reich, R. B. (2000) *The future of success,* A. Knopf: New York.

Scott, A. J. (2000) *The cultural economy of cities: essays on the geography of image-producing industries,* Sage: London.

Temple, J. (2002) 'The assessment: The New Economy', *Oxford Review of Economic Policy* 18, 241–264

Toffler, A. (1980) *The third wave,* Collins: London.

Ullman, E. (1997) *Close to the machine: technophilia and its discontents,* City Lights Books, San Francisco.

Watson, M. (2001) 'Embedding the 'new economy' in Europe: a study in the institutional specificities of knowledge-based growth', *Economy and Society,* 30, 504–523.

Williams, K. (2001) 'Business as usual', *Economy and Society,* 30, 399–411.

Wittel, A. (2001) 'Toward a network sociality', *Theory Culture & Society,* 18, 51–76.

Zook, M. A. (2002) 'Grounded capital: venture financing and the geography of the Internet industry, 1994–2000', *Journal of Economic Geography,* 2, 151–177.

Zook, M. A. (2004) 'The knowledge brokers: Venture capitalists, tacit knowledge and regional development', *International Journal of Urban and Regional Research,* 28, 621–641.

5 The New Old Thing: e-commerce geographies after the dot.com boom

Matthew Zook

Introduction

The origin of the Internet era of electronic commerce (e-commerce) can arguably be traced back to October 1994 when the first version of the Netscape browser was released to the public. Widely popular because of its speed advantage over the Mosaic browser, it also contained commerce-enabling software, i.e., the secure socket layer (SSL), that paved the way for secure financial transactions over this growing network (Reid 1997, Abbate, 1999, Naughton 2000). Although e-commerce had existed for decades prior, it was expensive, difficult and largely the purview of large corporations. The Internet greatly democratized the ability to conduct electronic commerce and paved the way for the tremendous expansion of e-commerce experimentation and failure (centred in the dot.com boom and bust at the turn of the 20th century), followed by the less visible, yet fundamentally more important, expansion of electronic commerce across sectors and around the world.

This chapter explores the ramifications of e-commerce on the geographies of the economy before, during and after the dot.com boom and bust. This period represents a key moment in the execution of e-commerce and resulting changes in geographies of production (e.g. supplier networks, logistics and sales), organization (firm types, MNCs and firm networks) and access/interaction (e.g., who can participate and from where). After introducing the concept of e-commerce, this chapter borrows from the title of Michael Lewis's (2000) book (*The New New Thing*) on the founding of Netscape, to review the dot.com boom (the New New Thing) and bust (the Old New Thing) and most significantly, how the introduction of e-commerce (the New) shapes and is shaped by existing economic geographies and firm structures (the Old), to make the New Old Thing.[1]

Introducing e-commerce

Although the term New Economy has fallen out of favour post-2000, it remains an important concept in understanding the development of e-commerce. During the 1990s the New Economy was theorized as provoking fundamental disruptions to the existing economic order and thus allowing a largely new set of firms to disintermediate and reintermediate industries and markets.[2] This in turn was theorized as the means of creating a new set of rules that would further perpetuate the new economy. There was no more forceful advocate for this position than Kevin Kelly (1998, 1) of *Wired* magazine who argued:

> No one can escape the transforming fire of machines. Technology which once progressed at the periphery of culture now engulfs our minds as well as our lives. Is it any wonder that technology triggers such intense fascination, fear and rage? One by one, each of the things that we care about in life is touched by science and then altered. Human expression, thought, communication, and even human life have been infiltrated by high technology. As each realm is overtaken by complex techniques, the usual order is inverted, and new rules established. The mighty tumble, the once confident are left desperate for guidance, and the nimble are given a chance to prevail.

Although the extravagant nature of these ideas is now abundantly clear, they loomed large in the popular and business imagination of the 1990s. While the rhetoric surrounding e-commerce focused on its 'newness' and most consumers (and small investors) equated e-commerce with web-based retailing, its history is much longer and scope much broader. As a practice, e-commerce or the sale of good or services electronically, has existed since the 1970s (through Electronic Data Interchange or EDI). Moreover, despite the great acceleration of retail e-commerce during the commercialization of the Internet, it remains a relatively small portion of total e-commerce sales (3.8 per cent) in the United States.[3]

As Table 5.1 illustrates, retail e-commerce sales (defined as B2C) have grown by almost 800 per cent from 1998 to 2002 but are a fraction of the size of e-commerce sales in manufacturing or merchant wholesaling (defined as B2B). Together these two industries represent 92.6 per cent of all e-commerce transactions in the USA (although this represents a small but real drop from a 96 per cent share in 1999). This strong showing in e-commerce usage 'reflects the long-standing use of EDI in manufacturing and wholesale trade. EDI is the exchange of computer processable data in a standard format between organizational entities' (US Census 2004). This finding is reinforced by the relatively high percentage of total sales via e-commerce in manufacturing and wholesale compared to services and retail (see Figure 5.1). Thus, despite capturing much of the public's and stock markets' attention during the 1990s boom, most of e-commerce remains concentrated within manufacturing and wholesale although increasingly these transactions are conducted via Internet (versus EDI) based tools.[4]

But focusing on e-commerce as simply a means of facilitating sales online masks the complexity of the forms and structures that e-commerce can take (Zwass 1996, 2003). For example, Internet enabled e-commerce has allowed new actors to participate in commercial transactions with important implications for the resulting geographies. An exclusive concentration on sales also

Table 5.1 E-commerce's sales by industry – millions of $ (US data)

1998		
Industry sector	*E-commerce sales*	*Share of total sales (per cent)*
Manufacturing	n/a	n/a
Merchant Wholesale Trade	173,903	7.3
Selected Service Industries	14,463	0.4
Retail trade	4,926	0.2

1999		
Industry sector	*E-commerce sales*	*Share of total sales (per cent)*
Manufacturing	729,563	18.1
Merchant Wholesale Trade	209,863	8.3
Selected Service Industries	24,182	0.6
Retail trade	14,667	0.5

2000		
Industry sector	*E-commerce sales*	*Share of total sales (per cent)*
Manufacturing	755,807	18.0
Merchant Wholesale Trade	248,400	9.1
Selected Service Industries	36,022	0.8
Retail trade	28,000	0.9

2001		
Industry sector	*E-commerce sales*	*Share of total sales (per cent)*
Manufacturing	724,228	18.2
Merchant Wholesale Trade	286,211	10.6
Selected Service Industries	36,045	0.8
Retail trade	34,263	1.1

2002		
Industry sector	*E-commerce sales*	*Share of total sales (per cent)*
Manufacturing	751,985	19.6
Merchant Wholesale Trade	319,755	11.7
Selected Service Industries	41,463	0.9
Retail trade	44,287	1.4

Source: E-commerce figures are based on data collected annually in the Economic Census, the Annual Survey of Manufactures (ASM), the Annual Trade Survey (ATS), the Service Annual Survey (SAS), and the Annual Retail Trade Survey (ARTS) (see US Census, 2004).

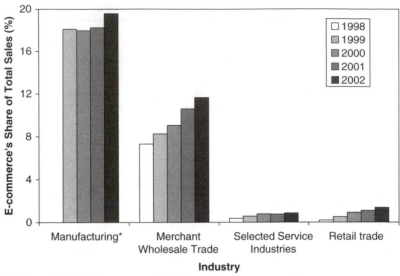

*1998 figures for Manufacturing are not available

Figure 5.1 E-commerce's share of total sales by industry (US data). Source: E-commerce
    figures are based on data collected annually in the Economic Census, the
    Annual Survey of Manufactures (ASM), the Annual Trade Survey (ATS), the
    Service Annual Survey (SAS), and the Annual Retail Trade Survey (ARTS) (see
    US Census, 2004).

obscures the potential of e-commerce to alter the structures, organization and
geographies of production through the use and leverage of the information
contained within any e-commerce system. Focusing on changes in the power
relations and structure of economic processes behind the increase of sales provides one with a much deeper theoretical understanding of the development
of e-commerce (Garcia 1997, OECD 1999, Porter 2001, Leyshon *et al.* 2005a).

Thus, e-commerce represents a means of value creation (through the reduction in inefficiencies or the rise of new types of interactions) for consumers
and firms whose constituency likely includes new actors who for reasons of
access, cost or complexity were previously excluded. This ability to create value
was a major driver of the dot.com boom of the 1990s, albeit often resulting in
spectacularly unsuccessful outcomes, highlighting the dangers of technological
determinism. For as Porter (2001) notes, simply implementing e-commerce
need not create value and as the dot.com era amply demonstrates, the process
of adopting e-commerce is a decidedly difficult and time-consuming task.

The New New Thing: the dot.com boom

The Internet was almost our WWII. It was a chance to make difference in
people's lives, change the world … and get really rich doing it. Former Chief
Evangelist for a dot.com firm interviewed in 2002.[5]

The story of the factors leading to the boom (and bust) of dot.com firms is told in more detail elsewhere (Hait and Weiss 2001, Cassidy 2002, Zook 2005) but it is useful to consider some of the factors behind it. Although now generally viewed as simply the preeminent example of capitalism and greed run amuck, there were compelling factors (beyond outright avarice) behind the irrational exuberance displayed by so many.

Chief among these were the inflated expectations and hype concerning the innovative nature of the Internet. Fueled by references to Schumpeterian theories of creative destruction, it was widely held that the Internet 'would change everything' and a new era of commerce via electronic networks was in the making. As one dot.com founder noted in late 2001, 'In order to start a company you need something REAL to invest in. It is usually pretty hard to see what it will be, but we KNEW that the Internet was the REAL THING.' While this interviewee no longer had the same confidence in his company (a difficult task given that he was interviewed after his company's bankruptcy) his statement aptly captures the hubris of the boom period.[6]

From this basic assumption much of the boom was driven. Risk capital was readily and cheaply available for dot.com companies, the media and many analysts provided a steady source of positive news on the topic and there seemed an almost insatiable demand by public markets for stock in companies with no profits and uncertain means on how profits could be achieved except through the often repeated mantra of 'Get Big Fast'.[7] As many company founders reported, 'It was hard not to drink the kool-aid' and the boom-driven expansion of e-commerce went forward at great speed (and contrary to the widespread rhetoric of the 'irrelevance of geography') concentrating in a few key locations, largely in the USA (Zook 2000, 2005).

While the boom was central in increasing e-commerce's visibility and size (particularly in the case of retailing) it was also unsustainable as the expectations for overnight transformation of markets and commerce quickly outran the pace of actual change. Moreover, since many of the firms formed during this time were built on little more than hype and hope there was little of value upon which to fall back when the public markets were no longer capable of sustaining the process (Feng *et al.* 2001). As one dot.com founder noted in late 2001, '99.9 per cent of the Internet companies shouldn't have existed … I include myself in this …We just had a lot of misplaced expectations.'

The Old New Thing: the dot.com bust

> Already, it is hard to fathom that just a couple of years ago many intelligent Americans believed that the marriage of computers and communications networks had ushered in a new era of permanent peace and prosperity. (Cassidy 2002, p. 1)

When the end of the boom finally arrived in early 2000 it came hard. Between March 2000 and April 2001 the NASDAQ index (where many of the public dot.com firms were listed) was down 68 per cent. Firms began a series of lay-offs in an effort to survive but many slid into bankruptcy and people outside the dot.com industry began to gleefully track, mock and predict the next dot.com crash (Kaplan 2002). Particularly spectacular was Webvan, an online grocery store, which had received more than $820 million in financing (both from venture capital and the public markets) but declared bankruptcy by July 2001. The cut-backs by dot.com firms had multiplier effects throughout the regions in which they were concentrated and no place was harder hit than the San Francisco Bay region where the unemployment rate rose from two per cent at the end of 2000 to seven per cent two years later (see, in addition, Walker 2005).

The dot.com bust, however, reflects the shortcomings of a particular type of e-commerce, i.e., massively funded companies trying to change the world overnight, rather than the shortcomings of e-commerce in general (Feng *et al.* 2001). As a long-time venture capitalist (who invested in several failed dot.com companies) remarked in the summer of 2002, 'With but rare exceptions, all the dot.com companies were built upon bad foundations. They tried to become tech companies but they never had it right … no one could get profits in front of revenues.'

Nevertheless this widely recounted failure of dot.com companies masks the simple yet important fact that some companies endured and retained the potential for 'changing the world'. As the founder of a surviving e-commerce company argued in early 2002:

> Not everything was bad. There was some great innovation, great opportunities and a great excitement in the air. What about eBay? What about instant news on the web? E-commerce and the Web have changed the way we use information in everyday parts of our lives.

The most telling example of the upside of the dot.com boom is that by the end of 2004 three companies, eBay, Yahoo! and Google, had a combined market value of $175 billion and are the dominant players in their respective e-commerce market niches. These valuations are well in excess of all the investment in dot.com companies during the boom period (Zook 2005).

The bursting of the dot.com bubble in April 2000 resulted in a marked decrease in rhetoric on the ability of the Internet and e-commerce to completely transform the economy. Moreover, Table 5.1 shows there was a drop in the total amount of e-commerce sales in manufacturing from 2000 to 2001. Despite this decline, e-commerce continues to grow and affect the way companies conduct business (Leyshon *et al.* 2005b). As the founder of a key e-commerce firm in Silicon Valley noted in 2002, 'I think the Internet is going to continue to have a long term transformative effect. The bubble didn't get the trend wrong, just the timing. Email doesn't replace phones but substitutes for them in certain ways. The same goes for e-commerce.' While it is no longer the heady stuff of instant companies and 20-year-old billionaires, e-commerce continues to have important implications for the development trajectories of individuals, firms and regions.

The New Old Thing: e-commerce geographies after the dot.com boom and bust

> The future is unbelievable with the technology of the Internet but it is going to take time. Dot.com founder in May 2002

> Some people view the Internet as over but the Internet is still early in its evolution. Sure, the gold rush is over but it will still continue to change the world. Dot.com founder in December 2001

A key lesson in analysing e-commerce after the dot.com boom and bust is the recognition of the brief history of Internet based e-commerce. David (1990), Fisher (1992) and Chandler (1977) provide cautionary lessons on the time scale over which a new technology (i.e., electric motor, telephone and railroads) affects the organization and spatial arrangement of the economy. This care contrasts sharply with the expectations of the 1990s. As one dot.com founder observed in May 2002, '…when something is new and exciting, people go nuts, and then there's a crash like we saw in 2000. The funny thing is that these huge expectations are eventually met but it is more gradual. I have no doubt that what we see over the next ten years will be much bigger than the big boom ever was.' With this long-term sensibility firmly in hand, this chapter focus on four ways in which e-commerce geographies (particularly those associated with the use of the Internet) are developing in the 21st century.

The first approach is an examination of the diffusion of Internet users and e-commerce globally. This demonstrates that the largely US and European concentration in the 1990s no longer holds sway as Internet use and e-commerce is increasingly prevalent around the world (OECD 2004). The second line of attack is an analysis of the way in which new sets of people (both in terms of location and background) are engaged in global e-commerce via the online auction website eBay. While admittedly relatively small-scale *vis-à-vis* manufacturing and B2B transactions, it nevertheless represents new sources of income and opportunities that had not existed prior to Internet enabled e-commerce. While eBay is not the only system for small scale e-commerce it is by far the largest and an analysis of the activities conducted through it demonstrates the spatial reach (connecting peripheral places and people to a global market) of Internet based e-commerce.

The third focus also highlights the provision of new opportunities for individuals via in Internet enabled e-commerce but via interconnections within a locality. The exemplar of this trend, the website Craigslist.org, developed largely as an online community focused on events, jobs and classified ads in the San Francisco Bay region. Building upon this localized design, Craigslist has since franchised to over 90 cities worldwide, each catering to its specific locality. The fourth and final way is potentially the most fundamental aspect of e-commerce geographies but also remains the most unstudied, i.e., how firms are adopting e-commerce in their operations and how this affects geographies of production, logistics and learning. Although a number of firm studies on e-commerce adoption have been produced by business school scholars, they remain largely silent on the spatial ramifications of this. This is arguably the most fertile ground upon which economic geographers can focus in the future.

Global diffusion of e-commerce

Although in many ways e-commerce remains centred in the United States, the 21st century marks its transition to a globally utilized network.[8] Measures of Internet use (users, hosts, websites, and infrastructure) are a good gauge of e-commerce diffusion although most closely associated with Internet enabled retail activities. As illustrated in Figure 5.2, the USA remains the largest concentration of Internet use but saw its share of the total Internet population drop from 69 to 22 per cent between 1997 and 2004. Simultaneously growth in Internet usage in non-US/European locations (particularly Asia) has grown enormously mirroring trends in IT goods production (OECD 2004). China grew from 0.4 per cent of all Internet users in 1997 to almost 12 per cent in 2004.[9]

The implications of this growth suggest an increasing importance in non-English and non-ASCII text on the Internet. While many of the technical and

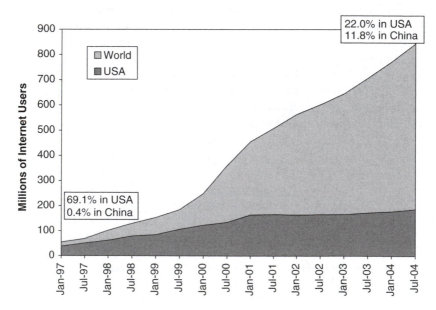

Figure 5.2 Growth of Internet users worldwide. Source: Longitudinal Data assembled by author from NUA's *How Many Online* and ClickZ Stats.

cultural trappings from the original Arpanet (such as the *lingua franca* status of English) remain embedded in Internet usage, there is a growing presence of expanded text encoding system, e.g., punycode, which standardizes the use of non-ASCII characters (Arabic text, Chinese characters, vowels with umlauts, etc.) in Internet protocols. Although still in the early stages, this has allowed for the wider use of these characters in Internet indexing (such as Google enabled searches in non-ASCII characters) and even the domain name system (Network Working Group 2003).

But simply looking at the growth of Internet users conflates use with engagement in e-commerce. As argued earlier (Zook 2001) it is both imperative and possible to examine this question with more nuance as this chapter does through data on the distribution of SSL licenses around the world as reported by Netcraft.[10] SSL (Secure Socket Layer) is a protocol developed by Netscape for encrypted transmissions and provides an indicator of the extent of retail Internet e-commerce.[11] Each web server running SSL has an associated certificate with a geographic location from which Netcraft has developed this database. The distribution of these licenses (excluding the USA) is illustrated in Figure 5.3. Interestingly, despite the increasing diffusion of Internet users, the USA remains the location of 63 per cent of SSL licenses.

This analysis is extended via an OLS regression in order to understand the factors important in determining the variation in SSL usage between countries. The regression is conducted at the national level and uses the number of SSL licenses per capita as the dependent variable.[12] Although a number of independent variables including measures of patents, exports,

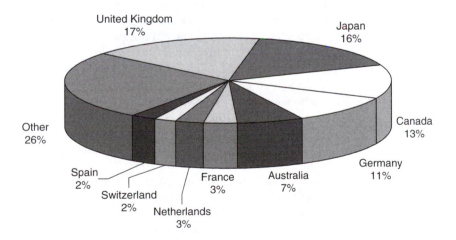

Figure 5.3 Distribution of SSL licenses (excluding the USA), 2004. Source: Number of SSL licenses (June 2004) Netcraft; The United States is the location of 62.7 per cent of all SSL licenses. This graph shows the distribution of the remaining 37.3 per cent.

Table 5.2 Regression results. Dependent Variable: SSL per capita, 2004 (Netcraft)

Independent variables	B	t
Constant	(55.68)	(2.59)**
GDP per capital (UNDP) – 2000	0.01	8.68***
Adult websites (Zook) – 2001	0.11	3.21***
Level of Spam Activity (ORDB) – 2004	(0.004)	(1.89)*
Adj R²	0.63	
n	65	
F	38.5	

Notes
*significant at the 0.1 level
**significant at the 0.05 level
***significant at the 0.01 level

expenditures on public education, etc. were considered, a combination of three independent variables do the best job of explaining the variability in the SSL data (see Table 5.2). These variables are (1) per capita income, (2) number of adult websites and (3) a measure of the level of spam-email activity in a country.

Per capita income is derived from UNDP data and is positively and significantly related to the distribution of SSL licenses. Moreover as Figure 5.4 illustrates, it is highly correlated with the dependent variable, accounting for almost fifty per cent of its variation. This finding is almost identical to those reported by Gibbs *et al.* (2003, 7) for a smaller group of countries and the percentage of their GDP represented by e-commerce sales. This suggests (not too surprisingly) that higher income countries are at an advantage in the adoption of e-commerce. More unexpected is the significant and positive relation between the number of adult websites in a country as of 2001 (derived from Zook 2003) and the per capita number of SSL licenses. Although the adult industry has been a leader in the adoption and commercialization of the Internet, it is not a sector that is generally supported or encouraged by governments. Nevertheless, this analysis (particularly the time lag between the independent and dependent variable) supports the contention that locations with an initial concentration in adult websites have the necessary skills and knowledge to later develop more mainstream e-commerce uses (Zook 2003).

The final independent variable is a measure of the level of spam related activity present in a country. These data are obtained from the Open Relay Database (ORDB) and measure the number of open SMTP relays, computers used by spammers to send email in bulk and anonymously, located in a country (ORDB 2004). This variable is significantly and negatively related to per capita SSL licenses suggesting that spamming (or at least the computers that are used by spammers) is associated with locations that do not have strong e-commerce development. While this may at first seem counter-intuitive given

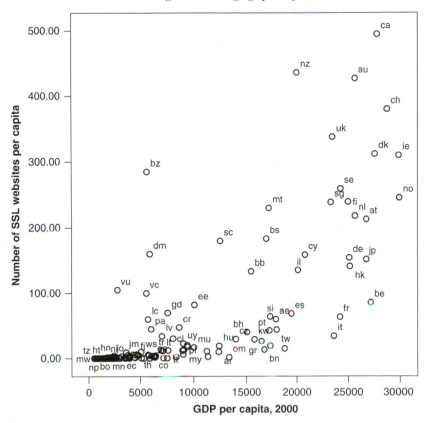

Figure 5.4 Scatterplot of SSL licenses per capita and GDP per capital. Source: Number of SSL licenses (June 2004) Netcraft; GDP per capita (2000), UNDP.

the positive relationship between SSL licenses and adult websites (another underground Internet activity) it suggests difference in governance structures. That is, any economic development requires a regulatory system in which people have confidence that transactions will conform to a set of rules or laws. After all, the owners of adult websites are interested in customers paying for content while spammers are simply interested in distributing their email (preferring as little governance as possible).

While this relatively simple macro–level analysis identifies some general characteristics associated with Internet based retail e-commerce adoption, there remain significant unexplained variation tied to any number of factors. Linguistic issues (e.g., the use of non-ASCII characters), economic and regulatory history (e.g., the presence or lack of non-store retailing) or cultural preferences (e.g. a preference for mobile vs. tethered digital networks) shape the manner in which e-commerce is adopted in particular locations (see Aoyama 2001, 2003, Gibbs *et al.* 2003, Zook *et al.* 2004).

eBay: making inefficient markets efficient

While the rhetoric during the dot.com boom surrounding e-commerce's ability to create frictionless markets has subsided, it is useful to note that at its heart was an element of truth. Namely, Internet based e-commerce can and does lower the cost of certain transactions and makes some markets possible. As Porter (2001, 67) notes, '… look at Internet auctions. Here, customers and suppliers are fragmented and thus have little power. Substitutes, such as classified ads and flea markets, have less reach and are less convenient to use.' Although theoretically anyone could buy and sell products out of his or her garage, the twin frictions of distance and trust prevented many people from successfully engaging in this type of activity. These barriers present particular difficulties for small operators and those without easy access to customers.

eBay has been remarkably successful in creating an online market place (with means of gauging the trustworthiness of unknown individuals) for transactions that likely would not have taken place.[13] Founded in 1995, by the 3rd quarter of 2004 eBay had over 125 million registered users and over a billion individual listings per year. Over $24 billion of sales take place via eBay each year providing it with an annual gross profit of over $1.8 billion (eBay 2004). Mirroring the trend towards the internationalization of e-commerce noted above, almost half of eBay's revenue comes from outside the USA with approximately 36 per cent coming from Europe (eBay 2004). This contrasts sharply with 1998 when 100 per cent of eBay's revenue came from the USA again mirroring the timeline in the history of e-commerce diffusion. This pattern also corresponds with the largely North American and European concentration of SSL licenses.

The size and distribution of this growth is particularly noteworthy given that much of the buying and selling that takes place on eBay is by individuals. Although detailed spatial and demographic data are not provided by eBay, there are over 143,000 eBay stores in operation (eBay 2004). While many of these stores represent existing retail businesses expanding into Internet sales (e.g., eValueville in Hattiesburg, MS), there are a number of anecdotal stories relating how people built businesses around eBay (shippingsupply.com located in Crawfordsville, IN) (Cohen 2002). While many of these operations are single individuals, the eBay platform provides a means through which a wider segment of the population located in more dispersed locations can engage in e-commerce. This potential and success has been noted by popular and academic researchers (Cohen 2002).

Much of the academic research to date, however, has concentrated on economic theories of price determinants, auction theory, and trust rather than the intriguing geographic implications of the eBay model, i.e., the ability for individuals and small scale businesses to market products worldwide via the eBay platform. While this is an advantage regardless of location, it has particular value for sellers without more ready access to buyers. In short, eBay is making small-scale, retail e-commerce possible in an expanded range of locations.

While the growing diffusion of eBay provides a ready indicator of its globalization, it is at the sub-national level within the United States where a

Table 5.3 US eBay cities

Size			Per capita		
Rank	City	Share of US eBay sales	Rank	City	eBay sales per 1,000 pop.
1	Los Angeles	8.0 per cent	1	Seattle–Tacoma	7.0
2	New York	6.8 per cent	2	Portland	4.8
3	Seattle–Tacoma	6.5 per cent	3	San Francisco	4.7
4	Philadelphia	4.2 per cent	4	Kansas City	2.9
5	Chicago	4.2 per cent	5	Indianapolis	2.8
6	Boston	3.1 per cent	6	Orlando	2.7
7	Dallas–Fort Worth	2.9 per cent	7	Nashville	2.6
8	Atlanta	2.6 per cent	8	Billings–Boise	2.6
9	Phoenix	2.6 per cent	9	Oklahoma City	2.4
10	Portland	2.3 per cent	10	Bismarck–Pierre	2.3

Source: Author survey reporting successful eBay sales (regardless of final sale price); *per capita* figures are rough estimates because eBay defined regions do not correspond to Census defined regions. MSA definitions for population figures were used in this calculation.

differentiation between regions becomes particularly pronounced. As Table 5.3 suggests the largest concentrations of eBay sales are strongly correlated with major population centres. When the data are standardized by population, however, an intriguing spatial pattern emerges (Figure 5.5). Although technologically strong regions such as Seattle and San Francisco are in the top quintile of places with high per capita usage, most of the remaining regions such as Bismarck-Pierre, Montana or Oklahoma City are not highly ranked on any index of technology regions (Zook 2000). Moreover the relatively smaller size of these cities and associated rural hinterlands suggests that eBay may be a particularly valuable means through which those in historically more remote locations can adopt and engage in e-commerce (see Figure 5.5).

Craigslist: grassroots globalization

An intriguing contrast and complementary example to eBay is the website Craigslist.org.[15] Also founded in the San Francisco Bay region in 1995, this no frills communitarian operation employs only 14 people but has a user base of 5 million and estimated annual revenues approaching $10 million (Hemple 2004). Craigslist, however, has a very different approach to e-commerce from eBay (and most other companies for that matter), which is arguably the reason behind its success. As founder Craig Newmark notes, the idea behind the website is simple:

> Craigslist is using the Internet to provide people with an opportunity to use it to do everyday stuff and make lives easier. Simple ordinary stuff like finding

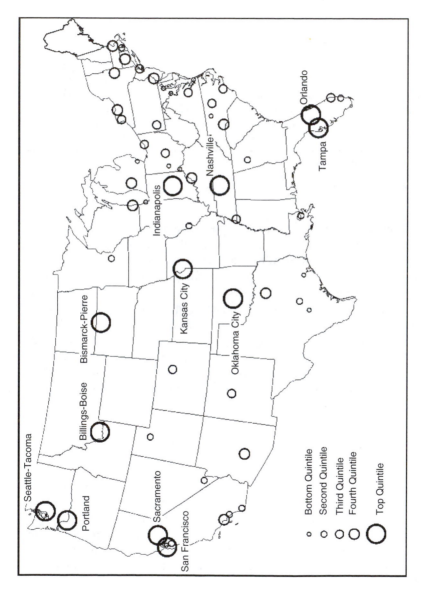

Figure 5.5 Cities rank by per capita sales on eBay. Source: author survey reporting successful eBay sales (regardless of final sale price); *per capita* figures are rough estimates because eBay-defined regions do not correspond to Census-defined regions. MSA definitions for population figures were used in this calculation.

an apartment, getting a job or finding or selling an old sofa … I'm not going to get rich but the development and deployment of the technology of the Internet during the 1990s provides the space for things like Craigslist which can ultimately be used to help solve human problems, big and small. (Author interview, April 2002).

This public service and philanthropic mindset including 'providing an alternative to impersonal, big-media sites' and 'being inclusive, giving a voice to the disenfranchised' (Craigslist, 2004) was and is a studied contrast to the style of e-commerce that emerged during the dot.com boom. Ironically taking the non-commercial path is likely crucial to Craigslist's survival and expansion as it was never burdened with the expectations and pressures that accompanied the massive capitalization of many dot.com companies (Feng *et al.* 2001). Alexa Research reports that Craigslist was the 107th most visited website in the world as of December 2004. This compares to its ranking of 131 in September 2003, 256 in May 2002, 409 in December 2000 and 616 in December 1999.[16]

Craigslist's approach resonates with Castells' (2001) argument that the network of the Internet provides the technical fabric in which both social and economic interactions are constructed and organized. While networks (such as those aggregated and leveraged by Craigslist) have long existed, they have hitherto been largely fragmented into a myriad of individual personal networks. Castells (2001, 2) asserts that the flexibility and widespread dispersion of information technologies such as the Internet have brought about an '… unprecedented combination of flexibility and task performance, of coordinated decision-making and decentralized execution, of individualized expression and global, horizontal communication, which provide a superior organizational form for human action.' This combination of the coordinated and the decentralized, the individual and the global, is an apt metaphor for the organizational structure of Craigslist.

The organization and largely non-commercial mindset, however, does not mean a lack of e-commerce as Craigslist supports its entire operation via charging fees for job postings in San Francisco, New York and Los Angeles. These charges (reminiscent of the historic subsidies structures within national telecommunications systems) allows the rest of Craigslist, consisting of message boards, ads for apartment rentals, personal ads, and event notifications, to operate free of charge. Furthermore, it has made possible the expansion of Craigslist into an increasing number of cities (see Figure 5.6). Exclusively a San Francisco Bay phenomenon from 1995 through 1999, Craigslist currently has city-specific sites in 66 US and 26 international cities.

While this expansion mirrors the globalizing trends seen in SSL licenses and eBay usage, the main attraction to Craigslist's city sites is paradoxically their local focus. As the instructions for the use of Craigslist (2004) note, 'The web is global, but Craigslist is local. You should post to the general geographic location of where you are located.' While not every firm that engages in

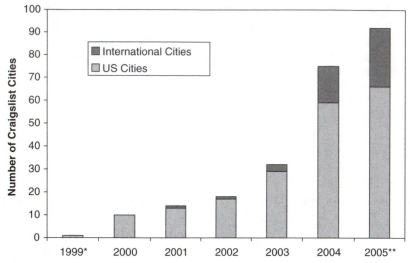

Figure 5.6 Growth of Craigslist, 1999–2005. Source: http://www.craigslist.org/about/

e-commerce will be as place focused as Craigslist, it highlights the corollary to the global diffusion of e-commerce, i.e., the value of localization.

Evolving firm value chains

The fourth and final aspect of the 'New Old Thing' is also arguably the most important component of emerging e-commerce geographies, i.e., how do firms integrate e-commerce into the existing spatial organization of internal and external business practices. Despite technophile rhetoric to the contrary (aptly demonstrated during the dot.com boom) this integration results not in simple substitution but a blending of the electronic and the physical (Graham, 1998, Aoyama 2001, Currah 2002, Couclelis 2004). E-commerce research within geography to date has often focused on consumer activities and/or a limited number of site and company cases (Aoyama 2001, Currah 2002, Aoyama 2003, Murphy 2003, Zook 2003) making this a fertile area for research such as French *et al.* (2004) and Leyshon *et al.* (2005a).

Although diffusion statistics indicate that firms and individuals increasingly have access to the Internet (see Figures 5.1 and 5.2), the use to which it is put is often limited to simple tasks such as communication through email, information gathering, or online banking. As the OECD (2004, 7) notes '... relatively few firms have comprehensively adapted their business concepts, value chains, organisation, and supplier and customer relations. Internal integration of electronic order systems with other functions (e.g. marketing) or external integration with suppliers and customers remains infrequent and is often found only in large firms.' The next stage of e-commerce adoption, encompassing a more comprehensive overhaul of business practice occurring over a time scale of years and decades, parallels the timing and transformations associated earlier technologies (David 1990, Fisher 1992, Chandler 1977).[17] The key question for economic geographers (particularly in light of the aspatial sensibilities of most business studies) is how this process affects geographies of production, logistics and learning across industries (Aoyama *et al.* 2005). An important variable in this development is the role of market power in determining the contours of e-commerce geographies. In the case of Covisint (an online marketplace designed for the US auto industry) Feng *et al.* (2001, 489) argue, '... first-tier auto parts suppliers had no choice in 2000 but to sign up for a B2B exchange which was set up and owned by the car assemblers, who ... announced terms and conditions for participation were unfavorable for suppliers. ... They had no choice because the assemblers privately insisted that they would buy only from suppliers who used the exchange'.

The challenge of e-commerce and the role of existing industry power structures is particularly intense in sectors whose products can be digitized and traded across the Internet. Leyshon (2003) argues that the idea of a 'gift economy', a system in which products are given away for free tied to the dot.com boom of the 1990s, is especially distressing for media industries. While most dominant media companies (including his case study of the music industry) have responded to the threat of 'free Internet e-commerce' by a reassertion of the power of copyright, it is not clear whether this is a viable long term strategy, particularly in light of the growth of peer to peer networking. Leyshon *et al.* (2005a) extend this analysis through an extensive set of existing firms and actors in the music industry, highlighting their reluctance to embrace the power of the Internet and software via a radical restructuring of business models. The extent to which this reflects firms' attention to Porter's (2001, 66) observation that e-commerce 'often comes at the expense of average profitability' or a 'cultural crisis' (Schoenberger 1997) within this industries' management remains to be seen.

While the spatial implications of e-commerce expansion are firm and industry specific, it is clear that differentiation is taking place. This is particularly evident when comparing the variation between urban and rural locations. Although rural firms are arguably positioned to accrue the greatest benefits from e-commerce adoption (akin to the advantages that eBay offers to individuals in rural locations) they are often at a disadvantage because of lower education levels and other capabilities (see Cuadrado-Roura and Garcia-Tabuenca 2004, Sambrook 2003). Additionally, because of the uncertainty around how best to implement e-commerce, it is likely that firms located in cities with better human resources and access to knowledge will be earlier adopters (Van Geenhuizen 2004). This divide (again based on resources and knowledge) is also likely to be evident between large and small firms and independent and branch plants (OECD 2004).

Moreover it is evident that the implementation of e-commerce depends on existing cultural, societal, institutional and economic characteristics (OECD 1999, Aoyama 2003, Gibbes *et al.* 2003, Kling *et al.* 2003, Fillis *et al.* 2004). As French *et al.* (2004, 69) argue:

> Simply stated, the form of the commodity, the organizational structures underpinning its production and consumption, and the spaces of its representation all matter fundamentally here, and produce a far more nuanced and culturally-inflected economic landscape than many existing accounts of e-commerce have suggest. The bi-polar narratives that dominate the literature (physical versus virtual, clicks versus bricks, material versus immaterial) seem to be less and less useful in describing and explaining the complex spatialities and temporalities at work ...

Finally, beyond the typical actors and factors associated with economic change, is the technological superstructure of e-commerce, i.e., code or software, which supports firms' expansion into this realm. Although often treated as a simple technical or infrastructure question, software codes (and the programmers who created them) have an important agency in their own right in structuring the potentiality of e-commerce systems (Leyshon 2001, Thrift and French 2002, Dodge and Kitchin 2005). Ranging from the relatively benign, e.g. the popularity of a widely used software package, to the blatant use of market power to establish a B2B marketplace, e.g., Covisint (Feng *et al.* 2001), to the extreme of software designed to disallow copying (Lessig 2004), the structure of code is an essential (if often unseen) part of e-commerce development.

Conclusions

This chapter outlines the development of Internet based e-commerce geographies during the past decade of decidedly strong hyperbole. Despite rhetoric to the contrary, geography remains an important variable in understanding the diffusion and use of e-commerce. In fact, far from removing geographic differentiation it seems more likely that e-commerce will contribute to the uneven nature of the capitalist space economy. French and Leyshon (2004, 285) note the increased importance of global centers in reintermediation and it is precisely the contours of reintermediation (within firms, industries, sectors and states) that they assert will determine '... whether core activities are indeed, under the auspices of e-commerce, moving into new spaces and place.' From the concentration exhibited during the dot.com boom to the ability of eBay and Craigslist to redefine the way in which people interact with those near and distant to the re-organization of industries, spatial relations and place continue to play central roles in the economy.

E-commerce was integral to the New Economy as conceived during the boom of the 1990s, but has not dissipated as have many of the superficial trappings associated with dot.com firms. E-commerce is clearly a central facet in the development of economic geographies throughout the 21ˢᵗ century as businesses and individuals reorganize the economic space in which they operate. Furthermore, the decline in the novelty and visibility of e-commerce reflects the pervasiveness of the practice. Leyshon *et al.* (2005b, 12) argue that '… it has almost become embarrassing to refer to a phenomenon such as e-commerce because its use and applicability is so obvious that it no longer warrants description.' After all, firms are not defined as phone-commerce companies simply because they make use of a telephone technology. Likewise, the concept of 'e-commerce companies' *per se* is fading as its use becomes a matter of course.

Nevertheless, the innovative potential of e-commerce due to the flexibility of its use, the increase in potential connectivity between actors and their ideas (Carlsson 2003) and its paradoxical ability to provide the means for both the agglomeration and dispersal of power, ensures its relevancy in the future. Thus, Internet based e-commerce, i.e., the new old thing, remains fertile ground in the experimental process of e-commerce adoption and the resulting changes in economic organization, power structures and economic geographies.

Acknowledgement

This paper has been made possible by a Research Grant '*Connecting the Cyberspace to Place: Understanding the Evaluation of Transactions and Value Chains in Electronic Commerce*' from the National Science Foundation (BCS-0454840).

Notes

1 Lewis's (2000) book, *The New New Thing*, refers to the constant search for the next innovation with the potential to reshape the economy. Jim Clark, the founder of Silicon Graphics, Netscape, Healtheon, and MyCFO, is presented by Lewis as the exemplar of this entrepreneurial mindset, albeit not without its downside. This chapter's reference to this term is based on the fundamental connection between the expansion of e-commerce and the Netscape browser although its treatment of 'New New Thing' and associated variations are the author's.
2 French and Leyshon (2004, 277) argue that this process is best characterized as 'reintermediation' because the circumvention of existing intermediatory firms was dependent upon the simultaneous creation of new intermediaries.
3 The US Census defines e-commerce as 'goods and services sold online whether over open networks such as the Internet, or over proprietary networks running systems such as Electronic Data Exchange [sic] (EDI).' (US Census, 2004). The data presented here reflect this definition.
4 It is also important to note that e-commerce's penetration into manufacturing differs considerable between specific industry sectors. The sector with the highest per cent of e-commerce sales is transportation equipment (NAICS 336) with 47.9 per cent and beverage and tobacco (NAICS 312) with 43.7 per cent of sales conducted electronically. The sector with the lowest percentage of e-commerce sales is printing and related support activities (NAICS 323) with 4.9 per cent and textile mills (NAICS 313) with

8.5 per cent. While it is not within the scope of this chapter to consider the full gamut of reasons for this variation, industry structure (particularly power relations between firms) is an important factor. For example, the three dominant firms of the US automotive industry have historically pushed EDI on their suppliers and have championed the centralized Covisint system which conducted more that $1 billion in trades per quarter in 2001 (Kadet 2001, Kandampully 2003).

5   The quotations presented in this chapter are from a series of interviews with dot.com company management and early stage venture capital investors which were conducted in 1999 ($n = 84$) and 2001–02 ($n = 53$). The majority of individuals were from the San Francisco Bay but the research also included interviews in New York City and Los Angeles.

6   Another dot.com founder interviewed in January 2002 provides a more e-commerce explicit expectation for Internet technology. 'We had convinced ourselves – and the world had convinced itself – that this was a whole new paradigm. We were not alone in believing that the world had permanently changed. The Internet and this new age of global communications would provide insight on customer demand, manufacturing inventory and would eliminate the huge swings in the economy caused by over-inventory. The collective wisdom at the time was that we would have perfect insight into customer demand because of the web.'

7   See Leyshon *et al.* (2005b) for an analysis on how the idea of 'e-commerce' was embedded in the economy through a process of virtualism in which idealized theories and material practices of capitalism construct new 'knowledge' about the economy.

8   While the number of Internet users has grown apace in certain areas of the world (most notably in China and Asia) there remain regions such as sub-Saharan Africa and Central Asia that have very low levels of use. See http://www.zooknic.com/Users/ for a time series of maps charting these changes.

9   This growth of users in China presents a particularly thorny problem for the ruling Communist party which wishes to both encourage technologically related growth as a means of economic development but also desires to control the information with which its citizens interact. Although the Internet is generally seen as beyond any governmental control, Zittrain and Edelman (2002a, 2002b) have documented the fairly successful filtering programs of the Chinese government. Moreover as Privacy International (2003) notes, efforts to censor citizens' access to information deemed undesirable by governments is increasing as more people and places come online.

10   In addition to Netcraft's measure of SSL licenses, the author also analysed the variation in the presence of e-commerce terms in a country's webspace. Utilizing a specialized API interface to the Google search engine, a series of 20 terms associated with e-commerce were each queried with 250 country and language restrictions (e.g., only webpages from China or Germany containing the term e-commerce would be returned for that particularly search). Analysis of the number of hits per country for the terms 'e-commerce' and 'Electronic Commerce' resulted in very similar results to the SSL data (e.g., more than 65 per cent of the hits were located in the USA and the top ten countries in terms of SSL licenses were all in the top 15 in terms of number of Google hits). Interestingly, the countries with a stronger e-commerce presence as measured by Google hits versus SSL licenses were China, Russia, the Czech Republic, Hong Kong (politically part of China but with a distinct Internet presence), and Taiwan. When these measures were used as the dependent variables in multivariate regressions, they showed a similar relationship with the independent variables although with lower adjusted R^2s and *t*-scores.

11   As noted in the discussion of US Census figures on Electronic Commerce, retailing (B2C) is a much smaller aspect of e-commerce use than sales between business (B2B) and it is likely that this extend into the international arena. Unfortunately there are fewer comparable measures of business to business e-commerce for all countries at the international level.

12 The USA is excluded from this analysis due to the high number of SSL licenses located there in order to be more representative of the overall global experience with e-commerce. Inclusion of the USA in the model results in similar findings.

13 eBay is by no means the only mechanism for these changes. Nevertheless, given its rapid growth, ease of use, large member base and dominance of its market segment, it is reasonable to focus upon it. It is interesting to speculate whether eBay's dominance of this market will in time be seen as the same type of damaging monopoly that other dominant companies (e.g., Microsoft) have been characterized as having.

14 The information presented in this paper is based on data collected from eBay's web-page on the Internet. Using a series of scripting programs, an algorithm was devised that takes a sample of eBay listings in a variety of categories for completed auctions to obtain the item id, a short description, final list price, whether the item sold, country of the seller, seller's id, seller's eBay rating, eBay subcategory. For sellers located within the USA sub-regional data were also available in approximately 75 per cent of the cases. Random stratified sampling techniques were used to obtain a sample of 708,461 items placed for auction in June 2002 of which approximately 45 per cent were successfully sold.

15 The relevance of this comparison deepened in August 2004 when Craigslist announced that eBay had purchased a 25 per cent stake in the company (Hemple 2004, Wingfield 2004). This sale took place because a minority shareholder in Craigslist was interested in liquidating their holdings rather than something pursued by Craigslist's management.

16 For comparison, eBay was the 11th most visited site in December 2004 and Yahoo! was the most visited site.

17 Furthermore, the effects of using e-business methods may not be immediate. For example, case studies for 2000–02 show the impact of e-business to be significant but consistently lower than expected, reflecting over-optimistic expectations and measurement difficulties (OECD 2004. p. 8).

References

Abbate, J. (1999) *Inventing the Internet.* Cambridge, MA, MIT Press.

Aoyama, Y. (2001) 'The Information Society, Japanese Style: Corner Stores as Hubs for e-commerce access', in T. Leinbach, and S. Brunn, eds, *Worlds of Electronic Commerce.* John Wiley & Sons, New York, 109–128.

Aoyama, Y. (2003) 'Sociospatial dimensions of technology adoption: recent M-commerce and e-commerce developments', *Environment and Planning A* 35, 7, 1201–1221.

Aoyama, Y., Ratick, S. and Schwarz, G. (2005) 'Business-to-Business Electronic Commerce and the Logistics Industry: A Conceptual Model', *Geographical Analysis* 37, 1, 46-68.

Carlsson, B. (2003). 'The New Economy: What is New and What is Not'. in J.F. Christensen and P. Maskell, eds, *The Industrial Dynamics of the New Digital Economy.* Edward Elgar Publishing, Cheltenham and Northampton.

Cassidy, J. (2002) *Dot.com.* Harper Collins, New York.

Castells, M. (2001) *Internet Galaxy.* Oxford University Press, Oxford.

Chandler, A. (1977) *The Visible Hand: The Managerial Revolution in American Business.* Harvard University Press, Cambridge. MA.

Cohen, A. (2002) *The Perfect Store.* Little, Brown & Company, New York.

Couclelis, H. (2004) 'Pizza over the Internet: e-commerce, the fragmentation of activity and the tyranny of the region', *Entrepreneurship and Regional Development* 16, 41–54.

Craigslist. (2004) *About Craigslist.* Available http://www.craigslist.org/about/ (10 December 2004).

Cuadrado-Roura, J.R. and Garcia-Tabuenca, A. (2004) 'ICT policies for SMEs and regional disparities. The Spanish case', *Entrepreneurship and Regional Development* 16, 55–76.

Currah, A. (2002) 'Behind the web store: the organizational and spatial evolution of multi-channel retailing in Toronto', *Environment and Planning A* 34, 1411–1441.

David, P. (1990) 'The Dynamo and the Computer: An Historical Perspective on the Modern Productivity Paradox', *American Economic Review*, 80, 355–361.

Dodge, M. and Kitchin, R. (2005) 'Code and the Transduction of Space', *Annals of the American Association of Geographers*. 95, 162–180.

eBay. (2004) *eBay Investor relations*. Available http://investor.ebay.com/index.cfm (10 December 2004).

Feng, H., Froud, J., Johal, S., Haslam, C. and Williams, K. (2001) 'A new business model? The capital market and the new economy', *Economy and Society* 30, 467-503.

Fillis, I., Johannson, U. and Wagner, B. (2004) 'Factors impacting on e-business adoption and development in the smaller firm', *International Journal of Entrepreneurial Behaviour and Research* 10, 178–191.

Fischer, C.S. (1992) *America calling: a social history of the telephone to 1940.* University of California Press, Berkeley, CA.

French, S. and Leyshon, A. (2004) 'The new, new financial system? Towards a conceptualization of financial reintermediation', *Review of International Political Economy* 11, 263–288.

French, S., Crewe, L., Leyshon, A., Webb, P. and Thrift, N. (2004) 'Putting e-commerce in its place: reflections on the impact of the Internet on the cultural industries', In Power, D. and Scott, A.J., eds, *Cultural Industries and the Production of Culture*. Routledge, London.

Garcia, D.L. (1997) 'Networked Commerce: Public Policy Issues in a Deregulated Communication Environment', *The Information Society* 19, 17–31.

Gibbs, J., Kraemer, K. and Dedrick, J. (2003) 'Environment and Policy Factors Shaping Global E-Commerce Diffusion: A Cross-Country Comparison', *The Information Society* 19, 5–18.

Graham, S. (1998) 'The end of geography or the explosion of place? Conceptualising space, place and information technology', *Progress in Human Geography* 22, 165–185.

Hait, C. and Weiss, S. (2001) *Digital Hustlers: Living Large and Falling Hard in Silicon Alley.* Regan Books, New York.

Hemple, J. (2004) 'A Talk with Craigslist's Keeper', *Business Week*. September 8.

Kadet, G. (2001) '*B2B Shakeout*' Available at www.computerworld.com/rckey52/story/0,1199,NAV63_ST059829,00.html.

Kandampully, J. (2003) 'B2B relationships and networks in the intern age', *Management Decision* 41, 443-451.

Kaplan, P.J. (2002) *F'd Companies: Spectacular dot.com flameouts.* Simon and Schuster, New York.

Kelly, K. (1998) *New Rules for the New Economy*. Penguin, New York.

Kling, R., Kraemer, K. and Dedrick, J. (2003) 'Introduction', *The Information Society* 19, 1–3.

Lessig, L. (2004) *Free Culture: How Big Media Uses Technology and the Law to Lock Down Culture and Control Creativity*. Penguin Press, New York.

Lewis, M. (2000) *The new new thing: a Silicon Valley story*. W.W. Norton, New York.

Leyshon, A. (2001) 'Time-space (and digital) compression: software formats, musical networks, and the reorganisation of the music industry', *Environment and Planning A*, 32, 49–77.

Leyshon, A. (2003) 'Scary Monsters? software formats, peer-to-peer networks and the spectre of the gift', *Environment and Planning D: Society and Space* 21, 533–558.

Leyshon, A., Webb, P., French, S., Thrift, N. and Crewe, L. (2005a) 'On the reproduction of the music industry after the Internet', *Media, Culture and Society,* 27, 177–209.

Leyshon, A., French, S., Thrift, N., Crewe, L. and Webb, P. (2005b) 'Accounting for e-commerce: abstractions, virtualism and the cultural circuit of capital', *Economy and Society,* 428–450

Murphy, A.J. (2003) '(Re)solving space and time: fulfilment issues in online grocery retailing', *Environment and Planning A,* 35, 1173–1200.

Naughton, J. (2000) *A brief history of the future: from radio days to Internet years in a lifetime.* Overlook Press, Woodstock, NY.

Network Working Group. (2003) *RFC 3492- Punycode: A Bootstring encoding of Unicode for Internationalized Domain Names in Applications (IDNA).* Available http://www.faqs.org/rfcs/rfc3492.html (10 December 2004).

Open Relay Database. (2004) *Open Relays by Country.* Available http://www.ordb.org/statistics/countries/ (8 June 2004).

Organization for Economic Co-operation and Development (OECD). (1999) *The Economic and Social Impact of Electronic Commerce: Preliminary Findings and Research Agenda.* OECD Press, Paris.

Organization for Economic Co-operation and Development (2004) *Highlight: OECD Information Technology Outlook.* OECD Press, Paris.

Porter, M. (2001) 'Strategy and the Internet', *Harvard Business Review* March: 63–78.

Privacy International. (2003) *Silenced: An International Report on Censorship and Control of the Internet.* London: Privacy International. Available http://www.privacyinternational.org/survey/censorship/silenced.pdf (10 December 2004)

Reid, R. (1997) *Architects of the Web: 1,000 days that built the future of business.* John Wiley & Sons, New York.

Sambrook, S. (2003) 'E-learning in small organizations', *Education and Training* 45, 506–516.

Schoenberger, E. (1997) *The Cultural Crisis of the Firm.* Blackwell, Oxford.

Thrift, N. and French, S. (2002) 'The automatic production of space', *Transactions of the Institute of British Geographers,* 27, 309–335.

US Census. (2004) *2002 e-commerce Multi-sector Report* Available at http://www.census.gov/eos/www/papers/2002/2002finaltext.pdf (10 December 2004).

Van Geenhuizen, M. (2004) 'Cities and cyberspace: new entrepreneurial strategies', *Entrepreneurship and Regional Development* 16, 5–20.

Walker, R. 2005. 'The Boom and the Bombshell: The New Economy Bubble and The San Francisco Bay Area', in G. Vertova, ed., *The Changing Economic Geography of Globalization.* London: Routledge.

Wingfield, N. (2004) eBay Buys Stake in Craigslist, *Wall Street Journal* August 13.

Zittrain, J. and Edelman, B. (2002a) 'Documentation of Internet Filtering in Saudi Arabia'. Working Paper. Berkman Center for Internet & Society. Harvard Law School. Available at http://cyber.law.harvard.edu/filtering/saudiarabia/ (27 October 2002).

Zittrain, J. and Edelman, B. (2002b) 'Documentation of internet filtering in China'. Working paper. Berkman center for internet & society. Harvard Law School. Available at http://cyber.law.harvard.edu.iltering/china/ (27 October 2002).

Zook, M.A. (2000) 'The web of production: The economic geography of commercial internet content production in the United States', *Environment and Planning A,* 32, 411–426.

Zook, M.A. (2001) 'Old hierarchies or new networks of centrality?: The global geography of the internet content market', *American Behavioral Scientist,* 44, 1679–1696.

Zook, M.A. (2003) 'Underground globalization: Mapping the space of flows of the internet adult industry', *Environment and Planning A*, 35, 1261–1286.

Zook, M.A. (2005) *The Geography of the Internet Industry: Venture Capital, Dot.coms and Local Knowledge*. Blackwell Publishers, Cambridge, MA.

Zook, M., Dodge, M., Aoyama, Y. and Townsend, A. (2004) New Digital Geographies: Information, Communication, and Place, In S. Brunn *et al.* eds. *TechnoEarth: Geography and Technology*. 155–176.

Zwass, V. (1996) 'Electronic Commerce: Structure and Issues', *International Journal of Electronic Commerce*, 1, 3–23.

Zwass, V. (2003) 'Electronic Commerce and Organizational Innovation: Aspects and Opportunities', *International Journal of Electronic Commerce*. 7, 7–37.

6 The New Economy and earnings inequalities: explaining social, spatial and gender divisions in the UK and London

Diane Perrons

Introduction

Understandings of the New Economy differ. Optimistic accounts focus on economic growth, technological progress, the increasing use of computing and information technologies, the expansion of knowledge goods, increasing opportunities, productivity, and well-being (Greenspan 1998, Coyle and Quah 2002). Manuel Castells (2001), for example, argues that we have entered a new technological paradigm – centred on micro electronics-based information/communication technologies (ICTs) and genetic engineering. As some of these accounts recognize, while the ICT revolution facilitates increasing global integration, it is also geographically uneven. In particular, Internet access is differentiated by location, social class, gender, ethnicity, age and education, collectively referred to as the digital divide (Quah 1996, Norris 2001). Other social theorists such as Ulrich Beck (2000) and Richard Sennett (1998) are more pessimistic. They emphasize deteriorating working conditions, increasing insecurity, and individualization associated with the demise of traditional systems of social support, including trade unions and state welfare policies. This chapter links these contrasting interpretations of the new economy through a conceptualization that recognizes some of the potential of ICTs, but foregrounds the widening social and spatial divisions of contemporary global capitalism. These are especially evident in neo-liberal societies where state moderation is muted. This analysis has been discussed elsewhere (Perrons 2004a); in this chapter it is linked more directly to economic analyses of rising inequality, and extended further to provide a more detailed analysis of spatial inequality.

The chapter begins with a discussion of rising inequality at a global scale, within countries and between women and men. It then develops an alternative explanation which synthesizes and extends some of the contrasting theorizations of the New Economy by explicitly incorporating a gendered and spatial perspective. Finally this analysis is very briefly illustrated by some contrasting experiences of work and life in the New Economy.

Rising inequality

The New Economy is associated with rising economic inequality both between (Milanovic 2002) and within countries (Sassen 2000, Atkinson 2003, Goos and Manning 2003, Hamnett 2003, Machin 2003, Piketty and Saez 2003, Beaverstock *et al.* 2004) and these developments are interrelated. Overall there has been a vast increase in social wealth in the last few decades, but existing levels of inequality on a global scale are stark and undisputed. Currently 2.8 billion people (44 per cent of the world's population) live on less than $2 a day, and around 1.2 billion on less than $1 a day, while the richest 1 per cent receives as much income as the poorest 57 per cent (UNDP 2002). Between 1990 and 2000, 57 countries became poorer and 21 moved backwards on the UNDP HDI measures (UNDP 2004). Whether the overall trend of inequality is increasing or decreasing is however a contested issue and different measures point in different directions.

Measuring inequality is complex and recorded inequality depends on the method of calculation in terms of the choice of statistical indicators, the spatial unit of analysis and the measure of income – gross domestic product, purchasing power parity, or some broader based measure of well being such as the United Nations Indices of human development.

In an analysis using GDP per capita, Branco Milanovic (2005) refers to three concepts of inequality, each measured in different ways, producing different findings about the scale and direction of inequality. On the first measure, Concept 1, each country is taken as a single unit and inequality is shown to have steadily increased since 1950. Treating countries equally is appropriate if the objective is to assess the effectiveness of different policies and theories of development. In terms of global inequality, however, this measure is rather limited; changes in the degree of inequality in small countries have an equal impact on the outcome as changes in the more populous ones. The second measure (Concept 2) correspondingly weights countries by their population. This more accurately represents what is happening to people on a world scale. On this measure, inequality has fallen over time. However it is very sensitive to what has been happening in China owing to its large share of the world's population, and where growth – especially in the recent decade – has been extremely rapid. If China is excluded, inequality on a global scale has been fairly stable: if anything it has increased slightly in the last decade. Milanovic argues that this measure is limited too, because it does not allow for inequality within countries, and so effectively measures international, rather than global, inequality. To get a measure of the true extent of global inequality it is vital to take inequality within countries into account, as this varies significantly and has been increasing in recent years in many countries, including the UK, USA and China (see also Beaverstock *et al.* 2004).

To take internal inequality into account and so obtain a more accurate measure of global inequality, Milanovic (2005) uses household survey data. So far he has data for only three years; while it is not possible to identify any trend, it is nonetheless clear that global inequality increased between 1988 and 1998, and – more significantly – the scale of global inequality is far higher than international inequality, i.e. inequality as measured by country averages.

Milanovic's (2005) comparative analysis of inequality within different countries has interesting implications for analysis and policy. He demonstrates, for example, that the richest third of Brazilians are considerably more affluent than the poorest decile of French people, while the poorest 5 per cent of Brazilians are poorer than the poorest 5 per cent of rural Indians. Recognizing the differential extent of internal inequality is important if the objective is to ensure that international transfers go from the rich of one country to the poor of another, and not vice versa, which could happen when national systems of taxation are regressive and redistributed funds appropriated by rich minorities in poorer countries.[1] This recognition is also necessary in order to accurately identify the processes generating inequality: the focus of this chapter is in demonstrating the connections between the New Economy and increasing inequality globally but more specifically within countries, with specific reference to the UK.

Given that income is not always distributed equally within households, a further measure of inequality, Concept 4, would also be required to take account of continuing inequalities between women and men. But obtaining data for this measure would be even more difficult. Existing research suggests that while there has been a feminization of the labour force on a global scale, gender inequality remains. This is primarily due to continuing job segregation between women and men, higher pay in jobs where men are over represented (ILO 2004), the contemporaneous expansion of informal forms of work – just at the moment when increasing numbers of women are gaining access to the paid labour force (Beneria 2003) – and the continuing unequal division of domestic work and childcare leading to gender inequality in time use. This is again found in all continents and for all countries where data exist (UNDP 2003). Overall, women represent 60 per cent of the world's 550 million working poor, earning less than $1 a day (ILO 2004).

Turning more directly to internal economic inequalities, it is clear that earnings inequalities have risen dramatically in the last three decades in many OECD countries especially at the top end of the distribution and among those following neo-liberal economic policies (Piketty and Saez 2003). Gosta Esping-Andersen (2005) points out that, while there is a trend towards earning inequalities throughout these countries, their impact on income is modified by state policy – especially in the more redistributive social democratic states of Northern Europe. Thus the most spectacular increases have been in the USA, where Chief Executive Officer earnings increased by 2500 per cent, moving from 39 times the pay of an average worker in the 1970s to over 1000 times at the end of the 1990s. Similarly, while the incomes of the top 1 per cent of families increased by 157 per cent there was only a 10 per cent gain for those in the middle of the distribution (Krugman 2002). In the UK the top 1 per cent share of total earnings has risen to nearly 6 per cent, having fallen historically from the 1920s to a low of around 3.5 per cent in the early 1970s (Atkinson 2003).

As far as empirically established links between inequality and the New Economy are concerned, this is nowhere more striking than in the USA, when the ninety-third consecutive month of growth recorded in December 1998 (the cornerstone of one interpretation of the New Economy; Greenspan 1998) was simultaneously the record year for redundancies (Benner 2002). As the incomes of the elite expanded dramatically those of ordinary workers were stagnating. In Silicon Valley, perhaps the icon of the New Economy, the average earnings of corporate executives increased by 2000 per cent between 1991 and 2000 while those of production workers experienced a 7 per cent decline; the earnings ratio between them moving from 41:1 to 956:1 (Benner 2002; see also Krugman 2002). There are several explanations for increasing inequalities, which will be outlined, before developing an explanation that links increasing inequality to the New Economy analytically.

At the global level, inequality is attributed to increased competitiveness, the widespread pursuit of neo-liberal policies (Krugman 2002) and uneven incorporation within the global division of labour. In this latter respect value chain analysis (see for example Gereffi and Kaplinsky 2001, Schmitz 2003) is useful to indicate how the contemporary organization of production allows a large share of the value of products to be appropriated by producer service functions, such as branding, marketing, and design, rather than direct production. This ability contributes to the rising relative wealth of OECD countries – where these activities are disproportionately located – and clearly impacts on the range of incomes and opportunities found there. In particular, control and command functions have created a range of high-income jobs in producer services, especially in global cities where these activities are concentrated (Sassen 2000).

Focusing on the internal distribution of income within countries, the growing significance of innovation and high technology or skill-biased technological change (SBTC) is said to have increased the relative demand for and relative wages of workers with high levels of education. However this explanation is incomplete because earnings inequalities have been increasing for over thirty years. During these years, increasing numbers of people have acquired contemporary skills, especially in ICTs. Further, demand has also increased for workers in low skilled or 'McJobs', but their relative pay has declined (Goos and Manning 2003, McDowell *et al.* 2005) thereby contributing further to the rise in inequality. Indeed, Maarten Goos and Alan Manning (2003) provide strong evidence to link earnings inequalities to different forms of work. They develop a categorization of 'good and bad jobs' from occupational and industry/sectoral categories and differentiate them by pay decile (good jobs with earnings in the top two deciles and bad jobs in the lowest decile) and then demonstrate growth in both between 1979 and 1999, especially in the former but declines in jobs in the middle of the distribution.

Recognizing the limitations of the SBTC analysis, Atkinson (2003, 20) turns to sociological literature and speculates that inequalities can be attributed to the nature of 'skills' rewarded in the contemporary labour market (his emphasis) with people-related rather than cognitive skills becoming more significant. Correspondingly, rewards are given less to skills acquired from formal education and more to those from socialization within more advantaged families and communities. This explanation has parallels with Pierre Bourdieu's (1990) notion of appropriate social and cultural capital. However, elite education is still mandatory for top jobs in the UK, but not a sufficient condition – owing to fierce competition – so people related skills and appearance are also drawn upon. The extent of competition for these jobs also calls into question whether the market determines their pay or not, and if indeed it is their positioning at the apex of the value chain that enables their firms to appropriate a large share of social wealth and so pay high salaries.

The significance of people related skills has also long been recognized in the feminist literature (see Hochschild 2003, first published 1983), but they are also required in a wide range of work including care work, sales and call centres which are not noted for high levels of pay.[2] Furthermore given the shortages that occur in these sectors – especially for elderly care, and in some cases of supermarket workers – it is curious that pay does not rise as the market would predict. Toynbee (2005) argues that in the UK in low paid sectors such as supermarkets and care homes the employers effectively operate as cartels to maintain low wages. Atkinson (2003) however refers to the idea of social codes setting the boundaries within which more conventional economic ideas about supply and demand operate. Krugman (2002) similarly turns to sociological concepts and specifically to the idea of social norms, because although he finds explanations based on SBTC, economic restructuring through the new global division of labour, and the 'superstar' effect all plausible, he maintains that none convincingly account for the dramatic widening of earnings inequalities in the USA and the acceptance of the super rich (see also Beaverstock *et al.* 2004). He argues that there has been a cultural shift towards greater financial permissiveness, a belief in charismatic leaders and in the effectiveness of incentives, which have combined to create new social norms, which in turn endorse inequality. Thus economists seem to be moving away from the idea of 'objective' measurable determinations of wage inequality towards 'softer' – less tangible – explanations. It can be argued that the development of new social norms and their embodiment of gender inequalities also require explanation.

Social theorists (Sennett 1998, Beck 2000, Reich 2001) have developed ideas about a new less regulated social system characterized by individualization and growing risks as well as opportunities, partly associated with new forms of work and especially their comparative insecurity. Ulrich Beck (1992) argues that welfare gains or losses are now attributed to individual successes or failure rather than wider social and economic processes linked with the region, locality or social class. So, this explanation may be complementary to the social norms argument, in the sense that greater toleration or acceptance of inequality could be linked to individualization arising from deregulation, the fragmentation of work, performance related individualized pay bargaining and more generally to the idea that individuals are responsible for their own achievements (as well as failures) and thus deserving of the rewards (losses). Danny Quah (1996) also suggests that because the New Economy appears to offer more scope for individual social mobility the poor accept widening social divisions, believing that they too have a chance of becoming rich. Quah's (1996, 2003) however develops an analysis of the New Economy that identifies analytically processes tending towards widening social divisions. This analysis is outlined below and this approach is extended to explain the gendered and spatial nature of contemporary social divisions.

Quah's (1996, 2003) analysis can be linked with explanations of employment change and extended by incorporating feminist analyses of the gender coding of jobs and earnings in order to provide a richer explanation (than social norms or SBTC) of rising inequality in general and for the regional and gender variations. Quah (2003) attributes widening social divisions to the economic properties of knowledge goods or 'bitstrings' that is goods that can in principle be digitized and which are becoming increasingly prevalent in the New Economy. Quah's definition of knowledge goods as bitstrings is technical rather than moral so as he points out Britney Spears is as much a knowledge worker as electronic traders as her products can be disseminated digitally. Thus the definition differs somewhat from Castells' (2001) self-programmable workers, although there are parallels. Knowledge goods are highly expansible, that is they can be replicated at very low cost, and they are non-rival; thus one person's consumption does not prevent another's. These properties should lead to greater equality in general and a more equitable distribution of income. But knowledge goods are also characterized by increasing economies of scale, thus large firms tend to dominate the market, and having done so they create a range of related products locking consumers in to their particular brand. A further economic property of knowledge goods is the superstar effect, which Quah links to consumers' preferences for producers/products of greater renown even though they may differ only marginally from their competitors. Given their weightless nature and related potential global reach, there are few constraints on market size, so these superstar producers are able to capture an increasing share of the market, thereby widening the earnings differential between themselves and other producers.

Correspondingly they are able to appropriate directly or through the firms that employ them high salaries. Quah (1996) refers here to the greater earnings dispersion between opera singers than between shoemakers, given people's preference for well-known singers. The earnings differential between JK Rowling, author of the Harry Potter books, and a less well known fiction writer would be another illustration – or the way that a minority of football clubs have risen to and sustain their dominance by virtue of their capacity to attract and retain what are perceived to be the very best players from around the world. Overall the analysis can be used to explain both the differentiation between firms and between employees. It can also account for the growth of large global corporations and the related global division of labour, including the concentration of top jobs in global city regions. Thus Quah's (1996, 2003) exposition of the 'superstar' effect, which is rather different from Sherwin Rosen's (1981) explanation that Krugman rejects, can explain the high earnings of the 'galaticos' and the high CEO's incomes, referred to earlier, as intensified competition and increased ease of 'switching,' i.e. transferring between suppliers, characteristic of the New Economy (Reich 2001), creates an imperative for firms to hire the best employees. As knowledge goods and knowledge workers become more important in the New Economy, social inequalities will correspondingly tend to increase, leading not only to widening inequalities on a global scale but also to earnings differentiation – between knowledge workers, and between the high earning knowledge workers and those in sectors such as care and personal services which have opposite economic properties and a different gender composition. These are discussed further below. Extending the analysis in this way, that is by combining the ideas of feminist researchers (Folbre and Nelson 2000, McDowell 2004) with those of Danny Quah (2003), it is possible to explain why these widening social divisions are also differentiated by gender.

Women continue to be globally over represented in generic/high touch work such as care, cleaning and personal services (ILO 2004; within the UK, Social Trends 2004), which are typically low paid, partly because they have opposite economic properties to 'knowledge work'. In general these services are not infinitely expansible or non-rival, so market size is limited, and they are inherently technologically unprogressive. Correspondingly, wages tend to be more uniform but low (Baumol 1967). Referring specifically to care work, although there are potential economies of scale, there are still fixed and relatively small limits to the number of people each worker can care for. New technologies may be able to transcend some of these limitations through electronic monitoring – such as temperature gauges in assisted housing, or replacing home visits by text message reminders to the elderly to take their medicine (Coyle 2004). But – in general – productivity is constrained unless, as in the latter case, the nature of the service is profoundly, and many would consider adversely, changed and correspondingly earnings tend to be low. Care is a also a composite good, consisting of guarding (making sure that no harm comes to the cared for) and nurturing (enhancing their well-being), but this latter aspect is difficult to measure (Folbre and Nelson 2000). Thus while nurturing aspects provide positive social externalities in terms of happier people and more rounded social citizens, they are typically unrecognized in the wages paid to employees. These properties also help explain why, unless market logic is challenged, these activities are either provided on a not-for-profit basis, in which case supply is limited by financial constraints, or else if provided by profit-seeking firms, prices are high even though employees are generally low paid. Thus although personal groomers for the elite may receive high hourly pay, or even retainers, to ensure 24 hour availability, their earning compared to the elite themselves are comparatively low[3] and workers in high cost private nurseries are still among the lowest pay decile in the UK. This analysis accounts for the low pay in these sectors but not for the over representation of women within them.

Feminists have long pointed out that the concept of skill is gendered, with stereotypical male occupations deemed skilled and so rewarded financially, while women's jobs often rest on their unrewarded 'natural' talents (Phillips and Taylor 1980). Moreover, when women do enter male spheres of work a glass ceiling seems to prevent them from reaching the top. One reason for this is long working hours, which are difficult to combine with family responsibilities which in practice continue to fall primarily on women (Harkness 2003).[4] However, in OECD countries some women continue to work very long hours and yet still fail to reach the top. This absence has been attributed to subtle and indeed less subtle forms of discrimination, sexual harassment and the prevailing macho culture, which reacts negatively to the presence of the female form and continues to thrive despite all of the equal opportunities and antidiscrimination policies. Indeed the labour market is a site of embodied performances and women's bodies are considered simply out of place in the cerebral world of finance (McDowell 1997). Likewise men's bodies could be seen as being out of place in care work but even here inequality remains in that when men do enter predominantly female spheres they tend to re-inscribe their roles as masculine and appropriate the higher paid, higher status niches. Thus in cleaning, men tend to work with machines and in nursing focus more on paper work rather than direct care, as well as the more macho branches for example, psychiatric nursing, which can involve restraining violent patients and thereby retains traditional masculine traits (Cross and Bagilhole 2002).

The New Economy and spatial inequality – 'superstar' regions

So far the analysis has outlined some of the processes leading to uneven development on a global scale, by a very brief reference to value chain theory, and in more detail the processes leading to earnings inequalities within OECD countries, and consequent gender inequalities. These explanations will now be linked to spatial inequality and the development of 'superstar regions'.

One of the mysteries of the New Economy is why space, place and distance continue to matter. Paradoxically, as the power of communications has increased so has the concentration of high-level economic activities in a small number of highly interconnected locations. A new economic landscape has emerged consisting of global cities and global city-regions, which could be collectively termed superstar regions, with lower order centres, industrial and agribusiness districts, in between, as well as areas of industrial dereliction and rural regions largely bypassed, but not unaffected by, global flows.

Considerable efforts have been made to define and measure these centres of affluence. Should they be termed world cities (Hall 1966, Friedman 1986), global cities (Sassen 1991, 2000) or global city-regions (Scott *et al.* 2001)? Which cities or regions merit this status and what is their relative ranking

(Taylor *et al.* 2002)? These measures are important to policy makers as many cities and regions aspire to join this global elite. The most comprehensive measurement effort to date perhaps has been the hierarchical inventory of world cities, based on the existence of producer service firms with a strong global presence and global connectivity (Taylor *et al.* 2002). Whichever definition is used however, the same two or three cities, London, New York and Tokyo, appear in the top ranks, with Paris, Frankfurt, Hong Kong, Singapore, Milan, Chicago and Los Angeles following and Seoul, Beijing, Mexico City, Buenos Aires, São Paulo, Sydney, Bangkok, Johannesburg, and Kuala Lumpur,[5] also making appearances in the top 20–30 depending on the precise measures used (see Hall 2001).

Global cities and global city-regions house the most dynamic elements of global capitalism and are where the corporate executives, government leaders and high level professional and technical workers, whose decisions and innovations shape the lives of people throughout the world, reside. In the UK the top 1 per cent of earners account for about 300,000 people who earn at least £100K and these high earners are disproportionately concentrated in London with 8.5 per cent of the taxpayers earning over £50K compared to 4.5 per cent for the UK as a whole (Inland Revenue 2004). It is the presence of high level, internationally oriented financial and business services that define global cities even though they may only form a relatively small volume of the total industrial activity.[6] At the same time they are typically the largest and wealthiest regions in the countries concerned and so have a wide range of industries and services associated with modern economies as well as the living spaces of their employees.

For Sassen (2000) global cities are the outcome of the asymmetry between the spatial dispersal of production and the continued centralization of control within large corporations. Global cities are where the key strategic and coordination functions take place and consequently they have become the 'command points in the organisation of the world economy' (Sassen 2000, 4). As decentralization becomes more extensive, the task of coordination becomes more complex and corporations subcontract some of the high-level producer service functions such as accountancy, law or public relations to specialist firms, which then become leading corporations themselves. These activities benefit from localization and urbanization economies. Being in the information loop is crucial to facilitate innovation and minimize risk and some activities still require a physical presence in these locations, especially for non-routine operations.

Sassen's (2000) analysis implicitly incorporates ideas from the new international division of labour theory developed in the 1970s, which specified how the vertical division of labour within the firm was being expressed horizontally over geographical space, with the high level or level 1 activities being located within the most developed regions (Hymer 1975). Global value chain literature could also be drawn upon to explain why these coordinating functions, and not routine production activities, are able to appropriate a large share of the value that enables them to pay the high salaries and the rents in these locations. The new economic geography literature on clustering helps to explain why – despite new ICTs – many of these high-level producer service firms are located in close geographical proximity.

By terming them superstar regions however, the aim is to encapsulate not only the processes leading to their formation but also the ensuing uneven spatial development and the internal inequality. This term also has the advantage of a negative or at least quizzical connotation by depicting their elitism and spatial exclusiveness. As a consequence it might overcome policy makers' uncritical desires to become global cities, irrespective of their negative side. The superstar concept is theoretical and so bypasses some of the difficulties of empirical definition arising from the dynamic and constantly evolving nature of economic organization and contemporary processes of urbanization. Furthermore it helps account for some of the growing inequality within them in a more analytical way.

The theoretical ideas about social divisions in the New Economy can be drawn upon to explain the income differentials between the high paid knowledge workers and the low paid workers who take care of their daily lives. This empirical division has been noted for some time; Castells (1989) for example refers to the information rich and information poor, or the symbolic analysts and generic workers. The analysis of these divisions presented here differs somewhat, not least because this chapter presents Quah's concept of knowledge goods which rests on technical economic properties and does not therefore imply that care workers, whose work and products have opposite technical properties in terms of being non-rival and expansible, are without knowledge or skill.

The key activities of global cities and global city-regions are quintessentially knowledge-based. Correspondingly they have equivalent properties to knowledge goods; that is they are weightless, with an almost infinite global reach, and in some respects they are infinitely expansible. These properties are clearest in software, but even consultancy or architecture, where each project may seem to be bespoke and will indeed differ in detailed content, nonetheless they still have many common features, allowing companies to realize some economies of scale. Consumers develop preferences for products and firms of greater renown or 'superstars', reinforcing their cumulative growth, as their market share and income will not be constrained by geographical distance. The replication of waterfront developments and architectural styles, albeit with added on local nuances, deriving from a small number of 'superstar' architects would be one example. Thus superstar firms in law, accountancy, consultancy and architecture materialize and locate in the global cities in a self-reinforcing way, as firms in London or New York, and are believed to be superior to ones located elsewhere and they correspondingly capture an increasing share of the market and continue to grow.

Producer services are extremely specialized and require highly skilled professional workers. As the work is decidedly pressurized, premiums are paid for people with proven talent, thereby bidding up salary costs and increasing the earnings differential between these and other workers in the locality, especially the low paid service sector workers and the workers in the more flexibly organized manufacturing activities that remain within these centres. The competitive environment also means that work is usually project based and employers draw in professionals as and when required on individualized short-term contracts to offset their risks. This insecurity in turn tends towards long working hours as both employees and employers take on projects as and when they are available (Reich 2000).

Correspondingly, knowledge workers have little time to manage their own day-to-day reproduction, which leads to a growing demand for a wide range of personal services. However, the inherent economic properties of this work, discussed above, together with its gender and ethnic coding, mean it is likely to be low paid. The social divisions in the New Economy are particularly visible in global cities where the highest paid workers are found, and these and low paid workers work and sometimes live in close proximity. In London for example social housing and million pound residences can be found alongside one another. Thus while there has been a professionalization of employment (Hamnett 1996) marked by the expansion of jobs in the professional and managerial categories, there has also been some expansion in personal services and a decline in manufacturing, suggesting that employment options are polarized (Sassen 2000). While there have been debates about the meanings of occupational categories (Bruegel 1996) and whether what has taken place is professionalization or polarization what is very clear is that earnings differentials have widened and as indicated below, there has been a deterioration in the relative position of low paid work in at least one global city, London.

Thus the New Economy is characterized by widening social divisions that take a gendered and spatial form. The processes outlined so far are largely theoretical and linked to the market but market processes develop differently in different places, depending on their history, the level of development of the country as a whole, prevailing macro economic policies, welfare regime and political philosophy as well as the precise nature of activities present. The role of the more developed welfare state in continental Europe and to a lesser extent in the UK is particularly important in moderating the extent of inequality found in large cities when contrasted with the USA (Hamnett 1996). Thus the specific forms of each and every global city or superstar region will be different so to consider in more detail how life and work are experienced in one such region the remainder of the discussion therefore relates to London.

Living and working in a superstar region

London has a higher proportion of residents in the top two occupational groups (which require a university degree or equivalent) than any other region in the UK. Between 1992 and 2000, full-time employment expanded further in these categories attracting young, highly qualified migrants from elsewhere in the UK and from other countries. Personal and protective services, which include caterers and care workers, was the only other occupational group where full-time employment increased, and this category – together with sales occupations – experienced the largest increase in part-time employment (GLA 2002). These changes in employment structure, together with the much slower rate of growth of earnings for low-paid occupations, have led to a widening of the earnings gap between the top and bottom deciles for both women and men. Figure 6.1 portrays the inter-decile range for men and Figure 6.2 for women for Great Britain, the South East Region, London and the City (in London) between 1981 and 2003, and show that earnings inequalities have been increasing in all of these areas with the highest levels of inequality in London and the City where the top jobs are concentrated.

The earnings distribution for men in London is wider than in the rest of the UK and wider than women's in all areas, reflecting both the existence of the highest-paid jobs in the London area and male dominance within these jobs, but also the continuing existence of low-paid male employment. Thus overall the scale of inequality is greater between men, owing to men's presence in the highest-paid jobs as well as those at the lower end of the distribution. Nevertheless there has been a growing duality between women, as a significant minority of women do work in high-paid sectors, if not in the very top jobs, while women overall remain vastly over represented in low-paid work, especially personal services.

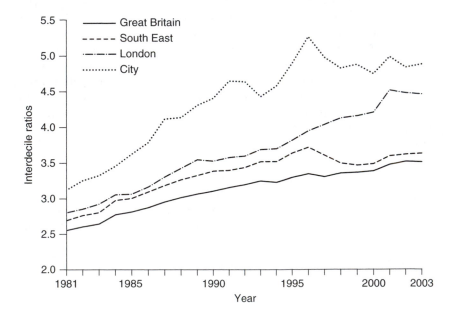

Figure 6.1 Earnings inequalities men.
        Source: New Earnings Survey (various years).
        Note: The data are for gross weekly earnings.

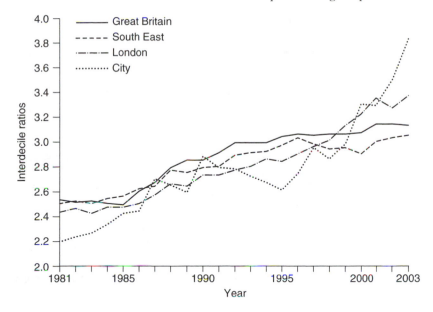

Figure 6.2 Earnings inequalities women. Source: New Earnings Survey (various years).
   Note: The data are for gross weekly earnings.

Figure 6.3 portrays the 90–50 earnings ratios and the 50–10 earnings ratios
for men and women just for London. The former measures the extent to
which the top decile has been moving away from the median and the latter the
extent to which the lowest decile has been falling away from the median.
Figure 6.3 demonstrates that inequality is increasing at a faster rate between the
median and the lowest decile indicating the change in employment composition and the expansion of low-paid work in London for both women and men.
This diagram indicates that rising inequality can not simply be attributed to
the super-rich or the 'top 1 per-centers' that are moving away from the rest and
so a problem of affluence but instead is linked to the expansion of jobs at the
bottom and disappearance in the middle tiers, in this respect suggesting some
support for the polarization thesis of Sassen (2000), rather than professionalization (Hamnett 1996). The prevalence of low-paid work also accounts for the
fact that London has a lower employment rate, despite the higher average pay,
compared to other regions of the country, as despite new tax credit policies the
high cost of transport and childcare in London make paid work economically
irrational for some groups of low-paid workers.[7]

   In addition to widening inequality however, there are other changes in the
labour market that are especially prevalent in the UK, where the government
has explicitly supported the development of a flexible labour market – and
trade unions have become less important. While the government has supported
some of the EU directives on Equalities and Parental leave, it has retained its

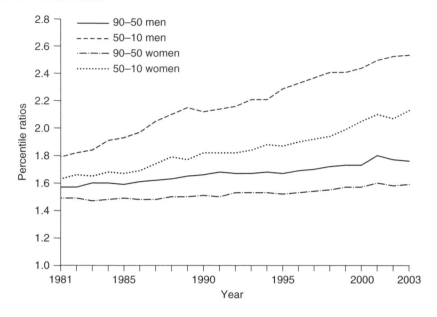

Figure 6.3 Earnings inequalities women and men in London. Source: New Earnings
Survey (various years). Note: The data are for gross weekly earnings.

opt-out from the working time directive and working hours for some of the
high-paid workers are extremely long. In addition it is now commonplace for
people to work unsocial hours, to work at the weekend, and to be employed
indirectly through a variety of agencies, even if working in public sector
institutions.

The expansion of employment in knowledge work, and caring work are
organically related – long working hours mean that high-paid workers, including women workers, increasingly demand marketized personal services and
care. These professional workers have limited social networks in the form of
family and friends, arising from the long hours spent at work, their own geographical mobility and more specifically the geographical distance from their
own parents. These people also wanted to spend their spare time in what they
perceived to be more exciting ways than cleaning and housework. For example, the ex-partner of Clare, one of the examples discussed below, employed an
au pair to take care of him on a regular basis as well as for the one day a week
when he took care of their child.

The remaining discussion draws on two iconic instances, important and
potentially enduring characteristics that symbolize key features of the New
Economy from a larger qualitative research project[8] to highlight how life is
organized at the upper and lower tiers of the earnings hierarchy in the New
Economy in London. People's lives are extremely diverse and their individual

circumstances are influenced by the way that their specific characteristics such as gender, ethnicity, education, partnership and parental status, stage of life course, as well as preferences, intersect with each other and with the context in which they find themselves. Thus every case is different and qualitative research can never be representative in a statistical sense. The instances referred to below have been selected because they seem to reflect some recurring patterns that perhaps signify some key aspects of contemporary life among people at opposite ends of the widening earnings hierarchy in the contemporary New Economy in London. The examples are drawn from 70 in depth interviews carried out in London analysed via a grounded theory methodology (Strauss and Corbin 1990) all of which contributed to the understanding of the New Economy presented above.[9]

Clare and Melissa are both working mothers and so both reflect the increasing participation of women in the labour market including mothers of young children (see Harkness 2003). Clare is now a single parent with one young pre-school child and a permanent full-time job in the knowledge sector while Melissa is married with three school-aged children and works part-time on a fixed-term contract as a nursery nurse in a local authority drop-in playgroup centre.

Clare encapsulates a number of features of the New Economy, both economically and socially. Economically, her earnings are in the highest female and male decile and she works in financial services – but in graduate recruitment. In fact her work involves searching for the superstars of the future. She is more in human resources than finance, in this sense reflecting continuing gender divisions in the New Economy. Indeed in her workplace 'it's really funny because this, this immediate team here is 95 per cent women, but you go over the road to the trading floors, and wherever else, and it's 95 per cent men ...'.

She also went on to say that the firm aims for political correctness and they are: 'very conscious that they don't have enough female employees' and that to get more and keep more that they need to be, 'umm, you know more facilitative in terms of childcare, flexible working arrangements, all that kind of stuff'.

She continues however by indicating that despite this formal stance:

> by the nature of the fact that this is mainly a sort of sales and trading organisation, it is very very male dominated, it's very full of egos, and there is a lot of sort of sexist banter or chit chat that goes on day to day. ... It's certainly no worse than any other bank, but, I think just because it is so male dominated, you do, you do encounter that, you, you, there'd be no point being a sort of shrinking violet girl working in an investment bank cos you get your head bitten off three or four times a week! ... So, if you're not comfortable with that you should probably go and work somewhere else.

Clare's statements are thus providing support for earlier arguments about women's under representation in these spheres.

Clare is not in a trade union and works long and fairly unpredictable hours and her job involves being away from home 'I mean I travel on business probably, ten days a month, um, and there'll be evenings where I don't get home until sort of 10, 11 … Oh I have a laptop at home that I work from regularly in the evenings anyway, an' I'm always on my mobile, so you know … 'Thus while her regular day is 8 until 6 quite often she works longer than this and regularly works from home in the evenings. She has a certain amount of flexibility as her work is measured by results and if she ever needed to be away from work she could make up the difference from home. As with the other high-paid mothers in the study, she valued proximity to her workplace so she could get home quickly if needed and made regular use of taxis for her journey to work.

In a social sense Clare similarly reflects many aspects of contemporary social life. She is a single parent – she separated from her husband when their child was 18 months old – and geographically distant from her own parents. She has a limited social network to draw on for support, not having had the time to develop one: 'I certainly don't have that mums' network thing going, 'cos I never did any of the sort of ante-natal classes and 'cos I was never off work long enough I never got to know anyone in that respect, so I kind of really lost out'. She uses a private nursery five days a week but also has a live-in au pair who fetches the child in the late afternoon and takes care of her until Clare arrives home, as well as doing all the child's cooking, cleaning and washing as well as errands for Clare such as fetching clothes from the dry cleaners. Clare depends on pre-prepared food and the microwave. Live-in assistance is essential owing to her long working hours and because she works away from home. Clare also makes occasional use of a baby-sitting agency and has used the emergency crèche at her ex-partner's workplace (also a city finance firm). Similarly if her usual arrangements break down she would call upon an ad hoc network created by her ex-nanny and her ex-partner's au pair, but all this would be paid support (see also Blair-Loy and Jacobs 2003). Her life is extremely busy and is not at all involved with any community or social groups. Thus Clare encapsulates the life of a high-earning parent in the New Economy, working long hours and drawing on a wide range of marketized services to sustain her existence.

At the opposite end of the earnings distribution is Melissa, who is a nursery nurse and lives with her husband and three children in local authority housing in Inner London but further out from the centre than Clare. Melissa works part time and her job is insecure. The nursery she works for belongs to the local authority but the funding for her job comes from the single regeneration budget and so she is on a fixed-term contract which has to be renewed periodically: 'Well, every year we've got to go through and ring them up and say "have you got money for Melissa to be working again next year?"' Her husband is a railway engineer, formerly employed by the public sector but now by the private sector company that manages the track.

He works shifts including days, nights and weekends. His usual working hours are around 40 but he can be called in to do overtime. Their combined earnings are considerably lower than Clare's though collectively they work a similar number of hours.

Melissa has always worked and her hours now correspond roughly with school hours and so she manages outside school childcare herself with occasional support from childminders. Melissa does the major share of housework and childcare, partly because her husband works longer hours and varied shifts. In the past she relied on friends and her own mother, who lived close by, for childcare. She would not have been able to afford to use a private nursery even had she wanted to. This inability to afford the service she is producing is another feature of the New Economy and differs from the Fordist era where the wages enabled people, albeit through loans, etc., to buy the goods they were making. The new class of low-paid service workers are providing services they themselves would not be able to afford. Melissa had to give up a full-time job owing to the difficulty of getting there on public transport, even though the distance was not great. Had she been able to afford taxi's from her earnings she might have been able to continue. Despite being a qualified childcare worker, Melissa and her husband's earnings are both in the lowest decile for women and men respectively. They would now qualify for the new child tax and working tax credits, which would clearly raise their incomes. However the question of why people doing valuable work, caring for children *and* maintaining vital infrastructure have to depend on state benefits does raise questions about the contemporary values of the New Economy.

Conclusion

This chapter has tried to develop an analytical explanation for the tendency towards inequality in the New Economy. To do so it has drawn on a range of existing theory and empirical research carried out in London. The main conclusion – that inequality is widening and gender divisions remain in the New Economy – may in some ways be predictable. It is interesting to note that even orthodox economists are concerned by the high levels of inequality and look towards social theory for explanation. Richard Layard (2005) has raised concern that the things that many people care most about in society are valued least highly through the market, thereby questioning the desirability of sticking too closely to the agenda of competitiveness. From other studies in this volume and elsewhere it is clear that the New Economy does offer considerable potential for raising social welfare. The technicians have in some ways done their job – it is crucial therefore for social scientists too to devise ways of organizing society differently, so that some of the gains that arise from these new ways of working can be shared more equally between regions and between women and men to achieve even the UK government's current goal of creating a flexible but fair society.

Notes

1   I am not suggesting that poor governance is responsible for the poverty of poorer countries simply highlighting the fact that transferred funds do not always reach the poorest
groups.
2   Care workers being amongst the lowest paid and call centre workers earning only 48 per cent
of average male or 65 per cent of average female wages. Figures calculated from IDS
(2003) and ONS (2003).
3   Thus Beyonce's (a popular singer) hair dresser on call 24/7 receives £200 per hour
(MTV Beyonce's millions).
4   Susan Harkness (2003) demonstrates the continuing unequal division of domestic work
and child care for the UK using data from the BHPS. Similarly Eurostat (2004) time use
data shows a similar pattern for a greater range of European countries.
5   Johannesburg and Kuala Lumpur are Gamma world cities on Taylor, Catalano and
Walker's (2002) definition, which means that they are global service centres for at least
two sectors (from accountancy, advertising, banking and law) and in one of these a major
centre.
6   See Dunford and Fielding (1997) for a discussion of the relative degree of sectoral and
occupational specialization in London and the South East Region in the 1980s and especially the high concentration of financial services and for information on employment
change by sector for the period between 1978 and 2000 see Buck *et al.* (2002).
7   For example, a lone parent with two children and childcare costs is better off returning
to work at the minimum wage outside London, but needs to earn £7.76 an hour in
London–i.e. almost 1.75 times the minimum wage in order to experience immediate
monetary gains from paid work (Bivand, Gordon and Simmonds 2003).
8   The qualitative research referred to derives from an ESRC-funded project (project reference no. R000239470) which was carried out jointly between the author, Linda
McDowell, Colette Fagan, Kath Ray and Kevin Ward. I would like to acknowledge their
assistance for this part of the chapter, Yiannis Kaplanis for gathering the quantitative data,
and Mina Moshkeri for the graphics. The in depth interviews were carried out between
2002 and 2004.
9   These interviews were carried out in the context of the ESRC project referred to above.

References

Atkinson, A. (2003) 'Top Incomes in the United Kingdom over the Twentieth Century',
Authors website http://www.nuff.ox.ac.uk/users/atkinson/TopIncomes20033.pdf, accessed
25 March 2005.
Baumol, W. (1967) 'Macroeconomics of unbalanced growth: the anatomy of the urban
crisis,' *American Economic Review,* 57, 415–426.
Beaverstock, J., Hubbard, P. and Short, J. (2004) 'Getting Away with it? The Changing
Geographies of the Global Super-Rich', *Geoforum,* 35, 401–407.
Beck, U. (2000) *The Brave New World of Work,* Polity Press, Cambridge.
Beck, U. (1992) *Risk society: towards a new modernity,* Sage, London.
Benería, L. (2003) *Gender, Development, and Globalization: Economics as if People Mattered*
Routledge, London.
Benner, C. (2002) *Work in the New Economy. Flexible Labour Markets in Silicon Valley,*
Blackwell, Oxford.
Bivand, P., Gordon, B. and Simmonds, D. (2003) 'Making Work Pay in London', Centre for
Economic and Social Inclusion GLA, London.
Blair-Loy, M. and Jacobs, J. A. (2003) 'Globalization, working hours and the care deficit
among stockbrokers', *Gender and Society,* 230–249.

Bourdieu, P. (1990) *The Logic of Practice* Polity Press, Cambridge.

Bruegel, I. (1996) 'Gendering the polarisation debate: a comment on Hamnett's Social polarisation, economic restructuring and welfare regimes,' *Urban Studies,* 33, 1431–1439.

Buck, N., Gordon, I., Hall, P., Harloe, M. and Kleinman, M. (2002) *Working Capital. Life and Labour in Contemporary London,* Routledge, London.

Castells, M. (1989) *The informational city: information technology, economic restructuring and the urban-regional process,* Blackwell, Oxford.

Castells, M. (2001) *The Internet Galaxy. Reflections on the Internet Business and Society,* Oxford University Press, Oxford.

Cox, R. and Watt, P. (2002) 'Globalization, polarization and the informal sector: the case of paid domestic workers', *Area* 34, 39–57.

Coyle, D. (2004) 'Getting the measure of the new economy', paper presented at the Resurgent Cities Conference, April, London School of Economics.

Coyle, D. and Quah, D. (2002) *Getting the Measure of the New Economy,* Isociety, The Work Foundation, London.

Cross, S. and Bagilhole, B. (2002) ''Girls' Jobs for the Boys? Men, masculinity and non-traditional occupations', *Gender Work and Organisation,* 9, 204–226.

Dunford, M. and Fielding, A. (1997) 'Greater London, the South-east Region and Wider Britain: Metropolitan Polarization, Uneven Development and Inter-Regional Migration', in H. Blotvogel and A. Fielding, ed., *People, Jobs and Mobility in the New Europe,* Wiley, Chichester.

Esping-Andersen, G. (2004) 'Inequality and the Welfare State in Europe', Ralph Miliband Lectures on Inequalities: dimensions and challenges, LSE.

Eurostat, (2004) *How Europeans spend their time. Everyday life of women and men, 1998–2002,* Luxembourg: Office for Official Publications of the European Communities.

Folbre, N. and Nelson, J. (2000) 'For Love or Money – Or both?' *Journal of Economic Perspectives,* 14, 123–140.

Friedman, J. (1986) 'The World City Hypothesis' *Development and Change,* 17, 69–83.

Gereffi, G. and Kaplinsky, R. (2001) eds, *Value of Value Chains,* University of Sussex IDS, UK.

GLA, (2002) 'London. Divided: Income inequality and poverty in the Capital', Greater London Authority, London.

Greenspan, A. (1998) 'Is there a new economy?' *California Management Review,* 41, 74–85.

Goos, M. and Manning, A. (2003) 'McJobs and MacJobs: the growing polarisation of Jobs in the UK', in R. Dickens, P. Gregg, and J. Wadsworth, eds, *The Labour Market Under New Labour* Macmillan, Basingstoke, 70–85.

Hall, P. (1966) *The World Cities,* Weidenfeld and Nicolson, London.

Hall, P. (2001) 'Global City-regions in the 21st Century', in A Scott, ed., *Global City-Regions,* Oxford University Press, Oxford.

Hamnett, C. (1996) 'Social polarization, economic restructuring and welfare state regimes', *Urban Studies,* 33, 1407–1430.

Hamnett, C. (2003) *Unequal city: London in the global arena,* Routledge, London.

Harkness, S. (2003) 'The household division of labour: changes in families' allocation of paid and unpaid work 1992–2002' in R. Dickens, P. Gregg and J. Wadsworth, eds, *The Labour Market Under New Labour,* Macmillan, Basingstoke, 150–169.

Hochschild, A. (2003) *The Managed Heart. Commercialization of Human Feeling,* University of California Press, Berkeley.

Hymer, S. (1975) 'The Multinational Corporation and the Law of Uneven Development' in H. Radice, ed., *International firms and modern imperialism: selected readings,* Penguin, Harmondsworth.

IDS (2004) 'Regional Pay. The realities of private and public sector practice' Income Data Services, London.

ILO (2004) 'Global employment trends for women', http://www-ilo-mirror.cornell.edu/public/english/employment/strat/download/trendsw.pdf.

Inland Revenue (2004) 'Income and tax, by region and country', http://www.inlandrevenue.gov.uk/stats/income_distribution/pi_t11_1.htm (accessed 25 March).

Krugman, P. (2002) 'For Richer' *New York Times Magazine* October 20, http://faculty.pnc.edu/arw/gbg344/For%20Richer.htm (accessed 28 June).

Land, H. (2003) 'Leaving care to the market and the courts', European Social Policy Association Conference, Copenhagen, http://www.sfi.dk/graphics/ESPAnet/papers/Land.pdf accessed 28 June.

Layard, R. (2005) *Happiness: lessons from a new science,* Penguin, London.

Machin, S. (2003) 'Wage inequality since 1975', in R. Dickens, P. Gregg and J. Wadsworth eds *The Labour Market Under New Labour,* Macmillan, Basingstoke, 280–290.

McDowell, L. (1997) *Capital Culture. Gender at Work in the City,* Blackwell, Oxford.

McDowell, L. (2004) 'Sexuality, desire and embodied performances in the workplace' in B. Brooks-Gordon, L. Gelsthorpe, M. Johnson, and A. Bainham, A. eds *Sexuality Repositioned,* Hart, Oxford.

McDowell, L., Perrons, D., Fagan, C., Ray, K. and Ward, K. (2005) 'The contradictions and intersections of class and gender: working women's lives in the global city', *Environment and Planning* A, 37, 441–461.

Milanovic, B. (2002) 'True world income distribution 1988 and 1993: First calculation based on household surveys alone', *The Economic Journal* 112, 51–92.

Milanovic, B. (2005) 'Globalization and Inequality Ralph Miliband Lectures on Inequalities: dimensions and challenges', LSE December. Available at, http://www.lse.ac.uk./Depts/global/eventsmiland2005.htm.

New Earnings Survey (various years), National Statistics http://www.statistics.gov.uk/statbase/Product.asp?vlnk=5749 (accessed 25 March.)

Norris, P. (2001) *Digital Divide Civic engagement, information poverty and the Internet Worldwide,* Cambridge University Press, Cambridge.

Perrons, D. (2004a) 'Globalization and social change. People and places in a divided world', Routledge, London.

Perrons, D. (2004b) 'Understanding Social and Spatial Divisions in the New Economy: New Media Clusters and the Digital Divide', *Economic Geography,* 80, 45–62.

Phillips, A. and Taylor, B. (1980) 'Sex and skill', *Feminist Review,* 6, 79–88.

Piketty, T. and Saez, E. (2003) 'Income inequality in the United States', *Quarterly Journal of Economics,* CXVIII, 1, 1–39.

Quah, D. (1996) 'The Invisible hand and the weightless economy', Centre for Economic Performance Occasional paper No. 12, LSE, London.

Quah, D. (2003) 'Digital Goods and the New Economy', (available from, www.econ./se.ac.uk/staff/dquah/dp-ozizhbne.html.)

Reich, R. (2001) *The future of success work and life in the new economy,* Heinemann, London.

Rosen, S. (1981) 'The economics of superstars', *American Economic Review,* 71, 845–858.

Sassen, S. (1991) *The global city: New York, London, Tokyo.* Princeton University Press, Princeton, N.J.

Sassen, S. (2000) *Cities in a world economy Second Edition* Pine Forge London, London.

Schmitz, H. ed (2003) *Local enterprises in the global economy. Issues of governance and upgrading* Edward Elgar, Cheltenham.

Scott, A., Agnew, J., Soja, E. and Storper, M. (2001) 'Global City-regions', in A Scott, ed., *Global City-Regions*, Oxford University Press, Oxford.

Sennett, R. (1998) *The corrosion of character*, WW Norton and Company, London.

Social Trends (2004) *Social Trends* 34, The Stationery Office, London.

Strauss, A. and Corbin, J. (1990) *Basics of Qualitative Research: grounded Theory Procedures and Techniques*, Sage, London.

Taylor, P., Catalano, G. and Walker, D. (2002) 'Exploratory Analysis of the World City Network', *Urban Studies*, 39, 2377–2394.

Toynbee, P. (2005) 'Gender Inequality: old patterns, new challenges', Ralph Miliband Lectures on Inequalities: dimensions and challenges LSE 3 February. Available at http://www.lse.ac.uk/collections/LSEPubliclecturesAndEvents/events/2005/20041216t17182001.htm

UNDP (2002) *Human Development Report 2002: Deepening Democracy in a Fragmented World*, Oxford University Press, Oxford.

UNDP (2003) *Millennium Development Goals A Compact among Nations to End Human Poverty*, Oxford University Press, Oxford.

7 Labour organizing in the New Economy: examples from the USA and beyond

Andrew Herod

Introduction

This chapter examines how the emergence of a 'New Economy' is impacting labour union organizing. First several aspects of the 'New Economy' which are having substantial impacts upon workers and their organizing strategies are outlined. Next, issues related to the spatiality of union organizing are explored and several models that various unions have adopted to address the geographic restructuring of contemporary capitalism are highlighted. Finally, what these different models mean for worker praxis is examined, the spatial relationships within which workers and their organizations operate is determined, and how the geography of capitalism is made is discussed.

Aspects of the New Economy as they affect workers

Four developments in contemporary capitalism have had significant implications for workers. First, there has been a transformation in the political and economic relationship between capital and labour. This has been marked by the replacement of labour with capital in the production process (e.g., the use of computer-aided manufacturing and design), threats (and actual practices) of capital mobility in the face of worker mobilization, and a growing anti-union attitude on the part of many employers, an attitude often encouraged by government.[1] Second, governments at the national and sub-national scales have become increasingly entrepreneurial in nature, fostering competition between communities to stimulate regional growth. This has made union organizing more difficult as unions are encouraged to temper militancy in the hope of fostering inward investment. Simultaneously, the privatization of public services and the growing spatial mobility of many public sector jobs (e.g., through 'tele-medicine') means that public sector workers (often heavily unionized) are being exposed to the disciplining aspects of neoliberalism. Third, new telecommunications and transportation technologies have enabled corporations to exploit the space–time compressions of the international division of labour. As a result, profits made overseas represent a growing proportion of all corporate profits and many workers in the advanced industrial economies are now forced to compete for jobs and investment with workers in the developing world.

Fourth, the model of business organization for many companies has radically shifted. In the 1950s the most common model arguably was one characterized by highly vertically integrated companies who conducted business with other firms through arm's length market transactions. Workers and management typically held long-term jobs within such firms and it was relatively easy to determine who was inside a particular firm and who was 'outside' it. Collective bargaining occurred between the inside management and a labour union representing inside workers (Wial 1994). In contrast, the past few decades have witnessed the growth of the 'networked firm' wherein many of the major elements of the former model have been replaced as activities previously conducted internally (e.g., provision of food services, manufacturing of components) have been sub-contracted out. Even within firms some activities may now be treated as quasi-independent, such that when the internal providers of services prove too expensive companies turn to outside contractors to do the job. Likewise, the formation of cooperative relationships (joint ventures, consortia, long-term alliances) with suppliers, customers and distributors in which one manufacturer may have direct influence over the production methods of another – regularly the case in the automobile industry – has resulted in workers in different firms often working in closer cooperation with each other than with workers employed by the same putative company. The result is that the boundary between those inside and those outside any particular firm has become increasingly blurred, which has made it more difficult for unions to identify which managers are actually responsible for making the decisions affecting workers' lives (see Wial 1994, Herod 1997a). Furthermore, market vagaries mean cooperative relationships between firms are frequently transitory in nature and have encouraged many TNCs to turn to part-time or temporary workers to achieve organizational flexibility.

There are, of course, myriad consequences of these transformations for workers. Three have particular resonance for unions. First, economic restructuring has meant the loss of millions of manufacturing and mining jobs, whereas employment in the service sector has increased, such that the low-cost retailer Wal-Mart is now the largest private non-temp agency employer in the USA. This shift towards service sector employment has been particularly significant for union organizing for several reasons: models of union organizing have typically been developed in the context of manufacturing and seem less suited to organizing service sector workers; manufacturing and mining have traditionally been the sectors out of which many labour movements grew; the geographical locations where new service sector jobs are being created are often not where manufacturing and mining jobs are being lost; and many of the largest service sector firms (e.g., McDonald's and Wal-Mart) are rabidly anti-union. Second, despite the rhetoric of how the New Economy will be a 'high-wage knowledge economy', for many workers the reality is that it is promising to be a low-wage service and manufacturing economy. Of the 25 million new jobs created in the USA during the 1990s, only 18 per cent paid more than the national average income (SOREDI 2001). Millions of workers have seen real wages decline during the past three decades – in the private sector they are still below what they were in the 1970s – whilst the growth of part-time and short-term contracts mean that the likelihood of workers holding long-term employment contracts with particular employers or of developing lasting contacts with other groups of workers (contacts often essential for labour organizing) has diminished.[2]

Third, for many workers the spatial relationship between the location of paid work and home has been transformed. Increasing numbers of workers today labour at home as telecommuters, industrial homeworkers, and home-based telemarketers, which has significant implications for unions' abilities to organize (Herod 1991). New geographical patterns of residence, consumption and sociability are emerging, such that growing numbers of workers work significantly farther from home than in the past. As a result, employees today are more likely to 'live a considerable distance from fellow-workers, possess a largely "privatized" domestic life or a circle of friends unconnected with work, and pursue cultural or recreational interests quite different from those of other employees in the same workplace' (Hyman 1999, 3). Consequently, the spatial basis upon which labour unionism has traditionally relied is being dramatically transformed for many workers as the geographical 'disjuncture between work and community [leads to] the loss of many of the localized networks which [historically] strengthened the supports of union membership (and in some cases made the local union almost a "total institution")'. Such geographical transformations in workers' lives are important because they have significant implications for the organizing strategies in which unions engage and for the types of strategies which already-unionized workers adopt when in struggle with their employers.

Spatialities of labour union activity

Declining levels of union membership – in 2001 only 9.0 per cent of all US private sector workers were union members, with state rates ranging from a high of 16.7 per cent (New York) to a low of 2.3 per cent (North Carolina) (*Statistical Abstract of the United States* 2002: Table 630) – have led to significant soul-searching by union organizers. There are two principal aspects to this soul-searching – how to organize greater numbers of workers into unions and how, once organized, unions can engage in more effective campaigns against employers. Significantly, in addressing these concerns many unions have begun to rethink how the changing spatial contexts within which workers live their lives have important implications for organizing strategies.

Organizing workers into unions and the spatiality of the workplace

The traditional model of labour organizing in the USA has largely developed in the manufacturing sector and has generally assumed that workers are full-time employees who work for a specific employer, often in a long-term relationship. As a result, it has relied on the following elements: identifying 'hot shops' in which an organizer is contacted by a group of workers who have decided they want to be unionized; organizers appeal to workers largely on the basis of wages and benefits and as employees of specific companies; unions tend to view organizing as a technical ability and not a shared process, such that workers are organized *by* the union; organizing strategies are premized on the existence of large, centralized workplaces with few entrance gates and regular shift changes, and with large, stable workforces; and the focus is upon winning 51 per cent of the vote in a National Labor Relations Board (NLRB) representation election as quickly and as inexpensively as possible (Green and Tilly 1987, Savage 1998).[3] Primarily, such strategies reflect the worksite orientation of US labour law and are based upon what were perceived to be the certainties of a Fordist economy (long-term, full-time employment and strict demarcation of job categories).

However, organizing the service sector and contingent manufacturing workers who are becoming an ever larger proportion of the labour force often entails dealing with quite different issues than when organizing Fordist manufacturing facilities. As Green and Tilly (1987) suggest, because service workers often have little experience with unions – many service workers are younger, are women, or are new immigrants, groups frequently seen as 'unorganizable' by older, white, male organizers – service sector workplaces are less likely than Fordist manufacturing facilities to develop hot shops. Given that service workers are more likely to come into contact with customers than are manufacturing workers, they may also be less concerned with traditional 'bread and butter' issues (especially if they are higher paid professionals, such as computer programmers or doctors) and more concerned instead with issues of product quality and job quality, such as how they are treated in front of customers. Equally, service sector employment is often characterized by small businesses with high labour turnover where part-time and temporary workers are regularly used.[4]

The physical layout of organizing service sector workplaces also usually makes them harder to organize than manufacturing facilities. Whereas leafleting may be an effective technique with large worksites where it is easy to identify workers and in which there are regular shift changes, this is usually not the case with service sector workplaces, where it is often more difficult to distinguish workers and managers through their dress (all workers, not just managers, may have to dress 'professionally'), where shifts may be more varied, and where smaller workforces may mean that organizers spend a lot of time leafleting but reach relatively few potential union members. Also, whereas manufacturing workers may often toil some distance from their foreperson, the design of shops and offices means that service sector workers often work very closely with supervisors (sometimes on joint projects), a situation which not only makes it difficult for union organizers to gain access to workers beyond the eyes and ears of their managers but which also frequently leads workers to feel that joining the union would somehow betray their boss (Berman 1998).

Even within the manufacturing sector conditions of work have changed such that the traditional organizing model is perhaps less appropriate than it once was. The growth of 'teamwork' in industrial production has blurred distinctions between supervisors and shopfloor workers, manufacturing plants tend to be physically smaller and employ fewer workers than in the days when Henry Ford's Rouge River industrial complex employed some 90,000 workers, 'batch production' of manufactured goods by flexible technology is more common, and the trend towards the reduction in the number of job classifications in factories poses challenges to traditional organizing models which rely upon the strict demarcation of work and controlling particular jobs via wage and seniority rules (see MacDuffie 1995).

In response to such issues a number of unions have attempted to implement different types of organizing in the workplace. The Harvard Union of Clerical and Technical Workers (HUCTW) has encouraged face-to-face meetings among workers and organizers rather than relying upon the distribution of leaflets. Instead of focusing immediately upon issues of wages, union organizers concentrate upon more open-ended concerns such as workers' ability to participate in a more democratic decizion-making process in the workplace. As Cobble (1996, 342) has indicated, 'collective bargaining sessions [at Harvard] took place in the style of the Polish Solidarity negotiations, with large numbers of small teams grouped around tables, working out compromizes on specific issues', rather than the more traditional model in which the union leadership bargains with management and then presents the collective agreement to the union membership as a *fait accompli* to be voted up or down.

Other unions have gone about organizing service sector workers by abandoning altogether the worksite-focused model of organizing (characterized by the traditional factory model and even HUCTW) and have (re)adopted instead an early twentieth century model of 'occupational unionism' which focuses upon organizing workers in a particular profession (such as waitressing, nursing, home-based clerical workers and home health-care aides). Such campaigns typically do not try to secure for workers job rights at particular worksites – frequently the goal in manufacturing – but stress employment security within the industry and offer portable rights and benefits associated with membership in the occupation which are retained even as workers move from job site to job site (Cobble 1991). Given that many service sector workers do not stay with a single employer long enough for traditional worksite-based union elections to be an effective option, such occupational unionism often draws on communitywide support networks to pressure employers to recognize unions voluntarily. Significantly, occupational unionism symbolizes a quite different spatial relationship between worker, union and worksite, as the locus of organizing is no longer a particular worksite but is workers employed in a particular occupation throughout the broader local or even national labour market. As a way of reinforcing unionized workers' access to certain occupations some unions have even begun making widespread use of union-run employment exchanges and job registries: thus the South Bay Labor Council in Silicon Valley, California, has set up its own non-profit temp agency (Solutions@work) offering union wages and a portable benefits scheme (Jayadev 2000).[5]

The changing nature of the economy, then, is forcing some unions to develop new models of organizing to recruit members, models that move beyond a focus upon the worksite to organize service and even manufacturing workers (e.g., industrial homeworkers). However, it is important to recognize that the spatial transformations brought about by the emergence of the New Economy pose challenges too for already-organized workers engaging in campaigns against their employers, though some of these issues clearly also impact unions trying to recruit new members. Significantly, these campaigns require unions to think strategically about the new spatial relations which contemporary global capitalism is bringing about.

Once organized: eight models of union campaigns in the New Economy

Model 1: traditional labour internationalism: worksite to worksite

The practice of labour internationalism, of course, is not new and can be traced to the early part of the nineteenth century, if not before (see Herod 1997b). However, the transnationalization of corporate investments means that workers are increasingly engaging in international campaigns to secure their goals. Frequently, such campaigns involve workers from one facility of a corporation providing aid to workers in another branch of the same corporation. On other occasions they involve a more general effort to link workers in one nation with those of another. In both cases, the goal is to overcome workers' spatial isolation by developing trans-spatial linkages. Given that such campaigns are becoming more common, it is worth exploring a number of aspects of such internationalism. In particular, whilst there has been a tendency to view international labour solidarity as inherently progressive, it is important to note that there is frequently a disconnect between appearance and reality: what seems to be an example of proletarian coming together across space may sometimes actually be a regressive political strategy.

This conundrum has been explored by Rebecca Johns (1998) in her distinction between what she calls 'transformatory solidarity' and 'accommodationist solidarity'. Specifically, Johns notes that whereas some trans-spatial solidarity actions are clearly designed to challenge the class relations of capitalism and to help workers overseas to better their lot for truly altruistic reasons (Johns calls this transformatory solidarity), other actions are actually designed to defend the privileged spaces of high-paid workers within the global economy: by encouraging others – often in the Global South – to organize to improve their wages, it becomes less likely these latter workers will undercut the wages of workers initiating the solidarity campaign, such that capital will be less likely to flee the Global North (accommodationist solidarity). In such a situation, the goal of those engaging in solidarity is to defend one group of workers' privileged position within the global spatial division of labour at the expense of another's, thereby dividing workers spatially under the guise of uniting them across space (Herod 2003). Of course, whilst in practice it may be difficult to determine exact motives for any particular trans-spatial solidarity action, it is clear that different motives may lead to quite different outcomes. As globalization leads to ever greater calls for workers to practise international solidarity, it is important both theoretically and politically to consider the goals of such activities, together with the varying implications for the geography of the New Economy that such divergent goals will have.

Model 2: Organizing along commodity chains, with multiple employers and worksites

The types of international solidarity campaigns outlined above are often waged against a single employer on a one-off basis as the need arises. However, as the global economy becomes more interconnected a number of unions are attempting to develop more permanent connections between workers in different countries. Again, such efforts are not new. Historically, there have been several permanent international labour organizations, of which the Global Union Federations (GUFs, what used to be called the International Trade Secretariats) and the International Confederation of Free Trade Unions (ICFTU) are probably the most well known (for more on these, see Herod 1997b, 2002). Such organizations typically work within the boundaries of particular industrial sectors (the GUFs) or are defined geographically (the ICFTU is made up of national trade union centres). However, as patterns of production and corporate ownership criss-cross the globe, frequently transcending both sectoral and geographical boundaries, some labour activists have begun to develop campaigns in which organization takes place not in particular sectors or across particular regions but in a manner which mirrors the commodity chain for particular products. Typically, such an approach involves workers from multiple employers, economic sectors and worksites.

For example, one GUF – the International Union of Food and Allied Workers' Associations (IUF) – has been associated with a project of the Transnational Information Exchange, based in Amsterdam and largely supported by the Dutch Federatie Nederlandse Vakbeweging (FNV) labour federation, to try to link cocoa plantation workers in West Africa with chocolate manufacturing workers and confectionary shop workers in Europe. Although this particular approach has faced the problem that working conditions for plantation workers and factory workers are vastly different, it has nevertheless provided useful educational insights for unionists in the confectionary sector in Europe and enabled them to gain a better understanding of the industry as a whole. Relatedly, the IUF has worked with its constituent member unions in an effort to combat child slavery in the cocoa producing regions of West Africa, an effort which resulted in the 'International Cocoa Initiative' signed between industry, government, consumer and labour representatives in 2001.

Although such approaches can provide immense problems for organizers who must develop linkages between workers whose employment conditions may have little in common, the growing economic and geographical diversification of many TNCs means that such strategies are likely to become increasingly common.

Model 3: International codes of conduct

A slightly different way in which trade unionists and labour activists have been trying to further workers' interests has been through efforts to establish international codes of conduct by which TNCs agree to abide. Unlike the activities described above, such codes are typically applied to whole companies, sectors and industries, rather than linking workers in individual worksites across the globe. Some of the first calls for codes came in the 1970s when several unions agitated for a United Nations Code of Conduct for Transnational Corporations, and unions were involved in the development of the Organization for Economic Cooperation and Development's Guidelines for Multinational Enterprises, which was adopted in 1977. In 1988 the first 'framework agreement' between an international trade union organization and a TNC was signed (see Wills 2002). Codes of conduct, though, have changed in form since the 1970s. Whereas the early codes were often implemented under the auspices of international institutions like the International Labour Organization (ILO), those established in the 1990s have more typically been developed by and for individual companies (usually under intense pressure from labour activists). Although such codes now frequently go beyond aspects simply of the workplace (the general focus of the former codes), the fact that they do not usually have the force of law behind them means that to be effective they require constant vigilance, usually through negative publicity for companies ignoring them.

Nevertheless, there have been some successes to ensure that corporations respect worker rights. For example, after much negotiating the IUF entered into an agreement in June 2000 with the Chiquita fruit company and the Co-ordinating Committee of Latin American Banana Workers' Unions under which the company agreed to grant union recognition to plantation workers. Significantly, the agreement mirrored the commodity chain atop which Chiquita stands as it also required the company's suppliers, contractors and joint-venture partners to comply with the code. This was the first agreement of its kind in the agricultural sector and committed Chiquita to abide by several ILO Conventions. A review committee, composed of banana worker, IUF and company representatives meets periodically to review the agreement's application. Other fruit companies, including Danone, Dole and Del Monte, have subsequently signed similar agreements with the IUF. Efforts involving coffee producing peasants, however, have been less effective. Thus, whilst Starbucks agreed in 1995 to adopt a code of conduct and to set up a pilot project in Guatemala, progress has been slow.

Model 4: Network-based organizing and bargaining

As Fordist models of economic organization have begun to be transformed through the growth of sub-contracting and the establishment between corporations of joint ventures, cooperative agreements, long- or short-term alliances and consortia, new challenges have arisen for workers. For example, sub-contracting exacerbates wage competition between 'core' and 'periphery' workers in firms, whereas joint ventures and cooperative agreements mean that managers of one company can often have substantial control over the activities of workers in their partner company, even though these workers are not employed directly by them. In response to such developments, a number of unions have begun to explore 'network-based bargaining' (Wial 1994). Specifically, such bargaining attempts to mirror the new organizational structures which have emerged in certain economic sectors and regions. Whilst some commentators have argued that unions should address the challenges that post-Fordist business arrangements bring by engaging in traditional industrywide pattern bargaining, advocates of network-based bargaining argue that this latter approach is likely to be more successful precisely because the new forms of business structure emerging in some manufacturing enterprises blur traditional distinctions between industrial sectors, thereby making it difficult to determine which companies should be included in any industrywide bargaining structure. Unlike the commodity chain organizing model, in which the sellers and purchasers of commodities (African cocoa farmers and European chocolate companies) are typically operating in the marketplace at arm's length, network-based bargaining, so its advocates claim, is particularly well suited to situations in which the lines of control between putatively independent companies may be hard to determine (such as when management from a component supplier takes its orders directly from the company it supplies, a situation increasingly common in the automobile industry).

Although commentators such as Wial advocate network-based bargaining as appropriate for post-Fordist forms of business organization, this model actually has its roots in the nineteenth century in industries such as garment manufacturing, where networks of manufacturers, contractors and jobbers in a particular geographical area bargained jointly and signed a single agreement with the appropriate union in which, typically, a uniform wage scale and other elements of the contract applied to all workers, regardless of their actual employer.[6] In the garment industry, particularly in New York City, such bargaining structures had two principal characteristics: (1) organizing, collective bargaining and contract enforcement were separate activities, and organizing was extremely flexible and could be conducted on the basis of employer, occupation, ethnicity and/or gender; and (2) unions frequently used secondary economic pressure (e.g., sympathy strikes) to enforce contracts, a tactic which encouraged parties to the union contract not to sub-contract work to non-union firms for fear of being struck (Wial 1994). In the case of the International Ladies Garment Workers' Union (ILGWU), for example, as few as seven workers could form a local branch union, though all unions within a particular geographical area were required to form a central labour board, which was responsible for negotiating with the various firms in the industry. Any grievances under the contract were handled by union representatives within the individual business establishments, a situation which allowed the ILGWU to decentralize worker organizing and contract enforcement within the overall structure of a more centrally articulated network.

In the contemporary period a nascent form of network-based bargaining has emerged in the automobile industry. Management at General Motors's Saturn

Corporation and its local United Auto Workers (UAW) union developed a system of bargaining allowing the union to organize across Saturn's network of suppliers. In this system local union representatives and managers jointly choose Saturn's suppliers, subject to approval by UAW national officials and GM headquarters – a process which gives the union some ability to exclude suppliers that compete on the basis of low wages rather than product quality. The union also successfully expanded its organizational reach to include employees of firms with which Saturn does business, such as its on-site food contractor and a trucking firm servicing the plant (Wial 1994). These developments show how network-based bargaining may emerge in situations in which a union negotiates with a single employer who occupies a dominant position in a network and who can impose particular conditions of work on its suppliers and service providers.

However, in situations where there is no dominant employer who can be pressured by a union to cudgel its business partners, slightly different models of bargaining have been developed. In California's Silicon Valley union organizers have artificially created a dominant employer by effectively 'amalgamating' myriad small companies into a single mass unit. Specifically, in attempting to organize companies that contract out much of their work, union organizers have pushed for industrywide master contracts but have adopted a two-tier approach. Recognizing that utilizing a traditional model in which one and then another workplace is unionized would be counterproductive because firms targeted earliest would become uncompetitive relative to non-union sub-contractors, organizers developed a strategy in which the goal was to get targeted sub-contractors to sign an interim agreement specifying that they would enter into an industrywide contract when at least 50 per cent of industry leading firms had agreed to the proposition. Such a two-tiered approach means that the first companies to sign onto the agreement will not be underbid by non-union competitors during the period in which the union is pressuring other contractors to do likewise and that, instead, key sub-contractors will unionize simultaneously. Furthermore, once the leading sub-contractors have been unionized in tandem, they will not only have sufficient pull within the market to demand more money from those companies for whom they sub-contract (money which can be used to improve workers' wages) but they will also have an incentive themselves to ensure (through employers' associations) that rival non-union sub-contractors adopt trade norms with regard to wages and working conditions.

Model 5: Organizing locally to thwart globally

Just-in-time (JIT) forms of production have become widespread in recent years. Key to JIT is the ability to deliver a component to the assembly line just before it is needed. This allows JIT users to avoid tying up their capital in components which otherwise might sit idly in warehouses for weeks. There are, however, important contradictions which have significance for workers at companies using JIT production. Specifically, adoption of JIT makes manufacturers vulnerable to disruptions in the delivery of components, a vulnerability that workers can exploit. Hence, in 1998 in a dispute between GM and the UAW, strikers at just two plants in Flint, Michigan, brought virtually the whole of GM's operations in the US, Canada and Mexico to a halt for several weeks due to the company's inability to secure components (Herod 2000). At its height, 144 of GM's North American assembly and component supplier plants had to close or cut back on production, which cost the company $1.2 billion (after tax) in the 3rd quarter of 1998. Only after GM reorganized its inventory control system could the corporation restart a number of operations.

The lesson here is that in an increasingly interconnected economy which is reliant upon JIT delivery systems, workers may not have to adopt traditional trans-spatial solidarity actions in order to cripple a company. Whilst workers may choose to implement traditional solidarity actions for ideological reasons, the fact that they are able to disrupt so completely a company using JIT through focusing their actions on perhaps only a single plant has significant implications for how workers choose to organize. Specifically, it suggests they would do well to understand how their particular workplace is networked within a corporation's broader structure and how certain locations within the production chain may serve as 'choke points'. Equally, the fact that the UAW strikers were able to halt GM's production for several weeks before the company succeeded in reorganizing its supply networks highlights that whilst shutting down particular choke points may give workers time to pressure a company, they will only have so much of it before a company can restructure its component delivery systems – that there is, in other words, an important 'chrono-politics' at work here in which workers must secure their gains before the impacted companies have time to reorganize their supply chains.

Model 6: From production spaces to consumption spaces

A sixth model of organizing which has been increasingly adopted recently is one in which the immediate focus of attention is not so much the workplace (what we might call the 'spaces of production') but, rather, the more public spaces of the streets or retailing (what we might call the 'spaces of consumption'). Such a spatial refocusing of tactics has been particularly utilized in labour disputes in the service and manufacturing sectors when it has proven difficult to identify a single employer or to organize them. Certainly, these tactics are not themselves new but they have become increasingly popular amongst some unions. Two industries in which such tactics have been used with some success are garment manufacturing and janitorial services.

With regard to the garment industry, in the 1970s labour activists and other commentators began to notice the resurgence of sweatshops in cities like New York and Los Angeles. Many had believed sweatshops a thing of the past, but with growing competition from overseas manufacturers growing numbers of domestic manufacturers turned to sweatshops and industrial homework as a way to remain competitive. Sweatshops and industrial homework locations, particularly those employing immigrant workers, however, have proven difficult for garment unions to organize. Not only are such workspaces difficult to locate physically – unlike many other manufacturers, they frequently do not require much equipment or space and so can be conducted in fairly anonymous buildings – but, once located, the ponderous requirements of US labour law mean that such facilities are frequently opened and shut before union organizers can hope to have a union representation election, never mind actually negotiate a contract. Equally, the structure of the industry has changed significantly during the past three decades. Whereas until the 1970s garment manufacturers were able to negotiate from a position of relative power with a diffuse retail clientele – a situation which meant that the garment unions could relatively easily exert pressure on manufacturers for good wages (who could then pressure retailers for good prices) – the growing concentration of the retailing market in the 1980s and 1990s means that the selling of clothing is now dominated by a handful of large retailers.[7] In response, garment union organizers have begun to rediscover some of the models of organizing which their predecessors used at the turn of the twentieth century.

Arguably, one of the most innovative campaigns in this regard has been that of the Union of Needletrades, Industrial and Textile Employees (UNITE) and the National Consumers League, who joined together in 1995 to initiate their 'Stop Sweatshops Campaign'. Three elements have constituted the body of the campaign: (1) it has focused not on the point of production but on pressuring the retailers directly (i.e., it is focused upon the point of consumption); (2) it is based on mobilizing not just union members but also consumers; and (3) it avoids privileging local workers at the expense of workers in other places, because it affects all workers in the production chain and not just those who would benefit in a more traditional workplace-by-workplace campaign (Johns and Vural 2000). Through focusing upon the spaces of consumption, UNITE avoids the problem of having to seek out each individual sweatshop and organize it. Instead, by pressuring retailers through highly visible 'public shaming' campaigns, UNITE hopes to compel retailers not to buy from manufacturers who operate sweatshops and who violate labour rights, whether those of workers in the USA or overseas.

Following this model, in 1997 a group of student interns working at UNITE founded United Students Against Sweatshops (USAS). As with the original Stop Sweatshops Campaign, the goal here was to shame universities who allow apparel with their names upon it to be produced in sweatshops. In January 1999 USAS members staged a sit-in at Duke University and won a commitment from the university to require full disclosure of all garment manufacturers with which it has licenses. Currently, USAS has over a hundred affiliates on university and college campuses across the USA and Canada. It was also a founding member of the Worker Rights Consortium, an independent global monitoring organization that works with religious groups, unions and NGOs in the USA and the Global South seeking disclosure of working conditions in apparel factories.

A similar campaign exerting public pressure on employers has been the Justice for Janitors (JfJ) campaign of the Service Employees' International Union (SEIU). Begun in 1987, JfJ attempts to overcome the problems encountered when using a traditional organizing model in an industry in which job sites are scattered and janitors may clean several buildings a night, in which types of cleaning can vary significantly across industries (which can affect work routines, making access to workers *en masse* difficult), in which janitors work for cleaning companies sub-contracted by building owners rather than for the building owners themselves, and in which the types of client–contractor relationships vary immensely. In response to such problems, the SEIU shifted tactics to focus upon what has been called 'geographical organizing' (Wial 1994). Rather than concentrating on organizing particular worksites or even particular sub-contractors, the JfJ campaign organizes across local labour markets to gain standard wages and benefits. Thus in Los Angeles, the union broke the city into several districts based on office markets and focused pressure on building owners in these areas through direct actions in public spaces (Walsh 2001). Taking into consideration geographical concerns, JfJ encourages each union to develop local tactics appropriate to its local labour market and situations. The SEIU's strategy depends upon organizing workers – which it does through visits to janitors' homes, churches, and workplaces (where possible) – and representing them before the union has official recognition as a collective bargaining unit. JfJ then pressures building owners through demonstrations and rallies in public spaces to encourage the cleaning companies with whom they sub-contractor to recognize the union without having to go through a lengthy representation election, and then to bargain with it. Other unions have adopted similar strategies – members of the Hotel Employees and Restaurant Employees Local 11 in Los Angeles initiated a 'Java for Justice' campaign in which hotel staff take over entire hotel dining rooms and order coffee, using the opportunity to explain their cause to hotel guests (Merrifield 2000).

Both the UNITE anti-sweatshop campaign and the JfJ campaigns, then, have attempted to use the public spaces of the street and of consumption to bring pressure to bear on employers in ways that direct action in the spaces of production do not seem capable of doing.

Model 7: Virtual organizing

One of the characteristics of the New Economy and of globalization has been the move towards the electronic world of e-commerce, e-mail, the Internet and what Quah (1999) has called the 'weightless economy'. Through utilizing new telecommunications technologies employers have been able to manage overseas facilities with no greater difficulty, it seems, than if they were located just next door. Significantly, after a slow start some unions are now beginning to use the Internet as a way of organizing workers and conducting corporate campaigns. One of the earliest such campaigns involved the Bridgestone/Firestone tyre company, possibly 'the first enterprise to be attacked on the Internet' (Hoskins 1996).

In 1994, Bridgestone fired 2,300 workers at five of its US subsidiaries and replaced them with non-union workers. In response, the NLRB ordered the company to reinstate the workers and pay millions of dollars in back pay, which Bridgestone refused to do. As part of an effort to force compliance, the United Steelworkers of America (USWA) and the International Federation of Chemical, Energy, Mine and General Workers' Unions (ICEM) GUF launched a 'cyber campaign' against Bridgestone. First, unionists used e-mail and electronic bulletin boards to communicate with supporters throughout the globe and to relay changes in the situation almost instantaneously. Workers and community activists coordinated activities at a global scale, making links between unions at Bridgestone's USA and South African subsidiaries. Through the use of web links they connected to myriad labour and progressive websites (such as *Labournet* in the United Kingdom and *VICNET* in Australia), thereby bringing attention about the dispute to a potentially huge global audience.

Second, union activists encouraged the public to bombard Bridgestone's feedback section on its own web page. Through union websites the USWA provided the general public with information about the company, including e-mail addresses of top Bridgestone executives, the locations of plants, subsidiaries and stockists worldwide, the names of banks and other investors with major financial interests in the company, and much other information of potential use. The ICEM also linked its own web page to the US National Highway Traffic Safety Administration's on-line form for filing complaints about defective motor vehicle equipment like tyres. Supporters were also encouraged to 'cyber-picket' websites Bridgestone established to publicize particular events in which it was heavily involved, such as sports car racing. In response, in September 1996 Bridgestone called back to work virtually all of the former strikers.

Whereas the Bridgestone case is an example of virtual organizing for a particular dispute, other groups of workers have used the Internet on an ongoing basis. Hence, groups of McDonald's workers have formed an international network of McWorkers – the McDonald's Workers' Resistance (www.mwr.org.uk) – through which they organized a 'Global Day of Action' (16 October, 2002) in which workers in numerous McDonald's restaurants in Europe, North America, Australia, New Zealand and elsewhere participated. The Internet has also been used to highlight labour abuses in China amongst workers making 'Happy meal' toys for the company. And, of course, although none would probably admit to doing so, the interconnectedness of the Internet means that groups of workers can readily spread viruses, trojan horses or logic bombs that may be used to attack particular companies' computer systems.

The adoption by workers of such strategies of virtual organizing raises significant questions. Not only does use of the Internet have spatial implications – information about disputes can transcend space more quickly than before, though in a quite geographically uneven manner, given global inequities in Internet access – but it also has organizational implications. Peter Waterman (1993), for instance, has argued that it augurs a change in the type of organizers relied upon by trades unions, from the union 'agents' of the twentieth century to the activist 'networkers' of the twenty-first, who may or may not be affiliated with a union but who are handy with a computer. This can have significant impacts upon some traditional union identities (such as the 'professional trade union organizer' and the 'international union official') as these positions may be usurped by workers who are not officially part of the organizational structure of their union but who are, nevertheless, developing contacts with workers in other parts of the world. Rather than being the preserve of professional agents, developing international union contacts may increasingly come to be done by shopfloor workers on a one-to-one basis, a situation which will make it a much more hierarchically 'flat' process (see Lee 1997 and Shostak 1999).[8]

Model 8: Living wage activism

A new model of organizing that has been popular in the USA during the 1990s has been the 'Living Wage' movement. First successfully implemented in Des Moines, Iowa, in 1988, the living wage movement has been spearheaded by a number of unions (notably the SEIU), churches and community groups, such as the Association of Community Organizations for Reform Now (ACORN), which claims to be the USA's largest community organization of low- and moderate-income families. To date, over 100 cities have adopted living wage laws, as have three private universities (Stanford, Harvard and Wesleyan) and a number of school boards. Essentially, such ordinances mandate that employers operating within particular geographical areas pay a living wage. Naturally, the actual amount of such a wage varies geographically, depending upon the local cost of living, but the goal everywhere is the same: to ensure that people who work can earn enough to raise themselves out of poverty. In some municipalities the laws apply only to public employees or the private employees of contractors using public tax monies, whereas in other municipalities the law also applies to employees of private businesses, regardless of whether they contract with the city or not. Most importantly, the living wage laws all mandate wages higher than the current US minimum wage rate of $5.15 per hour, a rate which even the federal government recognizes is below the poverty level.

Although the specific ways in which living wage laws work and the amounts they require to be paid vary considerably across the country, one commonality is that they typically have a dual wage level depending upon whether or not health benefits are offered by the employer – no health benefits requires a higher wage rate. Given that many part-time workers do not receive employer-provided health insurance, the establishment of a living wage with health insurance has been an important aspect of the organizing campaigns for such ordinances: for workers covered by the ordinance it makes no difference whether they are full-time or part-time employees. This is significant, for through living wage ordinances it appears that the labour movement and community groups who work on poverty issues have found a way to address, in part, the loss of health insurance coverage associated with the growth of temporary and part-time working.

Furthermore, such campaigns represent the adoption of a specifically spatial approach to bettering workers' lives. Much as UNITE's Stop Sweatshops campaign and the JfJ campaigns have switched tactics to focus upon the spaces of consumption, the living wage campaigns are geographically focused upon specific political jurisdictions. Interestingly, such a geographical approach to organizing takes us back to the mid-nineteenth century and the Knights of Labor, who favoured organizing along geographical lines, in contrast to the American Federation of Labor (which eventually became the USA's largest trade union centre) which favoured organizing along craft and industry lines.

Conclusion

This chapter has outlined how workers, labour activists and unionists are engaging with the economic, political and geographical realities of the New Economy. This conclusion draws back from the specific models outlined above to consider briefly some of the larger conceptual issues regarding labour, space and the geography of the New Economy. Three are particularly pertinent.

First, it is obvious that the new geographies of capitalism are bringing challenges for labour union organizers. Many of the old models upon which the labour movement traditionally relied and which incorporated certain assumptions about capitalism's spatiality appear to be less effective within the new post-Fordist space-economies. As new economic, political and spatial relationships have emerged unions are being forced to reimagine how they go about organizing, a process which will require them to be sensitive to the changed spatial relations within which their members live.

Second, following from this it is obvious that labour organizing strategies incorporate particular conceptions of space, regardless of whether or not the actual participants recognize this. For instance, workers seeking to develop trans-spatial solidarity networks implicitly comprehend that space can be used to hide social relations between workers and that solidarity is about opening up geographical links between spaces that may be thousands of miles apart. Equally, the JfJ, anti-sweatshop and living wage campaigns aim to overcome the increasingly fragmented, segmented and atomized economic surfaces of the built environment within which it is often difficult to organize individual worksites. Instead of developing campaigns that match the organizational spaces of the garment or janitorial industry – that is to say, campaigns that adopt a spatially atomized approach to organizing workers by seeking out each individual workspace in the urban landscape – JfJ, UNITE and the living wage campaigns have adopted a model of organizing in which the spaces of the built environment are overlain by an organizational and regulatory blanket covering whole expanses of territory.

Third, it is equally obvious that different models of organizing have different implications for how the geography of capitalism is made. If spatial relations shape social relations, the obverse is equally true. Hence, in the case of traditional international solidarity, workers' decisions concerning whether to engage in 'accommodationist' or 'transformatory' solidarity will impact flows of capital across the space–economy – in the former case it may result in capital staying in the privileged locales of the global economy whereas in the latter it may result in capital flight. The geographical scales at which workers choose to organize will also have impacts upon how the geography of capitalism is made. Thus, workers' decisions to engage in trans-spatial solidarity may have quite different implications than will decisions to strike only one or two key plants within a broader production chain, whereas their ability to carve out spaces within which standard conditions of work will apply – as in the case of the JfJ's differentiation of Los Angeles into various districts – imposes new structures and spatial orders upon the landscape which affect how local labour markets function. Not only, then, must unions and their members recognize how the new spaces of capitalism shape the possibilities for their own organization, but they should also be aware of how their own organizational activities shape the new spaces of global capitalism.

Notes

1   Bronfenbrenner (1997) notes that in the mid-1990s half of all US employers involved in private sector union elections threatened to relocate if workers voted in a union, and 12 per cent of employers actually followed through on this threat. Furthermore, she finds (Bronfenbrenner 2000) that during the late 1990s: 92 per cent of US employers, when faced with employees who wanted to unionize, forced these employees to attend closed-door meetings to hear anti-union arguments; 75 per cent hired management consultants to run anti-union campaigns; 75 per cent distributed anti-union literature in the workplace; 70 per cent mailed anti-union letters to their employees; 78 per cent held 'one-on-one' meetings between supervisors and their employees; and 25 per cent actually discharged union activists.

2   In 2001 there were 31.2 million workers in the USA (26 per cent of all employed workers) who worked fewer than 35 hours per week (*Statistical Abstract of the United States* 2002: Table 584). The median length of tenure with one's present employer has fallen from 6.6 years in 1987 to 3.5 years in 2000 (*Statistical Abstract of the United States* 1991 Table 654, and 2002 Table 583).

3   The NLRB is the federal government entity charged with investigating, interpreting and deciding violations of US labour law.

4   Wial (1993) calculated that the average service sector establishment in the USA in the early 1990s had approximately 13 workers whereas the average manufacturing plant had 51 workers.

5   As a non-profit agency, it can afford to pay higher wages than can for-profit agencies. Also, by charging companies lower fees it expects to attract a large pool of employers.

6   Manufacturers design and market clothing and may engage in some direct production; contractors specialize in actual production; jobbers focus upon design and marketing.

7   Such was the success of this model that mid-century garment workers secured some of the highest wages of all manufacturing workers, as high even as in auto and steel in some cases.

8   Whereas international campaigns have often been quite hierarchical – workers in a plant in country A contact their national union, which then contacts an international union organization, which contacts national union officials in country B, who subsequently contact the local branch union representing workers employed by that corporation in the second country – virtual organizing has the potential to put workers from different factories into direct contact with one another.

References

Berman, L. L. (1998) 'In your face, in your space: Spatial strategies in organizing clerical workers at Yale', in A. Herod, ed, *Organizing the Landscape: Geographical Perspectives on Labor Unionism*, University of Minnesota Press: Minneapolis, 203–224.

Bronfenbrenner, K. (1997) 'The effect of plant closings and the threat of plant closings on worker rights to organize', supplement to *Plant Closings and Workers' Rights: A Report to the Council of Ministers by the Secretariat of the Commission for Labor Cooperation*, Bernan Press: Lanham, MD.

Bronfenbrenner, K. (2000) 'Uneasy terrain: The impact of capital mobility on workers, wages, and union organizing', submitted to the US Trade Deficit Review Commission (available at www.ustdrc.gov/research/bronfenbrenner.pdf).

Cobble, D. S. (1991) 'Organizing the postindustrial work force: Lessons from the history of waitress unionism', *Industrial and Labor Relations Review* 44, 419–436.

Cobble, D. S. (1996) 'The prospects for unionism in a service society', in C. L. Macdonald and C. Sirianni, eds, *Working in the Service Society*, Temple University Press: Philadelphia, 333-358.

Green, J. and Tilly, C. (1987) 'Service unionism: Directions for organizing', *Labor Law Journal*, August: 486–495.

Herod, A. (1991) 'Homework and the fragmentation of space: Challenges for the labor movement', *Geoforum* 22, 173–183.

Herod, A. (1997a) 'Back to the future in labor relations: From the New Deal to Newt's Deal', in L. Staeheli, J. Kodras, and C. Flint, eds, *State Devolution in America: Implications for a Diverse Society*, (Urban Affairs Annual Reviews No. 48) Sage: Thousand Oaks, CA 161–180.

Herod, A. (1997b) 'Labor as an agent of globalization and as a global agent', in K. Cox, ed., *Spaces of Globalization: Reasserting the Power of the Local*, Guilford: New York, 167–200.

Herod, A. (2000) 'Implications of Just-in-Time production for union strategy: Lessons from the 1998 General Motors-United Auto Workers dispute', *Annals of the Association of American Geographers* 90, 521–547. [Publisher's erratum for figures published *Annals of the Association of American Geographers* (2001) 91, 200–202.]

Herod, A. (2002) 'Geographics of labour organizing in the New Economy'. Available at http://www.gees.bham.ac.uk/research/neweconomy/papers/seminar3/herod.pdf

Herod, A. (2003) 'Workers, space, and labor geography', *International Labor and Working-Class History*, 64, 112–138.

Hoskins, T. (1996) Statement by Trevor Hoskins, US Vice-President for Public Relations, Bridgestone/Firestone. Quoted in "Cybermanif" sur le web, *Le Monde*, 18 August.

Hyman, R. (1999) *An Emerging Agenda for Trade Unions?* Discussion paper DP/98/1999 published by the Labour and Society Programme, International Labour Organization, Geneva, Switzerland.

Jayadev, R. (2000) 'New ruling could give labor a toehold in Silicon Valley', *Jinn Magazine*, Issue 6.2, October 2–October 16, 2000. (Available at www.pacificnews.org/jinn/stories/6.20/001010-new.html).

Johns, R. (1998) 'Bridging the gap between class and space: US worker solidarity with Guatemala', *Economic Geography*, 74, 252–271.

Johns, R. and Vural, L. (2000) 'Class, geography, and the consumerist turn: UNITE and the Stop Sweatshops Campaign', *Environment and Planning A*, 32, 1193–1213.

Lee, E. (1997) *The Labour Movement and the Internet: The New Internationalism*, Pluto Press: Chicago.

MacDuffie, J. P. (1995) 'Workers' Roles in Lean Production: The Implications for Worker Representation', in S. Babson, ed, *Lean Work: Empowerment and Exploitation in the Global Auto Industry*, Detroit: Wayne State University, 54–69.

Merrifield, A. (2000) 'The urbanization of labor: Living-wage activism in the American city', *Social Text* 18, 31–54.

Quah, D. (1999) 'The weightless economy in economic development'. Working Paper, Department of Economics, London School of Economics.

Savage, L. (1998) 'Geographies of organizing: Justice for Janitors in Los Angeles', in A. Herod, ed, *Organizing the Landscape: Geographical Perspectives on Labor Unionism*, University of Minnesota Press: Minneapolis, 225–252.

Shostak, A. B. (1999) *Cyber Union: Empowering Labor through Computer Technology*, M. E. Sharpe: Armonk, NY.

SOREDI (2001) 'Where the Money is in Jackson and Josephine Counties'. Southern Oregon Regional Economic Development Inc., www.soredi.org/News.asp?NewsID=227

Statistical Abstract of the United States (various years) United States Census Bureau, Department of Commerce, Washington, DC.

Walsh, J. (2001) 'Organizing the low-wage service sector: Community and urban politics in the United States', unpublished Ph.D. thesis, Faculty of Architecture, Building and Planning, University of Melbourne, Australia.

Waterman, P. (1993) 'Internationalism is dead! Long live global solidarity?', in J. Brecher, J. Brown Childs, and J. Cutler, eds, *Global Visions: Beyond the New World Order*, South End Press: Boston, 257–261.

Wial, H. (1993) 'The emerging organizational structure of unionism in low-wage services', *Rutgers Law Review* 45, 671–738.

Wial, H. (1994) 'New bargaining structures for new forms of business organization', in S. Friedman, R. W. Hurd, R. A. Oswald, and R. L. Seeber, eds, *Restoring the Promise of American Labor Law*, Ithaca, NY: ILR Press, 303–313.

Wills, J. (2002) 'Bargaining for the space to organize in the global economy: a review of the Accor-IUF trade union rights agreement', *Review of International Political Economy* 9, 675–700.

8 New aspirations and old dilemmas: the New Economy and development in Southeast Asia

Michael Leaf

Introduction: the New Economy in Southeast Asia

The central concern of this chapter is with the practical question of whether the New Economy presents a viable development strategy for the nations of Southeast Asia. Certainly this is not a question which can be answered with a simple 'yes' or 'no', considering the wide variation in developmental conditions across the region. An economic development strategy for one nation may have little application when looked at from across the region overall. The broader issue therefore is with regard to where the New Economy fits in: to what extent and under what conditions does this present a new developmental strategy, and how might this differ from previous strategies? Phrasing the question in this way prompts a more basic question regarding the conceptual validity of the New Economy. As this is a concept that is derived out of the on-going developmental experiences of the advanced economies, does it have much purchase in those parts of the world that are still undergoing more fundamental economic and social changes? For example, to what extent is the presence of an advanced service economy (as one finds in the USA, Europe or Japan) necessary as a basis on which to develop the New Economy?

Constructing the inquiry in this way links the analysis into a long line of thinking regarding the planned inducement of national socio-economic development, arising, one may argue, from theories of modernization. The central notion here is that developing countries can advance step-wise through the transfer of technologies and institutions (i.e. the bases of advanced economic development) from the developed countries (Escobar 1995, Lewellen 1995). Beginning with the observation that the historical, 'natural' progression of national development in today's advanced economies has proceeded through the gradual advancement of increasingly higher value-added forms of production, attempts at accelerated modernization in less-developed nations have emphasized the transfer and establishment of the necessary conditions for this economic progression, from primary commodities, to manufacturing, to heavy industry, and on to advanced services (Hutton 2005). In this sense, the current recognition of the positive role of knowledge in increasing economic productivity – which is at the conceptual core of the New Economy – has now become a central tenet of international development thinking. The resulting bandwagon effect – what might be referred to as 'policy emulation' – can thus be seen as the latest chapter in the open book of planned modernization.

This, of course, raises questions about the nature of the New Economy – whether, for example, the emphasis on the production and utilization of knowledge is something qualitatively different from what has gone before, and whether one includes under the rubric of the New Economy the expanded application of knowledge to existing sectors of production (such as the increased automation of agricultural and industrial production), or whether one restricts the definition to wholly new, knowledge-based economic activities. The fundamental concept of the New Economy has indeed been contentious even in the context of the advanced economies, with challenges raised regarding the degree to which productivity advances and innovation truly characterize current economic developments (Gordon 2000, Pohjola 2002b) or whether there has been a meaningful positive effect on employment generation in the advanced economies due to new information technologies (Gadrey 2003). As it is not possible to deal with these fundamental debates here, this chapter will rely upon a fairly loose understanding of what constitutes the New Economy, and instead focus upon what have come to be seen as the pragmatic concerns for inculcating it into national development, including such issues as the attraction or development of an appropriate knowledge work-force and the importance of constructing sufficient regulatory regimes.

An important macro consideration here is the current phase of globalization and its effects on socio-economic interactions across the region. Certainly one interpretation of the increasing trans-border movements of ideas, capital, labour and so forth, is that globalization holds the potential for accelerating the transnational expansion of the New Economy (Pohjola 2002a). Hence, under increasingly neo-liberal trade regimes, national policies in recent years have actively promoted the attraction of transnational capital as one of the principal spearheads of advanced economic change. However, globalization has, in practical terms, also promoted greater differentiation between and across national economies, with different countries working to articulate local competitive advantages in their strategies for linking to the global economy. In the case of Vietnam, as one example, although globalization has meant the accelerated adoption of new telecommunications and information technologies, in macro-economic terms it has also meant the rapid expansion of more traditional forms of primary commodity production (such as rice and coffee) for sale to international markets. Thus, globalization may result in increasing differentiation and specialization, rather than narrowing or convergence across nations. Considering the diversity of conditions across the region, questions about the effects of globalization also translate into issues of regional interconnectivity, as seen, for example, in trans-border investment and cooperation between the more advanced economies, such as Singapore and Malaysia, and those at lower levels of development.

A further issue related both to the macro condition of advancing globalization and the potential for the inculcation of the New Economy is that of urbanization. Not only do cities (and increasingly, city-regions) constitute the primary nodes through which forces of globalization are articulated, they are also the locales in which higher value-added forms of production are concentrated (Sassen 1994, Bunnell 2002a). If the local expansion of the New Economy is to be built upon pre-existing sectoral conditions – deriving, for example, out of the local advanced service sector, or requiring a certain degree of development of domestic consumer markets – levels and forms of urbanization will have important implications for how the New Economy can develop.

In order to explore these issues across Southeast Asia, a quick survey of conditions across the nations of the region is undertaken, which of necessity emphasizes its diversity. As well, however, a few of the more relevant commonalities are drawn out. From this, the issue of how aspects of the New Economy have come into play in the developmental policy approaches of the nations of the region are revealed (the 'new aspirations' of the title), and the challenges implicit in this are discussed (the 'old dilemmas'). In conclusion, some ideas regarding what the future may hold for the potential role of the New Economy in the ongoing development of the region are presented. One could imagine that the short answer to the initial policy question posed is 'yes for some, no for others', though this is inadequate when account is taken of the growing inter-linkages throughout the region. Most likely the developmental benefits of the new economy will not be distributed on a strictly nation-by-nation basis, but will be articulated in an increasingly complex manner within and across the nations of Southeast Asia, as this is a region which historically and presently is characterized by tremendous interconnectivity and extraordinary porosity of borders.

Situating Southeast Asia

Diversity

Southeast Asia is a region characterized by great diversity, so much so that one might see it in certain respects to be a microcosm of the world. In cultural terms, this is a diversity borne out of the deep historical interactions between two great ancient imperial civilizations and myriad local cultures, resulting in a syncretic region with elements of both Indic and Sinic civilizations, to say nothing of more recent overlays from the dominance of Western imperialism in the colonial and postcolonial periods. It is a region of more than half a billion people, distributed very unevenly across eleven nations, from the world's fourth most populous (Indonesia, with over 200 million inhabitants, or 40 per cent of the region's total) to some of the least populous (Brunei, with 330,000 people, and East Timor – the region's newest nation-state[1] – with approximately 750,000 people).

Diversity is also evident in the region's political structures, which include a traditional monarchy, multi-party parliamentary monarchies, single party authoritarian states, and multi-party elected democracies with varying degrees of political openness and stability. In economic terms, one finds everything from high-tech and service-led economies, to economies based on more 'traditional' industrially led development, to plantation economies, to subsistence production and resource extraction, all shaped by the complexities of increasing (though quite uneven) integration with the global economy. Considering this wide diversity of economic conditions, it is not surprising to find tremendous disparities in wealth, both within and between the nations of the region. The two richest nations, petroleum-dependent Brunei and services-driven Singapore, both have annual per capita gross national incomes (GNI) in excess of US$24,000, some 70 to 90 times higher than that of the poorest nations (Cambodia, US$260; Laos, US$310; Vietnam, US$350) (Table 8.1).

Southeast Asia is a region characterized by ethnic complexity with considerable differences from country to country in the degree of homogeneity or heterogeneity of national populations. Multi-ethnicity or multi-culturalism in some cases arises from the effects of European colonialism (as in Malaysia and Singapore) and in other instances grows more out of postcolonial attempts to integrate disparate native populations (as in the island nations of Indonesia and the Philippines). Significant diversity can also be seen in national urbanization levels, with the city-state of Singapore at one extreme, contrasting with the predominantly rural nations of Cambodia (15.7 per cent urban in 1998), Laos (18.4 per cent), and Thailand (19.6 per cent). Urbanization level is roughly indicative of basic national economic structures (see Table 8.1) and correlates to a great extent as well with levels of national wealth.

Urbanization

Urbanization is, however, an extraordinarily dynamic field. As a generalization, one can say that those countries with still-low urban proportions tend to have the fastest urban population growth rates, indicative of both higher rural–urban migration rates and the general tendency of more fundamentally rural nations to have higher natural growth rates. For example, the region's fastest urban population growth rate is that of Cambodia, currently estimated at around 5.5 per cent per annum, a rate which will lead to a doubling of national urban population in little more than 12 years (United Nations 2002). Although Cambodia currently has the lowest urbanization level in the region (estimated at 15.7 per cent in 1998), this proportion will continue to rise quickly over the next few decades. Within these demographic trends one may discern important patterns of urban transition in the countries of the region; an important example is that of Indonesia which has risen quickly from a pre-transition level of about 12 per cent urban in 1950 (or a total urban population of around 10 million) to more than 40 per cent today (with close to 90 million urban dwellers). The proportion of urban population will only slowly begin to level off after at least another three decades with a national population more than 60 per cent urban, at which point the total urban population will be in excess

Table 8.1 Summary statistics for Southeast Asian countries

Country	Population (1998, in thousands)	Urban population (1998, per cent)	GNI per capita (1998, current US$)	Economic structure (1998, per cent of GDP): Agriculture	Industry	Services	Labour force in agriculture (1990, per cent) *
Brunei	321.7	71	24100	2.8	44.4	52.7	2
Burma	46554.7	26.9	–	59.1	9.9	31	73
Cambodia	11498	15.7	260	50.6	14.8	34.6	74
Indonesia	203678.4	38.7	660	18.1	45.2	36.7	55
Laos	5037.4	18.4	310	53.3	22.5	24.2	78
Malaysia	22180	55.9	3630	13.3	43.9	42.8	27
Philippines	72775.5	56.7	1090	16.9	31.5	51.6	46
Singapore	3923	100	24580	0.2	35.3	64.5	0
Thailand	59793.5	19.6	2110	12.7	37.8	49.5	64
Vietnam	76520	23.3	350	25.7	32.6	41.7	71
Total	502282.2	36.1					58

Sources: World Bank, World Development Indicators, 2002.

Notes: *Rigg, 1997.

of 180 million. Such trajectories in the long-term (80–100 years) urban transitions of the countries of the region raise significant questions regarding the nature of urban society in the not too distant future (Leaf 2005a).

For our purposes here, one important implication of the urban transition is the movement of labour out of agriculture in what have historically been predominantly agrarian societies. Despite the rapidity of these changes, there is still a high degree of dependence upon the 'materiality' of production, as indicated by the still high proportions of national labour forces in agriculture. In 1990, for example, it was estimated that approximately 58 per cent of the labour force across the region was still in agriculture which, in relative terms, is characterized by low productivity when compared to other economic sectors. In Thailand, for example, even with nearly two thirds of its national labour force in agriculture, the sector accounts for less than 13 per cent of national GDP. Despite modernization theory's assumption of a step-wise progression in economic development one should be careful not to see the movement out of agriculture as necessarily a movement into higher value-added forms of industrial and service production. Much of the recent population movement into cities has resulted in the expansion of lower-order services, so-called 'informal sector' employment (Moser 1984), or what has also been termed the 'urban subsistence economy' (Evers 1981). It should therefore not be presumed that the outcome of the urban transition in the countries of Southeast Asia will necessarily be comparable with the experiences of what are now the economically advanced or developed countries of the world, an observation that has implications for the potential future role which the New Economy may play in what are currently the poorer countries of the region.

Commonalities

The discussion so far has emphasized the diversity of conditions across the region with regard to their implications for future development trajectories. Cutting across this great regional diversity, however, one may also discern important commonalities. With regard to questions of policy setting, an important characteristic in this respect has been the role of the state in shaping economic development. As one would expect from the wide variation of political structures throughout the region, state developmentalism has taken a number of different forms, from outright state ownership of means of production to varying degrees of state-capital collaboration or collusion in linking national developmental objectives to market forces. If, in all this diversity, one may try to articulate a particular Southeast Asian 'model' of development, it would be one that is heavily state-directed, though certainly with varying degrees of success. In this respect, Singapore has come to be seen as the exemplar for the region, an observation with important implications for both political development and policy emulation in the region.

A further commonality might best be referred to as an established history of transnationalism throughout the region. Before the advent of European colonialism, this was a region of small kingdoms tied together by extensive local and long-distance patterns of trade, a major factor which underlay the attractiveness of the region in the 16th and 17th centuries to the economically expanding European powers (Reid 1988). This historic porosity of national borders – with regard to the movement of goods, people and cultures – was both a hindrance and a boon to the European colonial powers in the latter stages of territorial consolidation, and it has persisted in a variety of forms into the postcolonial era. Perhaps the most critical aspect of regional transnationalism in recent years has been the expansion and entrenchment of what is referred to by some as 'Chinese capitalism', an outcome of the trans-border networks of the numerically small, but economically important, immigrant communities of Chinese origin throughout the region (Chirot and Reid 1997, Ong and Nonini 1997, Suryadinata 2004). Chinese capitalism, in this respect, underlies many of the investment flows between nations in the region, such as those between Thailand and Burma or between Malaysia and Cambodia, whether informally or formally (as in the case of Singapore) supported by the institutions of the state. With the opening up of the People's Republic of China in recent decades, such regional interlinkages have been extended, with increasing investment from Southeast Asia into China. The 'modernization' of Chinese capitalism – traditionally seen to be derived from familial or place of origin linkages, but increasingly organized institutionally and managerially according to contemporary precepts of business practice – is indicative of the entrenchment of at least one aspect of regional transnationalism.

The risks associated with statist development in close collaboration with local capital, particularly transnational Chinese capital, were well illustrated in the effects of the economic crisis which hit the region in the late 1990s. Loss of investor confidence which initially triggered the rapid drop in local currency values, leading on to the financial and economic problems in many of the countries in the region was indicative, first, of the relative similarity of structural deficiencies in the financial sectors in the countries of the region, and, second, of the intra-region trans-border networks of investment flows. Debates over the 'contagion' view of the crisis were thus couched in terms of whether the root of the crisis lay in domestic structural problems or derived from the volatility of globalization. In effect, both of these roots of the crisis were closely interconnected, reflecting the particular forms that globalization has taken in the region.

For many countries of the region, the economic crisis exposed another common feature: the lack of sufficient social safety nets for those citizens hardest hit by the crisis. In one sense, this demonstrated a continuing reliance on what can be seen as traditional safety nets – informal social networks, intra-familial dependency, and so forth – despite the ostensible modernization of other social institutions (McGee *et al.* 2001). In another respect, however, this was also an indication of weak state regimes *vis-à-vis* social services and regulatory structures. In some cases – Indonesia being the extreme – the revelation of state weaknesses arising from the crisis has contributed to major political shifts and the recognition of the need for greater state intervention in the provision of improved social services. A further challenge in regard to ongoing political and economic developments in the region continues to arise from the volatility of globalization, as seen in recent years in the increasing flows of foreign capital to China in preference to Southeast Asia. Neo-liberal regimes for international trade and investment have done little to protect domestic economies and societies from the vicissitudes of global capitalism.

New aspirations: the New Economy as a developmental strategy

Exemplars and exceptions: Singapore and Malaysia

To broadly characterize the role of the state in national economic development in the region as being highly interventionist exposes a central contradiction to the neo-liberal underpinnings of the current phase of globalization. If the acceleration of globalization is fostered by the deregulation of transnational flows, how can national governments intervene in the interest of deriving the most benefits from globalization while preventing its most egregious social and environmental impacts? In this, the city-state of Singapore provides both an exemplar and an exception when compared to the other countries of the region. Over the course of its national development since the 1960s, Singapore has become both the primary positive example of the benefits of state developmentalism as well as the region's main nexus for globalization.

In retrospect, Singapore's national strategy can be seen as having started early in trying to actively engage transnational capital, at a time when other post-colonial, nationalist governments were wary of neo-colonialism through economic domination by foreign capital (Rodan 1989). Early establishment of Singapore as a base for foreign investment in the region was followed over time by a conscious strategy of 'ratcheting up' economic productivity, achieved through labour policy geared toward gradually increasing basic wage rates, coupled with foreign investment policy designed to over time move lower forms of industrial productivity off-island, and reinforced by highly interventionist strategies for human resource development through education policy carefully calibrated to produce the skilled (and more highly paid) workforce needed for advanced productivity. In this way, Singapore has continually reinvented itself over the past four decades and moved from a position of low-wage industrial production to an advanced service economy. In this way, it has achieved all that might be expected of a successful developmental state.

The developmental challenge since the 1990s has thus focussed on further internationalizing the Singaporean economy – through greater Singaporean transnational investment out of Singapore – with the goal of further strengthening the nation's position as the service centre for the region (Low 2001). Coupled with this, national development strategies have recently focussed on building up the Knowledge-Based Economy (KBE), as emphasized in popular campaigns. In this, there is the recognition that creative thinking needs to be promoted in human resource development for the New Economy, a recognition manifest in a number of ways, from the call for new approaches to basic education, to a new emphasis on the study of American-style entrepreneurialism, to a strong policy push to promote the arts in Singaporean life (Ong 2002). If human resource development in support of national development in the past has meant the privileging of sciences and engineering in local education, there is now a marked sea change in thinking, with the promotion of the arts as a means for instilling the creativity seen to be crucial for engaging with the 'constantly churning' New Economy (Atkinson and Court 1998).

The success of Singapore's development means that its policies are being carefully examined as the basis for policy emulation throughout the region. This role as regional exemplar needs, however, to be looked at relative to the country's exceptionality. As a city-state which has consciously and successfully used wage and land use policies to eliminate its agricultural sector, there is no longer a significant component of its citizenry who are dependent upon the materiality of primary production for their livelihoods. This is not to say that Singapore has 'dematerialized' its economy, but rather that its lack of national territory has led to a situation whereby its relationship with its immediate hinterland (Indonesia's Riau Province and the Malaysian State of Johor) is controlled through an international border. The lack of poor farmers (in relative or absolute terms) and dispossessed rural labourers among the Singaporean citizenry obviates the need for revenue redistribution between urban and rural sectors typical of most other countries in the region. Through the control of selective temporary migration (from Indonesia and Malaysia as well as further afield from Bangladesh and the Philippines), Singapore is able to gain the benefits of a rural reserve workforce without the associated costs (Coe and Kelly 2002).

Malaysia, Singapore's neighbour to its immediate north, can also be considered as somewhat of an exemplar and exception. In contrast to Singapore's unique position as a de-territorialized city-state, Malaysia has historically been something of a frontier territory within a highly populated region, as it is characterized by a relatively low rural population density and an economy based on agriculture and other primary commodity production which was only opened up in the latter years of British colonialism. The country's exemplar status derives from the extensive resources it has dedicated toward the development of high-tech and New Economy activities. Malaysia's policy obsession with IT-led growth has attracted quite a bit of interest in recent years primarily because of a series of government-sponsored mega-projects, initiated prior to the 1997 financial crisis. Key among these has been the Multimedia Super Corridor (MSC), a 15 km by 50 km swath of territory linking Kuala Lumpur to the new capital city of Putrajaya (designed to be the seat of 'electronic government'), the 'smart city' of Cyberjaya, a planned, high-tech research and development hub, and, further to the south in Sepang, a new international airport intended to compete with Singapore's Changi in attracting regional air traffic (Bunnell 2002b). Malaysia's policy emphasis on IT development since the 1990s has been interpreted as a politically astute move on the part of

Mahathir Mohamad, the nation's long-standing and recently retired Prime Minister to turn what had originally been seen to be a political threat – the expanded information flows associated with an increasingly networked society – into a political opportunity (Hilley 2001).

Such basic indicators as the ownership rate of personal computers and the proportion of Internet users nation-wide may be used to show the relative positions in the region of Singapore and Malaysia in terms of their potential for developing New Economy sectors.[2] In 2002, personal computer ownership in Singapore was far higher than anywhere else in the region, with more than 62 per cent of all Singaporeans owning their own personal computer, far ahead of second-place Malaysia at 15 per cent. Excluding the outlier of Brunei, with a rate of 8 per cent, the level of ownership of personal computers elsewhere in the region is strikingly low, with only about 4 per cent in Thailand, 3 per cent in the Philippines, and 1 per cent in Indonesia. This indicator of the breadth of the digital divide in the region is further reflected in the proportions of Internet users; Singapore is again the regional leader with close to 30 per cent of its citizens being Internet-connected in 2000, followed by about 16 per cent of Malaysians, 9 per cent of Bruneians, less than 4 per cent of Thais, and just 3 per cent of Filipinos. Although such figures indicate sharp disparities across the region in basic conditions favouring the expansion of the New Economy, it is also striking how state policies to build basic networks and get their citizens on line have achieved such rapid results (Than 2001). The number of Internet users in Malaysia has increased by more than 600 per cent between 1997 and 2000, comparable to the growth rates in Thailand and Indonesia, and yet out-paced by both the Philippines at 2000 per cent and Vietnam – the regional leader in this regard – with a user growth rate estimated at more than 6000 per cent over this three year period.

Strategies

State strategies for inculcating the New Economy go beyond the obvious emphasis on getting the IT and telecommunications infrastructure in place. Human resource development also comprises an important element in the equation. In terms of long- and short-term goals this is manifested in two somewhat different respects. For the long term, there is of course a strong emphasis on education – primary, secondary and post-secondary – in prepar-ing current and future generations for the New Economy. At a basic level, this has meant getting information technology into the classroom wherever possi-ble, although in the more technologically advanced nations of Singapore and Malaysia, emphasis has gone beyond technical competencies to stress the value of personal creativity in contrast to the rote learning approaches which have long characterized the region. In this, there is the recognition that the New Economy workforce of the future will need to be built not only on high-tech information skills, but will require creative workers with entrepreneurial values (Ng and Griffy-Brown 2001). In other words, it is understood that there is a requirement for a rather different sort of work force than that which has characterized earlier waves of industrial expansion in the region.

The emphasis on educational policy as a means to restructure the workforce for accommodating the needs of the New Economy reiterates the long-standing question of whether the risk-taking and creativity which underlie entrepreneurialism can be taught, or whether these are fundamental characteristics of individual personality. In this, one may see the partial recognition of the distinction between the 'information revolution' and the 'cognitive revolution'; that is, that the New Economy requires not only improved access to information, obtained through on-going technological advances, but also requires the ability to utilize information in new and innovative ways (Gadrey 2003). In spite of such concerns, state developmentalism must rely upon and build upon established policy strategies; hence, the view that education is key to building the New Economy.

Restructuring the domestic workforce through new approaches to human resource development is understood as a long-term strategy, however, and is thus insufficient for the immediate needs of the rapidly expanding knowledge-based economy. In Malaysia and Singapore, if not elsewhere in the region, planning for the New Economy also links into issues of population and migration policy. The emphasis here is not only on reversing any potential brain drain – that is, creating incentives to keep the best and brightest local talent – but a strategy as well of selective immigration to attract in appropriately skilled workers (Coe and Kelly 2002). There are parallels here to the technology transfer strategies of the past, whereby foreign skilled workers were enticed to relocate to newly industrializing countries in order to help establish the requisite skill bases for indigenous industrial and service sector development. In the new, globalized labour market, however, such skilled migrants need not come primarily from the advanced economies, but may be drawn from wherever talent can be found. Other developing countries, China and India in particular, are now targeted for recruiting, due to the international wage competitiveness of their IT-skilled workers.

In the case of Malaysia, this policy has been explicit, with efforts to attract 'extraordinary world citizens' to help build the New Economy at a time when the lower-skilled foreign workers are being expelled; social engineering is implicit in this drive, with targets set at sending home 20 foreign workers for every 'transnational knowledge worker' (TKW) recruited (Bunnell 2002c). The odd irony in this instance is that these TKWs are coming to Malaysia primarily from India and China, forcing the government to adopt a recruiting strategy quite at odds with historical patterns of social and political dispossession of the domestic Indian and Chinese communities. In comparison to pre-existing notions regarding policy approaches to national development through technology transfer, the new competitiveness to attract both foreign high-tech investment and its requisite skilled workforce places strong emphasis on quality of life and amenity value for expatriate workers, a situation which may have domestic political ramifications.

A further element in the policy palette for inculcating the New Economy is with regard to new institutional forms, emphasizing collaboration, market primacy and internationalization in the interest of promoting innovation. Collaboration, in this sense, stresses the need for both greater domestic state-capital interaction (often expressed as public–private partnership) and for expanded institutional connectivity to partners overseas, in the interest of attracting foreign direct investment and building the basis for research and educational linkages in support of knowledge-based development (Ong 2002).

All of these components of state policy – getting the infrastructure in place, building the domestic and expatriate human resource capacity, and developing innovative institutional forms – have distinct geographies, as expressed in what can be seen as place-marketing for the New Economy in the region. At one extreme – the national level – one can again point to the case of Singapore, which portrays itself to the world as the 'wired island' (Choo 1997). In Malaysia's case, the Multimedia Super Corridor is a specific sub-national region designed with similar intentions. In keeping with relative degrees of resource availability for promoting the New Economy, one can find similar although smaller scale undertakings in other countries of the region. One illustrative example is that of Saigon South, a 3,300 hectare project on the southern edge of Ho Chi Minh City, Vietnam. The site, master-planned by a consortium of foreign architecture firms led by the San Francisco office of SOM, and projected to contain an eventual population of up to one million, is intended to be much more than just a residential development. In addition to the range of amenities – golf course, international schools, medical facilities and so forth – meant to attract expatriate and well-off domestic buyers, the master plan contains extensive areas for 'science-based industrial parks', and the Vietnamese branch campuses of foreign universities, all served by state-of-the-art information technologies (Marshall 2003). In addition to the usual package of investment incentives, such as allowances for 100 per cent foreign ownership and simplified investment procedures, foreign firms are also now guaranteed full and direct Internet access, in contrast to the current state practices of establishing restrictive firewalls elsewhere in the country. In terms of state policies for building the New Economy in Vietnam, one can see Saigon South to be an intended locus for knowledge production and utilization, led first and foremost by foreign investment and foreign skilled workers, but with a clear vision of how this will feed into domestic development strategies. In short, Saigon South is a mini-Singapore contained within the national territory of Vietnam, and thus the spatial expression of regional policy emulation for the New Economy.

Countervailing tendencies (old dilemmas)

The challenges implicit in policy approaches to promote the New Economy in Southeast Asia are conditioned by a range of factors which, though differing from one national context to another, nonetheless may be broadly generalized for the region. Such countervailing tendencies may in some respects be seen as factors which have long hindered national development strategies, while others are more specific to the needs of the New Economy.

Statism

The region has long been characterized by certain political–economic factors that may arguably be interpreted as the negative consequences of state developmentalism (Leftwich 1994). The root factor in this line of analysis is seen in the necessarily close interconnections between the state and private capital implicit in statist development, which is manifested as a lack of public transparency in political–economic decision-making. Such conditions in turn allow for the persistence of clientelism in political culture throughout the region. At one level, such an analysis may be criticized for its culturalist overtones in that it emphasizes the continuity and persistence of pre-modern forms of personalistic governance. Yet James Scott, for one, interprets this not so much as the undifferentiated persistence of personalistic and clientelistic governance structures in the modern era, but rather as the re-invention or re-articulation of older forms and practices in light of the expanded state resources and consequent political pressures of newer, postcolonial regimes. One may thus distinguish between modern clientelism in reference to political goods in the modern economy and the older, more affective relations of pre-colonial agrarian societies (Scott 1977).

The implications of statist clientelism for national development are profound and multi-faceted. One particularly relevant example is the effect that this has had upon the functioning of banking sectors in many of the countries of the region. Although loan policies by both state and private banks ostensibly follow correct practices of fiduciary responsibility, political interference – that is, the direct consequence of high-level clientelism in determining access to loans – underlay excessive loan to asset ratios of banks throughout the region, a major contributory factor to the loss of investor confidence which triggered the regional financial crisis of the late 1990s.

One controversial, though in retrospect particularly prescient, analysis of these fundamental structural deficiencies is that of Kunio Yoshihara in the late 1980s. Yoshihara was highly critical of the nature of capitalist development in the region, and emphasized not only the problematic relations between political and economic structures at national levels, but also the non-productive 'ersatz' character of domestic capitalism which derived from it (Yoshihara 1988). Practices of rent-seeking, cronyism, and manipulation in financial sectors were thus seen as being inhibitory to the positive role that capitalism could provide for national development. One could perhaps argue that what Yoshihara was seeing were conditions which are broadly inherent to the evolving nature of capitalism in the world today, rather than something intrinsic to Southeast Asia, considering that his comparison was between 19th century Western capitalism and that of contemporary Southeast Asia. Nonetheless, the central role of political clientelism and its persistence in the aspiring developmental states of the region is indicative of the importance of political culture in shaping national developmental trajectories.

Related also to this analysis has been the particular nature of nationalism in some countries of the region, in that ethnic affiliation, and how this has been manifested in nationalist discourse, has often been a factor shaping inclusion and access to political goods. For Yoshihara, the fact that so much of the wealth of the region is controlled by Overseas Chinese, who, though residents and citizens of the nations of the region, are nonetheless often perceived and treated as foreigners, has contributed to the ersatz nature of capitalist development in Southeast Asia. Thus, although 'Chinese capitalism' is a critical aspect of trans-border connectivity, from nationalist perspectives its footloose character is nonetheless seen to be detrimental to building up domestic economies. Although it is possible that these relationships are being transformed by the exigencies of current processes of globalization, and in particular the opportunities which have followed upon the opening up of the People's Republic of China to the outside world, ethnic-based tensions between domestic Chinese minorities and majority populations still persist in many nations of the region (Suryadinata, 2004).

Needs of the New Economy

Thus the conditions of the current era merely recast and reconfigure older developmental dilemmas of the region. Regarding the specific needs of the New Economy, such old dilemmas underpin further challenges to state policy. As one example, one can point to what might be called the sociology of information, that is, the understanding that how knowledge and information are created and utilized within any socio-cultural setting will be shaped by social and political factors specific to that setting. In other words, the use of information is not neutral, in that it is socially embedded and therefore tends to reinforce prevailing power relationships. The potentially contentious generalization here is that Southeast Asian traditions of political culture are characterized by a strong emphasis on social hierarchy, which is manifest in differentiated constraints on information access and flows across hierarchies. Such tendencies are socially reproduced over time by educational systems which stress rote learning and conformism over creative thought and individual initiative, and by political and institutional forms which do not reward innovation but punish risk-taking.

A further specific challenge to the development of the New Economy derives from personalistic governance regimes. Here personalism should be understood in contradistinction to liberal notions of the rule of law in determining basic structures and processes for societal interaction. The persistence of personalism in political culture can be seen to undermine the functioning of impersonal legal frameworks, a situation directly related to the degree of 'informalization' as a characteristic of local regulatory regimes (Leaf 2005b). This is a governance issue with direct implications for the domestic deepening of the New Economy in that innovation in informational technologies is argued to be even more dependent upon guarantees of intellectual property rights than was the case with previous phases of technological change. The strengthening of domestic property rights regimes, in accordance with international pressures brought to bear through such institutional forms as accession to WTO membership, is thus understood as a prerequisite for both the transfer of foreign technologies and the fostering of necessary conditions for domestic innovation. Here one again sees the problematic nature of the persistence or reproduction of traditional forms – in this case, personalism and its outcome in the form of regulatory informality.

A final point with regard to the challenges of establishing conditions favourable to the New Economy as a development strategy relates to the role that foreign investment and the attraction of foreign expertise may play. Previous phases of transnational economic interaction – the earlier waves of industrialization in the region – were driven by the logic of the 'New International Division of Labour' and stressed such factors as low costs of labour, malleable workforces, and access to geographically proximate markets, a direct expression of the interests of Western transnationals in the globalization process. In the current phase of the globalization of informational technologies, however, geography is perhaps playing a less critical role in determining investment locations, while local amenity value is increasingly stressed (Douglass 1998). At one level, it is understood that the attraction of both a skilled expatriate workforce and the foreign managerial class which accompanies transnational investment requires good environmental conditions and a quality of lifestyle which may not have hitherto been available in the region; such an understanding underlies the production of environments such as Saigon South. Yet it is questionable whether this strategy is sufficient for establishing the requisite conditions for utilizing the New Economy as a vehicle for national development. As Douglass remarks 'the New Economy is not simply about constructing science parks or unleashing the entrepreneurial spirit. It is instead predicated on a number of social, political and economic relations that are very different from those put in place during Pacific Asia's era of accelerated industrialization of the late 20th Century' (Douglass 2000). National governments may be willing to engage with the material conditions needed for the New Economy, but are they willing to address implicit questions of governance related to informational society and the knowledge-based economy?

Outcomes and future potentials

Looking at these long-standing tendencies in the political economy of development in Southeast Asia relative to the state and societal aspirations at the heart of policy-making for the New Economy exposes the central dilemma of state-led development in the region. The basic approach, which has worked successfully in Singapore and is being emulated at varying scales elsewhere, has emphasized the technical and human resource needs of New Economy development, while failing to address more fundamental issues of governance. In this, we see continuity with other, previous strategies of state developmentalism; economic change and basic societal betterment are accepted as goals so long as they do not challenge the underlying political structures through which policy is set and carried out. Though such strategies have worked in the past – in the transition to postcolonial economies of the newly independent nations of the region, and then again in the drive to industrialize under export-oriented production – the nature of the New Economy as a knowledge-based and newly collaborative approach to economic development presents to the state previously unencountered challenges. Information needs implicit in the drive for the New Economy are forcing an opening up of state controls on the flows and utilization of information, as seen both in the awkward efforts to establish regulatory regimes for new information technologies and in the recognized need for building up a creative, entrepreneurial workforce. The recognition that the New Economy elsewhere is manifested primarily in the private sector – and is thus fundamentally linked to processes of globalization – presents further challenges to state developmentalism, as expressed in the search for new institutional channels for public–private cooperation and international engagement.

At one level, such an analysis raises questions which, in a certain sense, are technical; at another level, issues arise which are fundamentally much more political in nature. The core technical concern is with regard to the true potential for planning: can 'learning regions' be induced through policy and planning? The concept of the learning region is now being promoted as the spatial requisite for indigenous New Economy development, and has attracted significant research attention in recent years (Edgington 1998). In this regard, there is distinct scope for planning, as well as limitations. Policy and planning can ensure that necessary infrastructure is put in place, human resources are matched to perceived needs, and conditions are set to encourage high-tech, knowledge-based investment. Such strategies are geared toward building physical and human capital, but cannot ensure the formation of the social capital needed for the New Economy. In this sense, the question of whether a learning region can be planned is analogous to asking whether or not entrepreneurialism and creativity can be taught. The political question which this raises is in regard to the potential for the erstwhile developmental state to accomplish this. Is it implicit in the nature of state developmentalism to stifle social capital formation?

State developmentalism has in practice allowed for the persistence of older political cultures of personalism and clientelism, in contrast to the modern, liberal emphasis on the objective rule of law. The institutional needs of the New Economy, with regard to both the role that knowledge and information play and the need for a level regulatory playing field for public–private cooperation and transnational investment thus places new demands on the state. Whether in the face of these new demands the state can maintain its political position *vis-à-vis* society is an unresolved question. One should not perforce assume that economic change, as implicit in the drive to the New Economy, will trigger progressive political development. Developmental states have long histories of state–capital interaction; the unresolved question is how this will be transformed in response to the pressures for change prompted by the New Economy. Does the state need to change to accommodate these changes, thus leading to the establishment of new governance regimes or, consistent with the historic patterns of state developmentalism in the region, can states secure the benefits of the New Economy on their own terms?

The other, broader political question goes beyond the direct effects of building up indigenous New Economy sectors in Southeast Asia. If development policy is successful along these lines, what are the implications for society overall regarding social equity and the distribution of the benefits of the New Economy? Fundamentally, this is a question about the digital divide, which is variably manifest between nations and, perhaps more critically, between social strata within nations in the region. In international terms, one sees a clear pattern with Singapore as the region's unquestioned leader, though with heroic efforts on the part of other nations to catch up quickly. Paradoxically, perhaps the greater effect of this race to get online is the potential for increasing social and economic disparities within nations, with one outcome being the emergence of an informational elite whose connectivities across the nations of the region may exceed their connections and interactions domestically. This phenomenon may perhaps be understood as less an outcome of domestic policies favouring the New Economy than as a manifestation of corporate transnationalism in the region. Thus the New Economy might already be *in* a country such as Vietnam or Indonesia, but is it yet *of* these countries?

As emphasized before, most of the region is still characterized by large population segments dependent upon agricultural production for their livelihoods, and although the urban transition is continuing apace, this should not be assumed to be an expression of the even, upward movement of society along a trajectory of increasing economic productivity. The regional economic crisis in recent years has, if anything, demonstrated the ongoing subsistence nature of many urban economies, with the rapid expansion of so-called informal sector activities as coping mechanisms for those urban residents hardest hit. Agriculture still matters directly for more than 300 million people in Southeast Asia. And even for those large segments of society who have left farming behind to seek new opportunities in the city, the developmental promises of the New Economy are elusive at best. This is not to say that the New Economy doesn't matter, as clearly policy-makers across the region understand that linking to the international New Economy and working to derive an indigenous, domestic counterpart is a necessary and important strategy for building up modern national economies. Yet for the average citizen of the region the benefits of this will undoubtedly not be apparent for quite some time to come.

Notes

1   Due to lack of data, East Timor is excluded from comparative discussion here.
2   Figures on personal computers and Internet use are from *World Development Indicators* (World Bank, 2004).

References

Atkinson, R. D. and Court, R. H. (1998) *The New Economy Index: Understanding America's Economic Transformation*, The Progressive Policy Institute, Washington.

Bunnell, T. (2002a) 'Cities for Nations? Examining the City – Nation-State Relation in Information Age Malaysia', *International Journal of Urban and Regional Research*, 26, 284–98.

Bunnell, T. (2002b) 'Multimedia Utopia? A Geographical Critique of High-Tech Development in Malaysia's Multimedia Super Corridor', *Antipode, A Radical Journal of Geography*, 34, 265–295.

Bunnell, T. (2002c) '(Re)positioning Malaysia: High-tech Networks and the Multicultural Rescripting of National Identity', *Political Geography*, 21, 105–124.

Chirot, D. and Reid, A., eds., (1997) *Essential Outsiders: Chinese and Jews in the Modern Transformation of Southeast Asia and Central Europe*, University of Washington Press, Seattle.

Choo, C. W. (1997) 'IT2000: Singapore's Vision of an Intelligent Island', in P Droege, ed., *Intelligent Environments: Spatial Aspects of the Information Revolution*, Amsterdam; Elsevier, New York.

Coe, N. and Kelly, P. F. (2002) 'Languages of Labour: Representational Strategies in Singapore's Labour Control Regime', *Political Geography*, 21, 341–371.

Douglass, M. (1998) 'World City Formation on the Asia Pacific Rim: Poverty, Everyday Forms of Civil Society and Environmental Management', in M. Douglass and J. Friedmann, *Cities for Citizens: Planning and the Rise of Civil Society in a Global Age*, John Wiley, London.

Douglass, M. (2000) 'Re-inventing Cities for the New Economy – Strategies and Experiences in Pacific Asia after the Economic Crisis', paper presented in a public lecture, Bandung Institute of Technology, Bandung, Indonesia, November 7.

Edgington, D. (1998) 'Learning Regions: Lessons for Developed and Developing Countries', paper presented at *Global Forum on Regional Development Policy*, Nagoya, Japan, December 1–4.

Escobar, A. (1995) *Encountering Development: The Making and Unmaking of the Third World*, Princeton University Press, Princeton, NJ.

Evers, H. D. (1981) 'The Contribution of Urban Subsistence Production to Incomes in Jakarta', *Bulletin of Indonesian Economic Studies*, XVII, 89–96.

Florida, R. (1995) 'Toward the Learning Region', *Futures*, 27, 527–536.

Gadrey, J. (2003) *New Economy, New Myth*, London, Routledge, New York.

Gordon, R. J. (2000) 'Does the 'New Economy' Measure up to the Great Inventions of the Past?', *The Journal of Economic Perspectives*, 14, 49–74.

Hilley, J. (2001) *Malaysia: Mahathirism, Hegemony and the New Opposition*, Zed Books, London.

Hutton, T. (2005) 'Services and Urban Development in the Asia–Pacific Region: Institutional Responses and Policy Innovation', in P. W. Daniels, K.C. Ho and T. A. Hutton, eds, *Service Industries and Asia-Pacific Cities: New Development Trajectories*, Routledge, London, 52–76.

Leaf, M.(2005a) 'The Question of Boundaries: Planning and Asian Urban Transitions', in M. Keiner, W. Schmid, and M. Koll-Schretzenmayr, eds, *Managing Urban Futures: Sustainability and Urban Growth in Developing Countries*, Ashgate Publishers, Aldershot.

Leaf, M. (2005b) 'The Bazaar and the Normal: Informalization and Tertiarization in Urban Asia', in P. W. Daniels, K. C. Ho and T. A. Hutton, eds, *Service Industries and Asia-Pacific Cities: New Development Trajectories*, Routledge, London.

Leftwich, A. (1994) 'Governance, the State and the Politics of Development', *Development and Change*, 25, 363–386.

Lewellen, T. (1995) *Dependency and Development: An Introduction to the Third World*, Bergen and Garvey, Westport, CN.

Low, L. (2001) 'The Singapore Developmental State in the New Economy and Polity', *The Pacific Review*, 14, 411–441.

Marshall, R. (2003) *Emerging Urbanity: Global Urban Projects in the Asia Pacific Rim*, Spon Press London, New York.

McGee, T.G. *et al.* (2001) 'The Poor at Risk: Surviving the Economic Crisis in Southeast Asia', *Social Safety Net Programs in Selected Southeast Asian Countries, 1997–2000*, Project Final Report, UBC Centre for Southeast Asia Research, Vancouver, BC.

Moser, C. (1984) 'The Informal Sector Reworked: Viability and Vulnerability in Urban Development', *Regional Development Dialogue*, 5, 135–185.

Ng, C.-Y. and Griffy-Brown, C. (2001) 'Introduction: Knowledge-Based Economic Growth and Socio-Political Implications in East Asia', in Ng C.-Y. and Griffy-Brown C., eds, *Trends and Issues in East Asia 2001*, FASID, Tokyo.

Ong, A. (2002) 'Baroque Economy', paper presented at *Oikos and Anthropos: Rationality, Technology, Infrastructure Workshop*, Prague, April 27.

Ong, A. and Nonini, D. eds., (1997) *Ungrounded Empires: The Cultural Politics of Modern Chinese Transnationalism*, Routledge, New York.

Pohjola, M. (2002a) 'The New Economy: Facts, Impacts and Policies', *Information Economics and Policy*, 14, 133–144.

Pohjola, M. (2002b) 'New Economy in Growth and Development', Discussion Paper No. 2002/67, United Nations University, World Institute for Development Economics Research, UNU/WIDER, Helsinki.

Reid, A. (1988) *Southeast Asia in the Age of Commerce, 1450–1680*, Yale University Press, New Haven.

Rigg, J. (1997) *Southeast Asia: The Human Landscape of Modernization and Development*, Routledge, London.

Rodan, G. (1989) *The Political Economy of Singapore's Industrialization: National, State, and International Capital*, St. Martin's Press, New York.

Sassen, S. (1994) *Cities in a World Economy*, Pine Forge Press, Thousand Oaks, CA.

Scott, J. C. (1977) 'Patron-Client Politics and Political Change in Southeast Asia', in Schmidt, S.W. *et al.*, eds, *Friends, Followers and Factions*, University of California Press, Berkeley, 123–146.

Suryadinata, L. ed., (2004) 'Ethnic Relations and Nation-Building Southeast Asia: The Case of the Ethnic Chinese', ISEAS Publications, Singapore.

Than, M. (2001) 'New Economy and New ASEAN Member Countries', in C.-Y. Ng and C. Griffy-Brown, eds, *Trends and Issues in East Asia 2001*, FASID, Tokyo, 116–134.

United Nations, (2002) *World Urbanization Prospects: The 2001 Revision*. United Nations, Department of Economic and Social Affairs, New York.

World Bank, (2004) *World Development Indicators*, The World Bank, Washington, DC.

Yoshihara, K. (1988) *The Rise of Ersatz Capitalism in South-East Asia*, Oxford University Press, Singapore.

9   Russia's New Economy

Julian Cooper and Mike Bradshaw

Our economy is still very much dependent on raw materials exports. Of course, our natural resource wealth is Russia's natural competitive advantage, and this is not something we should be afraid of saying. But an even greater natural competitive advantage is the great intellectual potential our country possesses. This potential should be turned into a driving force that will take the Russian economy further in high-technology and high-revenue sectors.[1]

President Vladimir Putin, 2004

Introduction

If you visit President's Putin's website[2] you will find under the title 'priorities' the following four national priorities: the quality of life; towards the knowledge economy; towards an effective state; and national security. Elsewhere in this volume, others have commented on the confusion of terminology surrounding the notion of the New Economy. For most the idea of the New Economy is synonymous with the development of a 'knowledge based-economy' and this is seen as an almost natural progression in the development of largely Western developed market economies. In the context of a post-communist economy such as Russia, the idea of the New Economy takes on a double meaning. First, Russia, as a 'transition economy' is seeking to develop a new economic system that is based on market principles; and second, within that new economic system, Russia is also trying to promote the development of the 'new' or 'knowledge-based' economy as a means of securing sustainable economic recovery. As noted above by President Putin, Russia's economic recovery to date has been largely dependent upon the performance of the resource economy. International experience (Hutton and Ley's work on British Columbia for example) suggested that resource-based economic development is notoriously fragile and that resource-abundant economies should diversify their economies to protect against the inevitable downturn in the resource sector. President Putin clearly believes that Russia's diversification should be based on the development of a knowledge economy that harnesses the country's intellectual capital.

This chapter examines the progress made to date in Russia's move towards a more knowledge-based economic structure. Given the limitations on space, and the fact that this is not a book about transition economies, the reader is advised to consult other sources for an evaluation of Russia's progress towards a market economy (see, for example: Gustafson 1999, Aslund 2002, Sutela 2003, OECD 2004, World Bank 2005). As we shall see in a later section of this chapter, interest in the knowledge economy in Russia is a relatively recent phenomena; however, to appreciate the challenges that exist one must first consider the structural legacies left by the Soviet system and the impact of the 'transitional recession' of the 1990s on the structure of the Russian economy. Unfortunately, such an analysis faces severe data limitations and much of our early discussion can only examine the development of the 'service sector' as a surrogate for the growth of the new economy. This is not ideal, but the dominance of an 'industrialist view' of economic development during the Soviet period, and the immediate post-Soviet period for that matter, was such that the state statistical committee did, and does not, collect sufficient information on the service sector. To try to overcome this problem, case study evidence is used to evaluate the relative progress made by Russia's (new) knowledge economy. This brief introduction is followed by four substantive sections: first, there is a brief discussion of the structural legacies of the Soviet economy and the underdevelopment of the service sector; second, there is an analysis of the structural consequences of Russia's economic transformation during the 1990s, with a particular emphasis on the growth of the service economy. The third section then considers the development of the (new) knowledge economy in Russia. The final substantive section presents case studies of the growth of the Internet and ICT. The chapter ends with a short discussion that considers the possibility of an alternative path for Russia towards a knowledge economy and a conclusion that assesses its relative position in the global knowledge economy.

The service gap in Soviet type economies

> Progress towards a modern 'service economy' has been slow in the Soviet Union, and the level of provision of services remains low in comparison with Western countries at a comparable and lower levels of development. This situation, now much deplored by Mikhail Gorbachev, is the consequence of a development strategy over many decades that gave priority to the production of goods and skimped on provision of a service infrastructure. The consequent 'service gap', when compared both with the situation abroad and with domestic needs, is now large, and will be difficult to redress. (Schroeder 1987, 240).

Gertrude Schroder's 1987 analysis entitled: 'USSR: Towards the Service Economy at a Snail's Pace' is a rare analysis of the state of the service sector in the Soviet Union. It was written during the optimistic period of Mikhail Gorbachev's perestroika and represents a benchmark for the state of the service economy at the end of the Soviet period. However one measures it, in absolute or relative terms, the Soviet Union's service sector was woefully underdeveloped.

The reasons for this are well understood. From 1928, when the first Five-Year Plan was introduced, onwards industrialization was the priority in the Soviet Union's development strategy. A state ideology based on an interpretation of Marxism relegated 'services' to the non-productive sphere where they were systematically neglected. Consequently, the Soviet Union's service sector was enumerated as residual, in other words that which was left behind when the agricultural and industrial sectors were subtracted from production and employment statistics. This resulted in a very broad notion of services, which included transport and communications and commercial services that supported the so-called productive sphere; and consumer-oriented services, such as housing, health care and education that served the needs of the population. Finally, given the nature of the planned economy, there was a substantial science and administration sector that served the needs of the state. Table 9.1 details the relative size of each of these sub-sectors as well as the overall share of the service sector in terms of employment.

As these data indicate, the service sector grew modestly in the post-war period and while there was a slight decline in the role of transport and communications, consumer-oriented services only registered a small relative gain. Between 1950 and 1985 the level of urbanization increased from 39 per cent to 69 per cent, suggesting declining levels of service provision, particularly in the trade and finance sectors. Western visitors to the Soviet Union were immediately struck by the poor level of retail provision, both in terms of quantity and quality. Table 9.2 places the sluggish growth of the Soviet Union's service economy in international perspective. Again, this is based on Schroeder's 1987 analysis and it clearly illustrates the relative backwardness of the Soviet economy in structural terms. Japan and Italy are chosen as comparators. In 1980 the Soviet Union's service economy was below the level reached by Japan in 1960 and at the same level as reached by Italy in 1970. Thus, both in terms of meeting the needs of the Soviet population and in terms of international standing, it is clear that by the late 1980s a 'service gap' had emerged, in fact that service

Table 9.1 Employment in services in the USSR, 1950–1985

	1950	1960	1970	1980	1985
Services as a percentage share of total employment	22.0	26.7	32.8	37.3	38.7
As a percentage of total service employment					
Transport and communications	26.2	27.6	23.9	23.5	23.4
Commercial services	20.4	19.4	20.4	20.4	19.9
Consumer-oriented services	39.0	41.2	42.6	42.6	43.4
Science and administration	14.3	11.8	13.2	13.5	13.4

Source: Schroeder 1987, 243.

Table 9.2 The percentage distribution of the employed labour force by sector: USSR, Japan and Italy, 1950–1980

	Agriculture, forestry and fishing	*Mining, manufacturing and construction*	*Services*
USSR			
1950	53.9	24.1	22.0
1960	42.5	30.8	26.7
1970	32.2	35.0	32.8
1980	26.4	36.3	37.3
Japan			
1950	51.6	21.7	26.7
1960	32.5	27.8	39.7
1970	17.4	35.2	47.4
1980	10.4	35.3	54.3
Italy			
1950	43.9	29.5	26.6
1960	32.6	36.0	31.4
1970	19.3	43.4	37.3
1980	14.2	37.8	48.0

Source: Schroeder 1987, 246.

gap was first recognized in the early 1960s. Mikhail Gorbachev recognized the significance of the service gap and demanded 'decisive measures' to eliminate the gap between supply and demand for services (Schroeder 1987, 256). However, as Table 9.3 illustrates, the challenges facing the service sector in the late Soviet period were immense and the economy was not in a fit state to address them. Thus, we can conclude that by the end of the 1980s the Soviet Union had a poorly developed service economy and its economic structure was at odds with other national economies of equivalent levels of development. Mikheeva (2005, 74) presents data for the Russian Federation in 1990 that suggest that 32 per cent of GNP came from the service sector, compared to 45 per cent in Poland and 37 per cent in the Czech Republic. In the USA in 1990 the service sector accounted for 70 per cent of GNP. However, the problem was not just that Russia's (and the Soviet Union's before it) service sector was too small, it was also ill suited to the demands of the economy and the population. Furthermore, post-1991, however inadequate, it was clearly not designed to meet the needs of the market economy. Thus, a newly independent Russia not only needed to close the 'service gap', it also needed to develop an entirely new service economy, one that could support the emerging market economy.

Table 9.3 Schroeder's assessment of the challenges facing the Soviet Union's service sector in the late 1980s

---

1. A transportation network stretched tight and accident-prone and a road network that can only be described as archaic by modern standards.
2. A telephone system so backward that in 1985 only 23 per cent of urban families and 7 per cent of those in rural areas had private telephones.
3. A retail network employing backward technology, inefficient sales procedures and too few workers, and having too few outlets.
4. Repair and personal care facilities that are too few in quantity, poor in quality and the source of burgeoning illegal private activity to help fill the gap.
5. Poorly maintained and crowded housing that barely meets state-set minimum standards for health and decency.
6. A universal system of health care, whose poor quality and inadequacy are now being publicly blamed for endemic public health problems and unfavourable mortality rates.
7. An educational system that has probably over-supplied graduates relative to the ability of the economy to use them productively and failed to correctly match training with the economy's changing requirements.

Source: Schroeder 1987, 255–56.

The structural consequences of Russia's economic transformation

Sovietology is often accused of having failed to predict the collapse of the Soviet Union. While that may be true it was clear to all that by the late 1980s the Soviet economy was in deep crisis. Simple tinkering with the system could not bring about the radical transformation that was required; in the end the system could no longer sustain itself. The problems facing the service sector were symptomatic of a larger pathology, the centrally planned economy was simply unable to orchestrate the scale of economic restructuring required to create a modern internationally competitive economy. However, the collapse of the Soviet system exerted a heavy economic and social toll. Figure 9.1 charts year on year change in the growth of Gross Domestic Product (GDP) for the economies of Central and Eastern Europe (including the Baltic States) and the Russian Federation. The immediate consequence was so-called 'transitional recession' as the centrally planned economy collapsed, this came earlier in Central and Eastern Europe and the return to positive growth was achieved in 5 years, although there remains considerable variation within the region. In Russia, transitional recession followed the collapse of the Soviet Union in 1991 and was deeper and more protracted, with initial positive growth in 1997 being set back by the 1998 Russian financial crisis. However, since 1999 the Russian economy has experienced positive economic growth and is now out-performing Central and Eastern Europe. There is not the space here to discuss Russia's economic recovery in detail, for the purposes of the present analysis we are most interested in the impact the transitional recession had upon the structure of the Russian economy.

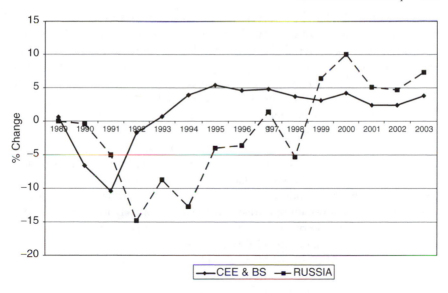

Figure 9.1 Annual change in GDP for CEE and Baltic States and Russia, 1989–2003.
Source: EBRD (2004, 38)

Table 9.4 compares the structure of employment in Russia in 1990 and in 2003. Because of the financial turmoil of the 1990s comparative data on the value of GDP by sector are not reliable, equally one should not expect consistency between different sources of information on the structure and performance of the Russian economy.[3] A number of trends are noteworthy: first, the 1990s witnessed a substantial absolute and relative level of decline in employment in industry, agriculture and construction; second, there appears to be a

Table 9.4 Changing structure of employment in Russia, 1990–2003 (percentage of total employment)

Sector (per cent of total employment)	1990	1995	2000	2003	Per cent Change in numbers employed 1990–03
Industry	30.3	25.3	22.6	21.9	−37.1
Agriculture and forestry	13.2	15.1	13.4	11.4	−24.9
Construction	12	9.3	7.8	7.7	−43.7
Transport and communications	7.8	7.9	7.8	7.8	−11.7
Services	33.6	39.4	45.3	47.7	+23.4
Other	3.1	3.0	3.1	3.5	−1.2
Total employment	100.0	100.0	100.0	100.0	−7.8

Source: Rosstat 2004, 141.

growth in the absolute and relative size of the service economy. Analysis of employment within industry reveals that it was the processing and manufacturing sectors that suffered the most, while the resource-producing sectors (with the notable exception of the coal industry) actually experienced an increase in employment. Thus, transitional recession not only brought about de-industrialization, within the industrial economy there was a process of 'primitivization' as the manufacturing economy collapsed and the resource sector proved more resilient. While the 1998 financial crisis, and subsequent devaluation of the Rouble, did promote import-substituting growth in the market-oriented sectors, such as light industry and food processing; it remains the case that the resource sector has been the engine of Russia's economic recovery. Much of the industrial economy that was destroyed by the transitional recession was not competitive and Russia is unlikely to regain pre-1991 levels of manufacturing output. Therefore, if the Russian economy is to follow the pattern of the industrialized West, the service sector should become the major employer and producer of value added.

Table 9.5 provides information on employment change within Russia's service sector. Overall, between 1990 and 2003 the service sector experienced a 23.3 per cent growth in the level of employment, during the same period the size of the workforce declined by 7.8 per cent. However, there were substantial differences within the service sector. Table 9.5 suggests that those sectors most closely linked to the growth of the market economy, wholesale and retail trade and finance and insurance, experienced the highest rates of growth; while those sectors associated with state service provision registered little or no growth. The dramatic decline in the sciences is discussed in the next section on the knowledge economy. It is also noteworthy that 'administration' also experienced a substantial increase in employment. The Federal and Regional Government apparatus has actually grown quite considerably as a result of marketization. Official data on the structure of output by sector in 2002, suggest that 38.4 per cent of total output came from industry and 39.8 per cent from the

Table 9.5 Changing structure of employment within Russia's service economy, 1990–2003 (percentage of total service sector employment)

Sector	1990	2003	Per cent Change
Wholesale and retail trade	23.2	35.3	+87.50
Housing and social services	12.7	10.4	+0.75
Health and physical culture	16.7	14.9	+10.24
Education	23.9	19.0	−2.06
Culture and arts	4.6	4.0	+7.21
Science	11.0	3.9	−56.60
Finance, credit and insurance	1.6	2.8	+115.17
Administration	6.3	9.8	+91.07
Total services	100.0	100.0	+23.28

Source: Rosstat 2004, 141.

service sector (Rosstat 2004a, 309). Thus, aggregate indicators suggest that there has been some progress towards a more service-oriented economic structure; first, because of the collapse of the manufacturing sector; and second, because of the growth of new 'market-oriented' service activities. Certainly, anyone who has visited Moscow on a regular basis since 1991 cannot help but have been impressed by the rapid growth of the city's service economy. But Moscow is not Russia and not all Moscovites can afford to shop at the designer outlets that now dominate the city centre. Regional data on economic structure highlight substantial regional variations in the role of the service sector; data on the size of the service economy in terms of employment and value of output do suggest that Moscow is an exceptional case. Regional variations seem to be inversely related to the resilience of the agrarian and industrial economies. In 2003, the service sector employed 50.9 per cent of the workforce in Moscow city, but only 39.5 per cent of the workforce in the Volga Federal District and 38.5 per cent in the Urals, both major industrial regions. The service accounted for 40.8 per cent of the workforce in Russia's most agrarian region, the Southern Federal District. Data on regional variations in the branch structure of gross regional product show even greater variation.[4] Using a somewhat different sectoral classification system, a sector of activity identified as trade and commercial activity accounted for 20.0 per cent of Russia's gross regional product, but for Moscow the share was 48.3 per cent, but this was exceptionally high. The only other regions with more than 20 per cent in this category were St Petersburg (21.0 per cent) and Nizhne Nogorod (20.1 per cent). Analysis of the employment figures for 2003 shows that the Central Federal District accounts for 28.5 per cent of Russia's employment in the service sector and Moscow city 10.5 per cent. Moscow's share of national employment in science is 34.4 per cent and the Central District's 52.7 per cent. Using 2001 data, Mikheeva (2005, 86) calculates the Central Region's share of the service sector's share of gross regional product as 44.9 per cent. Thus, the national figures are a balance between two or three outliers and the rest of the country.

If, as our analysis suggests, Russia's economic transformation has promoted a modest growth in the service economy, how far has it managed to close the service gap? Table 9.6 presents recent World Bank data on the share of GDP and employment contributed by the service sector for selected economies. Despite dramatic changes during the 1990s, in many ways the relative situation has changed little from the time of Schroeder's analysis in the late 1980s. While the service economy is reported to account for 60.5 per cent of Russia's GDP in 2002, this is lower than Poland and Portugal (President Putin has chosen Portugal as a benchmark for Russia's economic progress) and some way away from Italy and Japan. However, Russia's 2002 position is in keeping with the average for Upper Middle Income Countries, which is what Russia is classified as in 2005 on the basis of its level of GDP. Unfortunately comparative employment data are not available, but both the official Russian employment data and the GRP data suggest a lower share for the service sector for the Russian economy, possibly making the gap even wider. Furthermore, recent

Table 9.6 Share of services in gross domestic product for selected countries, 2002–03

Country	1990	2002
Australia	67	71
Belarus	29	60
Czech Republic	45	57
Italy	63	70
Japan	58	68
Poland	42	68
Portugal	42	66
Russian Federation	35	60
United Kingdom	63	72
Upper Middle Income	52	59
High Income	65	71

Source: World Bank (2005) *World Bank Development Indicators, Database*, Washington DC: World Bank.
http://www.worldbank.org/data/wdi2005/wditext/Section4.htm

analysis by the World Bank (2005) and the OECD (2004), suggest that there are reasons why the GDP data might overestimate the contribution of the service sector, or, put another way, underestimate the contribution of the resource sector.

During 2004 the World Bank mission conducted a series of research projects that examined the Russian economy, these were published in draft in 2004 and the final version was published as an official report the following year (World Bank 2005). One of the projects examined the sectoral composition of productivity changes and questioned the apparent dominance of the service economy. It concluded that the widespread practice of transfer pricing and differences between internal and external prices for commodities depressed the scale of contribution made by the resource sector (World Bank 2005, 59–63). Transfer pricing occurs when a company sells its output via controlled trading companies at artificially low prices. Without going into the detail, one consequence of this practice is to transfer the value of the output from the industrial sector, where it is produced, to the service (trade) sector, where the trading company operates. This then devalues the output of the resource economy and inflates the value of the service economy. Given the importance of the resource sector to the Russian economy, the cumulative impact of this behaviour is considerable. The World Bank study recalculated Russia's national accounts for 2000 using comparative data from Canada, the United Kingdom, the Netherlands and Norway, all of which are energy producing countries. As a result of this analysis, 13 percentage points of GDP are moved from trade to industry, which rises from 28 per cent to 41 per cent of GDP. Most of this adjustment (11 percentage points) accrues to oil and gas, which more than doubles in size to 19 per cent of GDP. The remainder is distributed across various industrial sub-sectors (World Bank 2005, 61). Using the classification of the 'service sector' that is employed by Rosstat, this sector's contribution to GDP then declines from 52.1 per cent of GDP (includes the category other in the service sector) to 36.4 per cent, this is due to a 12.7 per cent decline in the share attributed to the service sector. In their 2004 Economic Survey of the Russian Federation, the OECD (2004, 20) update the World Bank analysis for 2003 and reach the following conclusion:

> Official statistics suggest that Russia has a highly developed service sector, contributing roughly 60 per cent of GDP, which is only marginally below the 65–70 per cent typical of the most advanced OECD economies. This, however, seems counter-intuitive, given that most services in Russia are still relatively under-developed. Even the communications and banking sectors, arguably the most developed Russian service sectors, are relatively small when compared with countries that have developed service sectors. This apparent contradiction disappears when correcting for transfer pricing: the share of industry increases from 27 to 41 per cent ... At the same time, the service share drops from 60 per cent to 46 per cent.

The two studies use different data and generate slightly different results, but the general conclusion is clear, Russia's service economy is not as large as suggested by its national accounts. A measure of 46 per cent of GDP is lower than the average for low-income economies. Put another way, Russia's position as an upper-middle income economy, which is quite recent, is based on the revenue's generated by it resource economy, not the structure of the economy. If the true measure of the share of the service economy is below 50 per cent, then as the OECD (2004, 20) put it, 'there is scope for "catch-up" growth'. Our analysis has revealed a substantial 'research gap' when it comes to understanding the current structure and performance of Russia's service sector. Much more analysis is required to understand the current causes of the service gap and the possibilities for catch-up growth. In the context of the current volume, we have chosen to focus on the so called new or knowledge economy to assess its current status and to evaluate the prospects for catch-up.

Development of the New (knowledge) Economy

As noted in the introduction, there is a growing consensus in Russian policy circles that a diversification of the economy is an urgent necessity, reducing dependence on the energy and materials sectors, and increasing the role of a modern service sector. But, as we have seen from the previous section, progress so far has been rather limited. One particular option commands increasing support. This is the image of the future Russian economy as prospering in a globalized world by successfully exploiting its intellectual capital; Russia as a 'knowledge-based' economy.

The terms 'New Economy', 'Knowledge Economy' and 'Information Society' entered Russian discussion of alternative paths of development in the late 1990s. There is no surprise that Russian economists became interested in the issue. With the recovery of the economy from the 1998 financial crisis, awareness grew that GDP growth had become heavily dependent on the energy sector, making Russia's economic development dependent to a worrying degree on the level and stability of world oil prices. Interest in 'industrial policy' grew, although the liberally orientated Ministry of Economic Development and Trade (hereafter, MERT), led by Gref, was not well-disposed to the traditional 'picking winners' approach adopted by many of its advocates. In these circumstances, some economists more sympathetic to the approach of Gref and his colleagues began to explore alternative options, in particular the possibility that the active development of knowledge-based activities could provide a path of gradual diversification of the economy.

As noted in the introduction to this chapter, a distinction could be drawn between the new economy being created by new actors, in particular SMEs and through FDI, and one being created by new spheres of economic activity, in particular knowledge-intensive activities such as information and communications technology (ICT), high technology sectors such as aerospace, biotechnology, microelectronics and advanced materials, and new services, especially those possessing a high intellectual content. This is not a distinction usually drawn by Russian authors, who are inclined to focus on the latter interpretation. However, it is clear that the knowledge economy can involve both old and new actors. This is certainly the case in Russia, where much of the advanced R&D and higher educational capability was located in, or focused on, the military-industrial sector.

A major centre for discussion of the New Economy has been the State University – Higher School of Economics (HSE) in Moscow, the scientific leader of which is the eminent reform economist Evgenii Yasin. Leading figures are the rector, Yaroslav Kuz'minov, Andrei Yakovlev and Leonid Gokhberg, the latter director of the HSE's Institute for the Economics of Information. In a number of publications, some part of a series entitled 'New Economy – New Society – New State', they have discussed the significance of the 'new' or 'knowledge-based' economy and attempted to analyse Russia's current position and future prospects. These authors are evidently familiar with the literature on the topic of the international economic agencies, notably the OECD and World Bank. Their central concern is that Russia lacks a functioning 'national innovation system' (NIS) (Kuzminov *et al.* 2003). Concern that Russia's economy is inadequately innovative and, as such, ill-prepared for transition to a knowledge-based system, is shared by other specialists, in particular Irina Denezhina of the Institute for Economics of the Transition Period (Gaidar Institute) and a leading specialist on the R&D system, Irina Boiko of the Centre for Regional and Innovation Policy.

In addition to the work of the HSE, there are a number of projects and Internet sites devoted to the New Economy, innovation and related issues, three in particular are worthy of mention. The New Economy Foundation' (http://neweco.ru) was founded by the HSE, together with the Interdepartmental Analytical Centre (an important research centre for industrial policy), the Bauman Technical

Institute, the State Research Institute of IT and Telecommunications, and other centres in Moscow and St Petersburg, with a focus on ICT. The project Innovation – Investment – Industry (http://www.3i.ru) is more concerned with innovation-related issues, while the Centre for the Development of an Information Society (http://www.riotsentr.ru), an independent non-commercial organization, founded a number of research institutes, including the nuclear industry's Kurchatov Institute, Moscow Technical University of Communications and Informatics, and the Institute of International Economic and Political Research of the Russian Academy of Sciences, with a general interest in post-industrial society in general, and the role of ICT in particular.

Problems of the innovation system

Russia is still in transition from a command-type innovation system to a market-based system.[5] Some essential features of the current National Innovation System (NIS) include:

- An R&D system still dominated by large, inflexible, academic and state establishments divorced from the business sector and habituated to state funding on a substantial scale. In the case of the Academy, also exhibiting a striking reluctance to accept any proposals for meaningful reform.
- Weak development of the SME sector, including small hi-tech companies. According to MERT, only 2 per cent of SMEs are involved in innovation-related activities.
- Research in the higher education sector is still weak and divorced from business, although there are now some signs of positive developments.
- Inadequate intellectual property rights legislation.
- An almost total lack of venture finance and other funding for innovation.
- Inadequate management skills: in the words of the UN Economic Commission's report on Russia's readiness for a knowledge-based economy, 'Resolving the management problem for the new innovation economy is critical for the start-up stage, and is a key task for Russia' (UN ECE 2002).
- Lack of domestic demand for innovation, partly relating to weak competition in many sectors of the economy.

In addition, the inherited R&D system has contracted sharply in scale: total domestic spending on R&D in 2003 was less than 45 per cent of the 1990 level and the number of researchers little more than 40 per cent (Table 9.7). For a country of Russia's level of per capita income spending on R&D as a share of GDP is relatively high, but this is largely because Russia still devotes more than half total spending on research to military purposes. MERT has set a goal of R&D spending as a share of GDP of 2 per cent by 2010 (MERT 2005, 221).

But it is not only the weakness of the national innovation system that gives rise to concern; there is also the related issue of the quality of human capital. In both Russian and Western writings on post-communist Russia it has

Table 9.7 Research and development in Russia: expenditure and personnel

	1990	1992	1995	1996	1997	1998	1999	2000	2001	2002	2003
R&D spending as per cent GDP	2.03	0.74	0.85	0.97	1.04	0.95	1.00	1.05	1.18	1.25	1.28
R&D spending 1992=100[1]	340[2]	100	77	85	93	80	89	103	121	135	148
No of researchers (000)	993	804	519	485	455	417	420	426	422	415	410

Source: 1992–2003: Rosstat (2004, 359).

Notes:
1 In constant 1989 prices, using GDP deflator.
2 Approximate: calculated from Tsentr issledovanii i statistiki nauki, *Nauka Rossii v tsifrakh 1998*, M., 1998, p. 42 (also source of 1990, GDP share and researchers).

become something of a cliché to assert that the country possesses a comparative advantage in having a highly educated labour force, regarded as a favourable pre-condition for diversification towards more knowledge-based activities. However, as a number of Russian specialists have argued, this advantage should not be overstated. Firstly, the country's scientific labour force has contracted sharply over the past fifteen years and has aged to a considerable extent. Thus the number of researchers has fallen from just under one million in 1990 to 410,000 in 2003 and the average age of doctors of science has reached 60 and of candidates of science 53, with very little new recruitment of younger scientists over recent years.[6] Every fifth Russian scientist is of pensionable age. Clearly, low rates of pay in the sphere of science and higher education have played a significant role, but also the lack of meaningful reform in the Academy of Sciences system and to a lesser extent in higher education. In these circumstances it is not surprising that there has been a sizeable brain drain of talented young scientists, above all to the USA and Western Europe. Secondly, as Kuz'minov has argued, the educational system is still not able to provide forms of training appropriate to a New Economy, partly because of the still strong Soviet-era tradition of excessive specialization. Thus there is a shortage of IT specialists with all-round training of a kind promoting adaptability to fast changing technology.

Has thinking about the New Economy influenced Russian economic policy? There is mounting evidence that for Putin's second term economic strategy is indeed being shaped by concern to promote the development of a knowledge-based economy, with a new emphasis on human capital and on the creation of conditions fostering a more competitive and innovative economy. This new emphasis emerged most clearly in the document, 'Basic Directions of Activity of the Government of the Russian Federation during the Period to 2008', adopted in late July 2004.[7] A principal focus of this document was the creation of new sources of growth in the sphere of high technology and the 'economy of knowledge'. This orientation has also been a feature of recent programmatic documents issued by Gref's Ministry. Since visiting the leading Indian IT Company 'Infosys' in Bangalore in December 2004, President Putin has also on a number of occasions spoken of the importance of diversification and the critical role of information technology and other knowledge based activities.[8]

As some Russian economists are well aware, the development of a knowledge economy will face serious obstacles:

- The weakness of the NIS
- The need for substantial state investment to upgrade the educational system
- The need to create effectively functioning capital markets
- The need to promote genuine competition and a dynamic SME sector
- An all-pervasive lack of trust in the economy and society at large[9]
- The problem of reconciling the institutional requirements of a knowledge economy with traditional Russian security concerns and a predisposition to state intervention.

Case studies – The Internet and ICT

In this section we examine the development in Russia of one of the most significant manifestations of the New Economy, namely information and communications technology (ICT), taking as exemplars the Internet and cellular mobile phones. For each the development of the technology in Russia is reviewed, with analyses of the factors promoting and/or hindering their adoption, the diffusion of the technologies across the regions of the country is investigated, and Russia's relative progress considered in a comparative context, permitting an assessment of future prospects.

The Internet

In the Russian Federation use of networked computers and later the Internet developed at a relatively early date, mainly through the efforts of individual enthusiasts taking advantage of the relaxation of the Soviet system in the late Gorbachev years and its subsequent collapse. Much of this initial activity involved personnel and institutions of the defence industry. The domain name 'su' was registered in September 1990 and in 1993 the name 'ru', giving birth to what became quickly known as 'Runet', the Russian language zone of the global Internet galaxy.[10]

As can be seen from Table 9.8, the estimated number of regular Internet users expanded rapidly from approximately 1,000 in 1992 to 500,000 by 1996–97, 1.5 million by 1999 and 10 million by 2003. Taking the widely used indicator of number of users per 10,000 population, Russia reached 15 by 1995, 50 by early 1998, 100 in 1999 and over 1000 in 2004. At the same time, the number of hosts in the .ru domain grew steadily, from a mere 1.5 per 10,000 population in 1995,

Table 9.8 Internet use in Russia, autumn 2002 and spring 2005

	Autumn 2002	Spring 2005
Number of Internet users (mn)	8.7	18.9
per cent population 18 years old and over	8	17
per cent all men using Internet	10	21
per cent all women using Internet	6	13
per cent all with higher education using Internet	26	46
Per cent population using Internet by Federal District		
Moscow city	27	44
Central (ex Moscow)	6	13
North-Western	10	23
Southern	6	16
Volga	5	13
Urals	7	13
Siberian	7	15
Far Eastern	8	16
Place of use of Internet (per cent)		
Work	41	40
Home	32	48
Place of study	17	16
Internet café	9	12
At friends and other	24	24
Per cent age group using Internet		
18–24	21	42
25–34	13	28
35–44	8	18
45–55	4	10
55+	1	2

Source: http://www.fom.ru

to almost 20 in 1998 and about 80 in 2004. Within the Commonwealth of Independent States, Russia maintains the lead in terms of hosts, but now lags behind both Belarus and Moldova by Internet users per 10,000 population.

There are difficulties in measuring the development of the Internet. Much depends on the definition of a 'user' and measurement of the number of hosts in a given country has become less precise over time as the use of non-country domain names (e.g. .com, .org, and .int) has expanded, although in Russia until now there has been a distinct preference for the .ru domain. The Foundation for Public Opinion (FOM) in Moscow now publishes regular surveys of Internet use based on the widely employed Nielsen/Net Ratings method. This provides useful demographic details of the Russian user community. Some of the evidence is summarized in Table 9.8, which shows data for spring 2005 compared with the first such survey in autumn 2002.

The patterns of diffusion of the Internet by gender, age and education follow standard international trends. In the initial period of Internet development in

Russia usage was concentrated heavily in Moscow and St Petersburg, which were also dominant as centres for the establishment of Internet service providers (ISPs). Over time use and the provision of ISPs spread to other major regional centres, in the early years often those with well developed facilities for higher education and research (Perfil'ev 2002). Figure 9.2 shows the level of regional concentration of hosts in the .ru domain in 2001. Unfortunately, data for more recent years are lacking.

In order to establish the factors accounting for the differential regional diffusion of the Internet in Russia, statistical analysis was undertaken. This analysis suggests that in 2001 the most important factor influencing the regional diffusion of the Internet was the availability of telephone lines.[11] Additional factors were the overall level of social-economic development of a region, the highly educated personnel, using the number of R&D personnel as a proxy, and the availability of personal computers. These findings accord broadly with the results of analysis of the factors responsible for the differential diffusion of the Internet between countries, in particular for those undergoing post-communist economic transformation. Here an additional factor has been found to be the extent of economic reform and liberalization, but an indicator of this type is not available for the subjects of the Russian Federation.

While the development of the Internet in Russia has been very respectable by the standards of CIS countries, a broader comparative perspective raises doubts as to Russia's ability to match the performance of other countries of a comparable level of economic development, let alone the rates and level of development of OECD-member, or EU-member, countries. Table 9.9 presents data for Russia and three countries of comparable GDP per capita in purchasing power parity terms (Mexico, Brazil and Turkey) two rapidly rising nations of lower per capita income (China and India), two other ex-communist countries (Poland and Estonia, the latter the most highly developed ex-USSR economy), and two more wealthy countries (the UK and Finland), the latter one of the world leaders in Internet development.

In recent years a number of organizations have elaborated comparative measures of overall Internet 'readiness'. Table 9.10 shows Russia's standing in two of the most authoritative rankings, with the position of some other comparator nations, indicating that there is still some way to go before the country can be considered a fully fledged 'information society'. The evidence also suggests that Russia is in danger of falling behind such rising nations as China and India, with Indonesia one of several countries that is moving up the rankings.

In these rankings, Russia is weak in connectivity (the backward telecommunications infrastructure) and in business and consumer use of the Internet. In particular, electronic commerce is still at a very modest level, though growing rapidly. Here a major problem has been the lack of dependable systems of payments in a society that still has a deep-rooted distrust of the banking system and credit card use. According to estimates of the National Association of Participants of Electronic Trade (NAUET, Moscow), the volume of B2C

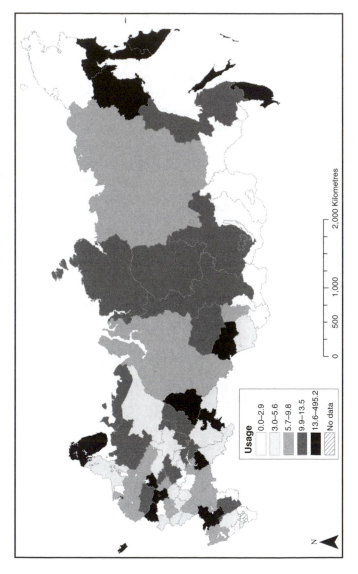

Figure 9.2 Internet usage in Russia's regions in 2001 (number of registered .ru domains per 100,000 population). Note: Grouped data: Nenets with Arkhangelsk, Komi-Permyak with Komi, Khanty-Mansi and Yamal-Nenets with tyumen, Evenk and Taimyr with Krasnoyarsk, Ust-Orda Buryat with Irkutsk, Agin Buryat with Chita, Koryak with Kamchatka. Source: Goskomstat Rossii.

Table 9.9 The development of the Internet, 1995–2004

	GDP p.c. $PPP	PCs per 1000	Internet users per 10,000 population			Internet hosts per 10,000 population		
	2003	2002	1995	2000	2003	1995	2000	2004
UK	27,690	406	188	2644	5919	75	281	746
Finland	27,460	442	1371	3723	5338	417	1022	3649
Estonia	12,680	210	270	2721	4441	24	284	1785
Poland	11,210	106	65	725	2325	6.0	88	644
Mexico	8,980	82	10.0	512	1200	1.5	57	175
Russia	8,950	83[1]	14.9	197	683[2]	1.5	22	79
Brazil	7,510	75	10.9	294	939	1.3	52	211
Turkey	6,710	45	8.1	306	849	0.9	11	84
China	4,980	28	0.5	174	633	0.02	0.5	1.2
India	2,880	7	2.7	54	175	0.01	0.4	2.5

Source:
GDP: http://devdata.worldbank.org/wdi2005/Table1_htm (accessed 19 April 2005).
PCs and Internet user and hosts per 10,000 population: data of ITU.
Forecasts: MERT (2004, 105).

Notes:
1   2004: 100; MERT forecast (8/04): 2007 – 243–250
2   MERT forecast (8/04): 2007 32 million users, c.2250 per 10,000 population.

Table 9.10 Network readiness indices, 2004

	World Economic Forum Network Readiness Index 2004 (104 countries)		EIU E-readiness ranking 2004 (64 countries)	
1st	Singapore	1.73	Denmark	8.28
UK	12	1.21	2	8.27
Finland	3	1.62	5	8.08
Estonia	25	0.80	26	6.54
Poland	72	−0.50	36	5.41
Mexico	60	−0.28	39=	5.33
Russia	62	−0.36	55	3.74
Brazil	46	0.08	35	5.56
Turkey	52	−0.14	45	4.51
China	41	0.17	52	3.96
India	39	0.23	46	4.45

Sources: WEF: http://www.weforum.org
EIU: Economist Intelligence Unit, *The 2004 e-readiness rankings* (http://www.ebusinessforum.com).
Notes: Countries ranked by GDP per capita (PPP), 2003.

(retail) e–commerce increased from \$218 mn in 2001 to \$660 mn in 2004; of B2B transactions from \$99 mn to \$440 mn, and of B2G (government) from zero to \$2,130 mn. However, 2004 retail on–line sales were still less than one per cent of all retail sales.[12]

There is certainly a strong government commitment to the development of the Internet, including measures to harness for the improvement of the quality and efficiency of government itself. The \$2.6 billion federal programme 'Electronic Russia 2002–2010', adopted in 2002, provides for a comprehensive and ambitious set of measures to develop the Internet infrastructure, create an Internet-friendly regulatory and institutional framework, and to develop rapidly e-government and e-education. A major focus of this programme is on initiatives at the regional and local levels.

In many developed countries, plus China, the most significant Internet development of recent years has been the rapid adoption of high-speed broadband access. In this respect, a new developmental gap is threatening to emerge: broadband is becoming available in Moscow and a few other major centres, but the pace of development is modest in comparison to China, Brazil, and West European countries.[13] Overall, it can be concluded that, with respect to the Internet progress has been made, but in an extremely dynamic global context.

Telecommunications

The USSR possessed a relatively backward telecommunications system, at least for general public use. The Party-government elite and the military-security establishment had their own 'closed' communications networks and there is little doubt that the development of these priority systems took precedence over general provision. Thus in 1990 Russia had only 14 main telephone lines (on the public network) per 100 inhabitants, compared with just over 44 in the UK. Since the collapse of communism terrestrial telecommunications have undergone development to the point that by 2003 Russia had 25.3 main lines per 100 people, but still far below developed West European levels, e.g. 59.1 (2002) in the UK, 65.7 in Germany and almost 75 in Sweden.[14] The infrastructure for international and inter-city terrestrial telecommunications was retained in state hands, with a near monopoly for the company 'Rostelekom'. In these circumstances, it is not surprising that mobile phone technology developed from the mid-1990s to fill the gap, with the dynamic being established by new private companies. Table 9.11 shows the diffusion of mobile phones.

This very rapid growth continued into 2005: by the end of the first quarter the number of cellular mobile phone subscribers had reached 85.2 million, almost 60 per 100 population.[15] One factor promoting rapid diffusion is competition. Whereas long-distance terrestrial telecommunications remains a state monopoly, in the mobile field there are some ten sizeable operators, although a dominant role is played by three GSM companies: 'MTS', which leads in the regions, 'VympelKom', which leads in Moscow and 'MegaFon', which leads

Table 9.11 The development of mobile phone use in Russia, 1991–2004

	1991	1995	1996	1997	1998	1999	2000	2001	2002	2003	2004
Mobile phone subscribers (000)	0.3	88.5	223	485	747	1371	3263	7750	17609	34423	72000
Mobile phone subscribers per 100 population	–	0.06	0.15	0.35	0.51	0.93	2.22	5.28	12.0	24.9	50.2

Source: 1991, 1995–97: International Telecommunications Union, Yearbook of Statistics (1988–1997), Geneva, January 1999, p.137; 1998–2002: <http://www.itu.int> (accessed May 2005. 2003, 2004); <http://www.minsvyaz.ru> (accessed 5 July 2005).

in St Petersburg. VympelKom was founded by former defence industry personnel. As for the mobile phones themselves, these are all imported, with the usual firms predominating – Motorola, Samsung, Siemens, Nokia and Alcatel. In 2002 the average price of a phone was $133, with a bias towards more expensive models in Moscow and St Petersburg, but cheap, basic models in the provinces.[16]

As with the diffusion of the Internet, mobile phone use was initially concentrated in the cities of Moscow and St Petersburg, but since the late 1990s has rapidly spread to other large regional centres, then to smaller towns and villages. As shown in Figure 9.3, by 2004 the major centres of mobile phone use, besides Moscow and St Petersburg, included Krasnodar krai in the South, Samara, Kaliningrad, Murmansk, Yaroslavl, Ryazan' and Tomsk oblasti. In an attempt to clarify the factors responsible for the differential rate of take up of mobile phones in the regions of Russia, a statistical analysis was undertaken. This indicates that the most significant factor is the overall level of socio-economic development of each region as measured by MERT's 'complex estimate'.[17]

Taking a broader view, notwithstanding rapid growth, Russia still lags behind comparator countries in the development of mobile phone technology, as shown in Table 9.12. The low level of average personal incomes is clearly an important factor, but also probably the relatively slow development of a vibrant small business sector and, more generally, the underdeveloped civil society, with a middle class of still modest scale. Further statistical analysis may shed more light on the role of these factors.

Taking the two cases of the Internet and mobile phones, the conclusion is clear: in relation to other CIS countries Russia's performance has been relatively strong, but if account is taken of other countries at a comparable level of economic development, the position is much less promising, raising the possibility that Russia's standing in world rankings relating to the New Economy will fall unless relevant policy measures are adopted and implemented. The same applies to a third field of new economy activity, the development of software, in particular so-called 'offshore' software development.

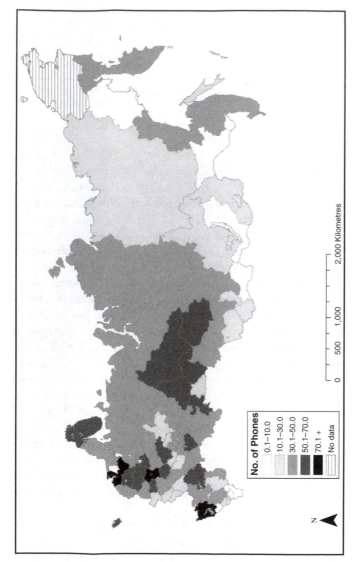

Figure 9.3 Mobile phone usage in Russia's regions in 2004 (number of users per hundred population). Note: Grouped date: Nenets with Arkhangelsk, Komi-Permyak with Komi, Evenk and Taimyr with Krasnoyarsk, Ust-Orda Buryat with Irkutsk, Agin Buryat with Chita, Koryak with Kamchatka, Moscow with Moscow oblast, St. Petersburgy with Leningrad. No data for Chukotka. Data for Krasnodar are incompatible but as indicated on the map, suggest very high mobile dispersion. Source: Mininfsvayz.

Table 9.12 Mobile phone subscribers, 1995–2003

	Mobile phone subscribers per 10,000 population			Per cent total telephone subscribers
	1995	*2000*	*2003*	*2003*
UK	979	7270	9120	60.5
Finland	2010	7200	9010	64.8
Estonia	205	3870	7770	69.5
Poland	19	1750	4510	58.6
Mexico	7	1420	2950	63.4
Russia	6	222	2493	49.7
Brazil	8	1370	2640	54.4
Turkey	71	2470	3940	59.6
China	3	658	2150	50.6
India	1	35	247	34.8

Source: http://www.itu.int (accessed 5 July 2005).
Note: Countries ranked by GDP per capita (PPP), 2003.

Software

It is generally acknowledged that Russia has advanced skills in software development and in some spheres of computing. However, these sectors do not play a very significant role in the economy. So-called 'offshore' software development (by programmers working in Russia to the orders of foreign firms) has evolved, but its scale is still very modest, in 2004 reaching an estimated volume of $760 million, compared with India, $8 billion.[18] There is also a sizeable sphere of activity of the so-called 'sharovarshchiki', working in shareware, mainly individuals and very small companies working to one-off orders. Finally, there are a number of specialized Russian software companies in niche fields such as pattern recognition, anti-virus software, games, and business information systems. However, the software business faces many obstacles, especially when attempting to export its products, when it faces many bureaucratic obstacles, in part relating to security concerns.[19] In relation to software development, Russian analysts have engaged in much soul-searching, seeking to establish why India has been so much more successful. In computing, while Russia possesses research skills in the field of high-speed computers, little is left of the computer industry inherited from Soviet times. However, a new computer industry has been growing in recent years, based on the assembly of imported components. In time, this could evolve into a viable sector able to compete successfully with foreign suppliers on cost grounds.[20]

Discussion: another path to a 'knowledge economy'?

A possibility now sometimes mentioned by Russian and Western specialists is that Russia could develop a knowledge-based economy by a somewhat different route than others, as a spin off from its energy-materials sector. This would be a path to a new economy in which old institutions will play a prominent role. In the words of former science minister Mikhail Kirpichnikov, in part at least this could be through the development of what he terms 'heavy hi-tech', i.e. technologies developed to exploit Russia's resource wealth such as pipeline transport, nuclear waste processing, environmental technologies, and deep, under-water, drilling in hostile Arctic conditions, requiring advanced materials, new manufacturing technologies, control systems, etc.[21] To date such developments have been on a limited scale and the state and private companies of the energy and materials sector have not been to the fore in R&D and innovation. However, there are some straws in the wind: in 2004, for example, 'Noril'sk nikel', part of the 'Interros' holding, established a new R&D unit with a substantial budget, contracting research from Academy and other institutes under a $120 million three-year programme for the development of new hydrogen power technologies.[22] At the same time, Gazprom has been devoting more attention to research into new environmental technologies.[23] It may also be relevant that the leading actors in B2B, commercial Internet buying and selling, are the electricity company RAO 'EES Rossii", and services linked to the oil and gas, metals and timber industries.[24]

Conclusion

Russia has made a start, with growing government recognition of the desirability of moving in the direction of a knowledge-based economy. However, practical policy measures for its promotion have so far been modest. Much remains to be done and transition to a New Economy is likely to be slow, with a strong possibility that Russia will lag behind other countries of a comparable level, and, more worrying for the Russian political elite, even behind countries currently of an inferior level of overall economic development.

Notes

1   Speech to Election Campaign Supporters, February 12, 2004. Available <http://president.kremlin.ru/eng/priorities/group70561.shtml> (accessed 29 July 2005).
2   <http://president.kremlin.ru>
3   For the most part this upon relies on statistics from the Russian Federal Statistical Service for domestic indicators and international organisations, principally the World Bank for comparative data.
4   These data are available from the State Statistical Service website: <http://www.gks.ru/bgd/free/bo1_19/lswPrx.dll/stg/d000/i000500r.htm> (accessed 1 August 2005).
5   For a concise summary of the Soviet NIS and transition to a market-based system, see Dezhina and Saltykov (2005).
6   http://www.carnegie.ru/ru/pubs/media/0160Ros_nauka_sovrem_tendentsii.ppt, 26 April 2005 (L M Gokhberg).
7   http://www.pravitelstvo.gov.ru/data/structdoc.html?he_id=100&do_id=1621, 28 July 2004.
8   See, in particular, speeches made during a visit to Novosibirsk Akademgorodok, January 2005 (http://www.kremlin.ru/events/detail/2005/01/82434.shtml, 11 January 2005).

9   This is recognized by leading Russian scholars, e.g. Ya I Kuzminov, A A Yakolev, L M Gokhberg *et al.*, *op.cit.*, p.7.

10   For the history of the Internet in the USSR and Russia, see http://www.nethistory.ru

11   Correlation of the log of the number of .ru domains per 100,000 people in a region with the number of telephone lines per 1000 people gives a Pearson coefficient of 0.617, at a 0.01 per cent significance level. Data on.ru domains from Perfil'ev (2003, 228-31); telephone lines, http://www.minsvyaz.ru/img/uploaded/2003021411144985.xls).

12   http://www.nauet.ru accessed 5 June 2005. Note: 2004 B2B and B2G data for January to November.

13   See International Telecommunications Union, Europe's telecommunications/ICT markets and trends 2003/2004 (http://www.itu.int, June 2005); <http://www.point-topic.com/content/operatorSource/profiles/Russia/Russia%20Broad> 4 March 2005.

14   International Telecommunications Union, Yearbook of Statistics (1988-1997), Geneva, January 1999 and <http://www.itu.org> May 2005. The Ministry of Economic Development and Trade's forecast for 2010 is now 40 telephones per 100 inhabitants (MERT 2005, 224).

15   http://www.minsvyaz.ru Accessed 5 July 2005.

16   *Vedomosti*, 18 March 2003.

17   This index for 2004-05 correlates quite closely with the number of mobile phone subscribers per 100 population (2004), with a Pearson coefficient of 0.667 at a 0.01 per cent level of significance (0.69 if outliers are removed – Moscow city and region, St Peterburg and Krasnodar krai). For the MERT index, see MERT (2004, 174-180); mobile phone subscribers by region: <http://www.minsvyaz.ru>.

18   <http://www.cnews.ru.ru> (accessed May 2005). MERT (2005, 224) has forecast software exports of $3 billion by 2010.

19   <http://www.izvestiya.ru/tech> (accessed 29 July 2004). In the words of HSE specialists, the procedure for obtaining permission to export software 'has been complicated to the point of absurdity.' Ya I Kuzminov, A A Yakolev, L M Gokhberg *et al.* (2003, 9).

20   According to Russian Business Consulting, in the third quarter of 2004 Russian national PC brands (e.g. Aquarius, Depo Computers, Formoza, R&K and Kraftway) accounted for 25 per cent of the home computer market, and locally assembled regional brands, 30 per cent <http://www.cnews.ru, 11> (accessed April 2004).

21   <http://www.opec.ru> (accessed 24 May 2005).

22   <http://www.cnews.ru> (accessed 29 June 2005).

23   <http://www.gazprom.ru/eng/articles/article8940.shtml> (accessed July 2005)

24   <http://cnews.ru> (accessed 10 May 2005).

References

Aslund, A. (2002) *Building Capitalism: The Transformation of the Former Soviet Bloc,* Cambridge University Press, Cambridge.

Dezhnia, I.G. and Saltykov, B.G. (2005) 'The National Innovation System in the Marking and Development of Small Business in Russia', *Studies on Russian Economic Development,* 16, 184–6.

EBRD (European Bank for Reconstruction and Development) (2004) *Transition Report 2004: Infrastructure,* EBRD, London.

Gustafson, T. (1999) *Capitalism Russian Style,* Cambridge University Press, Cambridge.

Kuzminov, Ya. I, Yakolev, A.A. and Gokhberg L.M. *et al.* (2003) *Novaya ekonomika-shans dlya Rossii, Tezisy,* Moscow State University-Higher School of Economics, Moscow: Preprint WP5/2003/01.

Mikheeva, N.N. (2005) Servsniyi sector v Rossiyeskoi eknomike: mezhotraclevoi analiz, Problemy Prognozirovaniya, 1. Available at HTTP http://www.ecfor.ru/fp/index.php? pid=archive/2005_1.

MERT (Ministry of Economic Development and Trade) (2004) *Prognoz sotsial'no-ekonomicheskogo razvitiya Rossiiskoi Federatsii na 2005 god I osnovnoi parametry prognoza do 2007,* MERT, Moscow.

MERT (2005) *Programma sotsial'no-eknomickeskogo razvitiya Rossiskoi Fedratsii na srednes-rochnuyu perspektivu* (2005–2008), Proekt, MERT, Moscow.

OECD (Organisation for Economic Cooperation and Development) (2004) *OECD Economic Survey of the Russian Federation,* OECD, Paris.

Perfil'ev,Yu. (2002) 'Development of the Internet in Russia: Preliminary Observations on its Spatial and Institutional Characteristics', *Eurasian Geography and Economics,* 43, 411–421.

Prefil'ev,Yu. (2003) *Rossiiskoe internet-prostranstvo: razvitie i struktura,* Gardariki, Moscow.

Rosstat (Russian State Statistical Service) (2004a) *Rossiiskii statisticheskii ezhedognik,* Rosstat, Moscow.

Rosstat (2004b) *Regiony Rossii: Sotsial'no-ekonomicheskii pokazateli,* Rosstat, Moscow.

Schroeder, G.E. (1987) 'USSR:Toward the Service Economy at a Snail's Pace', in *Gorbachev's Economic Plans:Volume 2,* Joint Economic Committee, Congress of the United States, U.S. Government Printing Office,Washington DC, 240–260.

Sutela, P. (2003) *The Russian Market Economy,* Kikimora Publications, Helsinki.

UNECE (United Nations Economic Commission for Europe) (2002) *Russian Federation: Towards a Knowledge-based Economy, Country Readiness Report,* Geneva: UN ECE. Online. Available HTTP: http://www.unece.org/ie/enterp/assesreport.htm (accessed 3 August 2005).

World Bank (2005) *From Transition to Development: A Country Economic Memorandum for the Russian Federation,* Washington DC/Moscow:World Bank Report No. 32308-RU. Available HTTP: http://worldbank.org.ru.

Index